Praise for Wordsmith

"Al Smith's boyhood began in Sarasota, then a tattered circus tent of a town. Hard times moved his coming of age to a scant farm scavenged from family holdings in Depression-era Tennessee. After the Army, he abandoned two college scholarships for drinking years in New Orleans as a young reporter covering madams and murderers. Recovered from whiskey in the state where they make it best, Al came back as a weekly newspaper owner, radio host and TV commentator. *Wordsmith* isn't just the who, what and where, but also the why and how Al Smith became modern Kentucky's leading citizen-journalist, a force for progressive causes and an advocate for rural America."

—Mark Neikirk, Civic Engagement,
Northern Kentucky University;
former Managing Editor,
The Cincinnati Post and *The Kentucky Post.*

"Like the author himself, the many-layered story that unfolds is informed, inspiring, and, most of all, interesting. The man who rose and fell in New Orleans, later owned a string of newspapers, hosted a weekly TV show, and headed the Appalachian Regional Commission. Here he tells a personal history that includes despair and delight, demons and determination, tragedy and triumph. It is his story, but, in truth, it is the human story—it is our story."

—James C. Klotter,
State Historian of Kentucky
Author of *A New History of Kentucky*

"Al Smith's long-awaited memoir provides a revealing look into the life and politics of the twentieth century South. Smith is a master storyteller whose anecdotes and analysis of state and national leaders, backroom deal making, and political skullduggery are both humorous and insightful. He overcame adversity to become one of the leading voices for progressive change in the modern South."

—Ron Eller, Distinguished Professor of
History at the University of Kentucky
Author of *Uneven Ground: Appalachia since 1945*

Praise for Al Smith

"A man dying from alcoholism fifty years ago, Al Smith recovered by working the twelve-step AA program. He has been a wonderful role model and example for thousands of recovering alcoholics—giving us hope, encouragement, and inspiration."

—Gordon L. Hyde, MD
Emeritus Professor of Surgery,
University of Kentucky
Past Executive Director
of International Doctors in AA

"Al Smith's essential ingredients are his never-dimming curiosity, his passion for politics and news, and his storyteller's soul."

—Jamie Lucke
Lexington *Herald-Leader*
editorial staff

"Al Smith created a unique spot for himself in Kentucky politics and journalism with *Comment on Kentucky.* He informed, cajoled, agitated and, yes, entertained thousands of Kentuckians for over three decades. We are richer for his vision."

—Ferrell Wellman
Host of *Comment* since
Al's retirement in 2007

"Al has done much for Kentucky but also for many individuals. We differ in our politics, but his encouragement and help have opened wonderful opportunities for me."

—John David Dyche
KET Election Night analyst
and Louisville attorney

[handwritten inscription:] For Dr. Gant White my new friend

WORDSMITH

My Life in Journalism

[handwritten inscription across page]

By

Al Smith

[handwritten signature] Al Smith Nov 16, 2013

clark legacies llc

Pied Type Press

This is a work of nonfiction. The experiences and events detailed in this memoir are true, and they have been faithfully recounted to the best of the author's ability. The names of some, however, have been changed in consideration for families and friends.

Order your copy today at http://www.clarklegacies.com

ISBN: 978-0-9832639-6-8

Library of Congress Control Number: 2011939700

CLARK LEGACIES LLC and PIED TYPE PRESS FIRST EDITION, 2011

Cover and photo layout and design by Sid Webb
Text layout and design by Michal Smith-Mello
Cover photo by Steve Shaffer, courtesy of KET
Cover photo (back) courtesy of The Courier Journal

For Martha Helen, as promised

Contents

Preface

AS I ENTERED THE DINING ROOM AT THE SPRINGS MOTEL in Lexington with Larry Forgy, then a young Republican aspirant for governor, I spotted Happy Chandler sitting at the head of a table surrounded by Dawahares. Lunch with Happy was a monthly ritual for the eight Dawahare brothers, whose family chain of department stores was started in east Kentucky's mountain coal camps.

Twice governor of Kentucky, a former U.S. senator, and the commissioner of baseball who helped Branch Rickey integrate the game with Jackie Robinson, Happy had aged in the decade since I'd interviewed him on KET, the state's PBS network. But that winter day, he still greeted me as "Albert Benjamin"—not my name, which is "Albert Perrine," but his, bestowed on me long ago in jest. In a state where everyone called him "Happy," he said, he enjoyed the rare sound of "Albert Benjamin," even if it came from his own lips.

Bidding goodbye to the old man, I left him chatting with Larry while a waiter showed me to a corner table for two. Seated, I saw Happy glance my way as he whispered a question to which Larry smiled and shook his head. Then Larry leaned down and kissed Happy on the head.

"That was a pretty scene," I scoffed as Larry rejoined me. "Right out of *The Godfather*."

"Want to know what he asked?"

"Well, yes," I replied.

"'Larry,' he said, 'Do you trust that little son of a bitch?'"

YEARS LATER, AT NATURAL BRIDGE STATE PARK, I listened at dinner as another former Kentucky governor, Bert Combs, complained that then-Governor Wallace Wilkinson was neglecting the state's nationally popular parks, which Combs had developed or improved during his tenure. Then the conversation switched to another governor.

"You knew Earl Long when you were on the New Orleans papers?" Combs asked me. "Sure did," I said. "I covered him through two elections."

"Then you know Earl was a bit crazy," said Combs. "I met him at the Kentucky Derby in 1955. He was making two or three bets on every race—big bets. He stopped me and said, 'You the fellow runnin' against Happy Chandler?' When I said that I was, he whipped out a check, scribbled something on it and handed it over."

Combs leaned in. "Al," he said, "that check was for $5,000. And Governor Long told me, 'Anybody can beat that son of a bitch is my friend.'"

Fearful the check would bounce, Combs said he deposited it early Monday and held his breath. It cleared. But Combs—"the little mountain judge," as Chandler called him—lost to Chandler anyway. He had begun his race calling for new taxes to support a host of improvements.

"It was the only campaign in state history that opened and closed the same day," Happy later jeered. But four years later, a wiser candidate Combs won the governorship on a second try.

HOW DID I—born in Sarasota, raised in Florida and Tennessee, and for ten years a reporter and editor in New Orleans—come to know Chandler, Combs, and Forgy in Kentucky?

When I came to Russellville to edit a weekly paper in 1958, my story was that I had left a good position in New Orleans to be near my Tennessee relatives. The truth was I had no place else to go. The only employer desperate enough to hire me was an elderly widow publisher in Russellville, a courthouse town of six thousand in rural Logan County some sixty miles north of Nashville. I was thirty-one, and just another tramp newspaperman who drank too much. After losing two jobs on daily papers in New Orleans, I was profoundly depressed and didn't much care if the next thing I lost was my life.

Russellville fooled *me*, the fooler, who had deceived himself through a long and intense pursuit of self-destruction. It took five more years to win my battle with the bottle, but in a small town that I had once scorned as nothing, I finally found everything. With my sobriety came a new role in the news business, as an "engaged journalist" who was both a teller of and a player in the story.

My early mention here of Chandler, Combs, and Long is just a reporter's trick to capture the reader's attention. Certainly those men were important in their time, and each did good work, even the mad Earl of Louisiana (rogue governor of the movie *Blaze*). But I mention them in these pages because their back stories, as well as that of two-time gubernatorial candidate Forgy and many others, are richly connected to the journalism, people, and politics I followed in Tennessee, Kentucky, Louisiana, and Washington, D.C., as well as to my early years in Florida.

As head of the Appalachian Regional Commission, spending hundreds of millions of dollars in Washington under two presidents from different political parties, I partnered with thirteen governors.

Impressive? I thought so then.

Now, just an old man with stories, those dollars count for less than the excitement of earlier times—gawking at the Flying Wallendas in circus winter quarters; awed by a Tennessee grandmother who fought women's suffrage, then voted first on Election Day in Nashville; and laughing at Jailer Joe Gunn Gregory, rescued from reelection defeat by Happy Chandler.

"My state job?" Gregory chuckled. "Check that sign in Russellville that pointed to Paducah, check every week to see if it was still there," Joe said.

The hero of Robert Penn Warren's masterful novel *All the King's Men* is not Willie Stark, the fictional governor resembling Huey Long of Louisiana, but instead Stark's assistant, the former reporter Jack

Burden. Like that novel, in my story the many political figures I've known seem almost like supporting players compared to those who served them and to my family, friends, fellow workers, and others. With all of them, I've shared vivid adventures in unique situations and different parts of the country. This book is about our collective experience: *their* unforgettable lives and *our* days together in a changing America.

As for Governor Chandler's question, "Can you trust the little son of a bitch?" Well, memories and memoirs are tricky, so reader, beware. But here's my story as I remember it.

PART ONE

The Thirsty Years

From one extreme to another, my early life went up and down:
From a child in a mansion on Sarasota Bay
to a teenager in a ramshackle house
on a poor farm in Tennessee.
From winner of a top national scholarship
to Vanderbilt dropout.
From dreams of fame as a fiction writer in the French Quarter
to copyboy at *The Times-Picayune.*
From a quick rise on two New Orleans dailies
to hung-over days on a weekly paper
and conflicted nights in a firetrap hotel in Kentucky …
I saw the highs and lows.
I wonder I didn't die.
The next fifty years were different:
a lot of sober journalism;
talking, writing, always a cause.
A lot of gratitude and a family to love.
I owned papers.
I served presidents.
But before Kentucky,
before New Orleans,
before the poor farm in Tennessee,
there was Florida,
my hard-luck parents,
and the boom-time promise of easy riches.

-1-
The Acacias

MY FATHER, ALBERT SR., WAS A CLERK in an Arkansas law office when a friend told him, "All you need to get rich in Florida is a pair of plus fours and a set of golf clubs." That was all it took. Albert and my mother, Elvira "Muff" Mace Smith, set out for Sarasota, Florida, in 1925.

My parents weren't alone. In the early 1920s, Florida was going crazy over real estate. Thousands of newcomers flowed into the state each month; fortunes were made, and sometimes lost, in a day. Speculators were scrambling for a piece of the boom.

My parents' timing could not have been worse. The boom finally peaked in October 1925, just as they arrived. By 1926, Sarasota's business leaders knew the boom was over; hurricanes and continued over-speculation brought an abrupt end to the prosperity. But my parents were confident the downturn wouldn't last. In 1927, when Lindbergh lifted the nation's morale by flying the Atlantic in the Spirit of St. Louis, I was born.

Though my parents must surely have felt despair by that point, my earliest memories are not colored by their worries. Instead, when I think of my early childhood, I remember The Acacias.

A magical, unkempt place of orange and grapefruit trees, sea birds and squirrels, oleanders and mossy oaks, The Acacias was a home perched on a bluff by Sarasota Bay. With its tree-lined drive circling an Indian mound that was topped by a crumbling concrete gazebo, it was a magical place where I lived until I was ten.

We moved to The Acacias in 1934, when my father, who came to Sarasota as manager of the Sarasota Abstract Guarantee Company—he later became a partner in the firm with Sarasota's mayor—contracted to sell the estate. We Smiths were agents to occupy, maintain, and market the property for Sarasota's own nobility, the Princess Julia Dent Grant Cantacuzene.

The Princess possessed a dazzling pedigree; she was the granddaughter of President Ulysses Grant and the niece of Berthe Honore Palmer, the wealthy Chicago widow (her husband had owned the Palmer House Hotel), who became much wealthier by virtue of timely investments in Sarasota real estate. Julia's husband, Michael, a Romanov prince, had escaped the Russian revolution with his head and his title but little else. Despite their lineage, the Cantacuzenes couldn't afford the upkeep of the three-story mansion and its eleven acres of grounds and outbuildings. Like most of us in Sarasota, the prince and princess were living on the margins.

The Acacias had seen a lot of history before we moved there. It had been built on a site called Yellow Bluffs, so named by Bill Whitaker, a settler who homesteaded there in 1840. It was from Yellow Bluffs, in June 1865, that Judah P. Benjamin, the brilliant Jewish Confederate treasurer with a price on his head, escaped in disguise to Nassau on a sloop provisioned by Whitaker. When Louisville relatives of Berthe Palmer built a new house on the Whitaker homestead in 1911, they christened it The Acacias.

By the time we moved there, The Acacias was a ghostly mess of creaky stairs, cracked windows, and dusty walls. Above a basement full of empty champagne bottles and forgotten luggage, the house was a derelict sleeping off the Florida boom days. Like the rest of Sarasota, The Acacias had foundered on a shoreline of busted dreams.

Yet, despite the gloom, I remember a childhood of mostly sunny days. I spent hours with my sister, Robin, and my black friend, Cornelius, playing in a tropical forest, shouting at the dolphins in the bay, and slapping at mosquitoes.

The servants' apartment on the third floor of The Acacias was unoccupied. Our help came from Cornelius's parents and sisters, who lived rent-free in a cabin on the grounds. My father paid the family

$20 a month to clean the house, wash clothes, build the fires in winter, and mow and rake the yards. In those hard times, before welfare checks and Social Security, our families—white and black— shared a lot at The Acacias. There were vegetables from the garden, eggs from a henhouse guarded by a fussy rooster, oranges and grapefruit from our grove, birds and rabbits my father shot, and fish caught in the Gulf or from the bridges that spanned Sarasota Bay.

As a friendly little boy with blond curls, I must have seemed more winsome than many whites to Cornelius's father, Ward, as I tagged along after his son, who was bigger, and strong enough to carry pine logs inside for fires on winter mornings. One day when I imitated our preacher quoting Jesus as He said "feed my sheep," Ward took the pipe from between his teeth, stooped down and kissed me on the cheek. Then he gave me a reflective look and said, sternly, "Don't tell your father I did that."

THOUGH MY GRANDMOTHER ELLA MACE, who lived with us at The Acacias, was stooped with age, she'd don an old-fashioned sunbonnet and work alongside my mother to help raise me and my sister. My mother, her dark hair at that time cut in a flapper style with bangs, was the youngest of Ella's five children, a "surprise" baby born when my grandmother was forty-five. The two women cooked together in an enormous kitchen next to the two dining rooms, one for everyday and one for special entertaining.

When the sunny days turned to drowsy nights, my grandmother read to me. Generally she favored chapters from books about a boy named Tom Sawyer, a dog named Beautiful Joe, and a horse called Black Beauty. But while she smoked her lone Chesterfield of the day after supper—always bummed from my father ("Al, give me a coffin nail!")—she read cowboy stories aloud from *The Saturday Evening Post.*

Grandmother Ella, as I usually called her, was born in Tennessee in 1857, when James Buchanan was President. Eight years old when the Civil War ended, she remembered seeing Union soldiers from occupied Nashville. She told of how her grandfather, Green Babb Cook, who had lost a leg when he campaigned with Andrew Jackson, brought the news from town about Abraham Lincoln's assassination. Stumping from the stable on his pegleg, my great-great-grandfather had yelled, "Old Abe Lincoln's killed! Old Abe Lincoln's dead!"

Ella grew up in a family of prosperous landowners who had built their own Methodist church, Cook's Chapel, near Lebanon, Tennessee. She became a Campbellite (Church of Christ) when she married Brice Martin Mace, who himself had inherited land and money. Book-smart and dreamy, Grandfather Mace was a poor manager who was too innocent for the sharp traders who came around. When he paid $5,000 for a prize jackass to enhance the breeding stock he raised, there was talk in the neighborhood. But three decades later, my grandmother always mentioned the high price, even when she reckoned it had been a mistake.

Grandmother Mace also told a scary story of how her husband's horse bucked at the sound of an oncoming train and threw him onto the track where a wheel mangled his leg. When the train crewmen brought my groaning grandfather to the house and laid him on the dining table, my mother, then six, hid screaming under the table until he was taken back and placed on the train. After a special run to Nashville, a surgeon amputated his leg and saved his life. According to my mother, "Mr. Mace" would not have survived had he not been so physically strong and regularly shunned tobacco and alcohol. (Mother liked a story with a moral.)

After that accident, my grandparents sold their farm and moved to Lebanon, where my grandmother set up a boarding house for law students at Cumberland College, and my grandfather started a career as a teacher. He went on to become superintendent of schools and a member of the state House of Representatives.

When a fire leveled the boarding house, Grandmother Ella was ruined. As with the Cantacuzenes, Sarasota offered my grandmother a place to escape the past and perhaps to convert personal history to a narrative recollected at a distance and without tears.

OUR PREACHER IN SARASOTA, Brother Anderson, was also our chiropractor. He was from Nashville, which my mother referred to as "the Jerusalem of the Church of Christ."

My father led the singing in Brother Anderson's little church. Dad had grown up a Presbyterian, but when he converted to the Church of Christ for the love of my mother, he earned extra respect from my Grandmother Ella. She wouldn't say a word against him, even when the Four Roses was getting the best of him. My favorite hymn was "Love Lifted Me"; perhaps its vivid images of "sinking deep in sin, far from the shore" spoke to a small child growing up on the Gulf. I felt comfort when the congregation sang, *"But the Master of the Sea heard my despairing cry, and from the waters lifted me, now safe am I. Love lifted me, lifted me ..."*

Granny Ella was never without a nickel or a dime to drop in the collection plate on Sunday. My grandmother's other children each sent her a little money when they could: checks from her two sons in Washington, D.C., and Michigan, and dollar bills or coins, carefully wrapped in toilet paper to conceal them from mailbox thieves, from her daughters in South Carolina and Illinois.

Although Brother Anderson's sermons all sounded alike to me, my grandmother complimented him each week before we drove home in the Essex to the same Sunday lunch: pot roast or baked chicken, string beans, iceberg lettuce and tomatoes or a Jell-O salad, and a pie or baked custard. After lunch, my grandmother read the funnies to me, and then we had naps and playtime. Sunday night suppers were cold roast beef sandwiches with lettuce, tomatoes, and homemade mayonnaise, eaten as we listened on the Philco to Jack Benny with Mary Livingston, Eddie "Rochester" Anderson, and the jovial announcer—"I'm Don Wilson."

These homey Sundays at The Acacias were often preceded by Saturday night poker games. On Sunday mornings, I frequently found my parents clearing ashtrays and bottles from a side porch. If I asked who had made the mess, they named guests like Slim Haley, who managed the circus, or one of baseball's Dean brothers, Dizzy or Daffy. Even "Mike"—aka Prince Cantacuzene—sometimes came to play, as did Karl Wallenda. Mr. Wallenda defied death at the circus by riding a bicycle on a thin cable high in the sky. When I asked my father why Mr. Wallenda was cross-eyed, Dad explained, "You know—from watching those wires."

Ty Cobb's brother Paul, who sold real estate, was a poker regular, as was Bob Robbins, a fishing pal who ran a title company in Tampa. Bob and his wife, Pearl, drove a flashy red Oldsmobile, their fishing rods sticking out from a side window, when they came down for weekends in our guesthouse. Pearl slipped me oatmeal cookies and fried the fish Bob and my father caught while Bob drank whiskey and read pulp fiction magazines, at least when he wasn't fishing.

MY SISTER ROBIN was born on August 29, 1932. The morning of her birth was the beginning of a memorable day. Alone except for a hired nurse, I managed to dress myself in my Indian costume, the first time I had accomplished this feat on my own. Putting on an Indian costume wouldn't be all that remarkable for most almost-six-year-olds, except that I was born with little physical dexterity.

Not for me the Lincoln Logs and Tinkertoys. The Boy Scouts dropped me for flunking knots; I lagged at riding a bicycle and driving a car. I never managed to tie a decent fishing hook, play a musical instrument, or hammer a straight nail. My handwriting is nearly illegible, and I have hunted and pecked my way with two fingers on keyboards through a lifetime of journalism. Nonetheless, I have imagined myself as accomplished in nearly every human endeavor. The birth of my sister, for example, was the day I almost slew a shark.

With a son dressed for a gunfight and a new daughter in a hospital crib, my father loaded Grandmother Ella and me into the Essex and drove us to a fishing spot on the bridge to Siesta Key. While grandmother and father waited for a nibble, my imagination got the best of me. Suddenly, I began to envision a shark attack …

My father yelled for help as he went under. Then the thrashing shark went after my grandmother! My mission was clear: It was up to me to kill this shark. I would stab the monster with my toy rubber dagger! …

But in my earnest attempts to save my family, I dropped my knife. Over the rail it went, spiraling into the water, where it was swept away in an instant under the bridge, gone forever.

This was a real loss. The rubber dagger was a treasured gift from my parents' friend Bob Robbins. I began to cry.

"Never mind, Albert," my father said. "I will buy you another dagger."

"You can't," I sobbed. "You can't. I heard you tell Granny our money is all locked up!"

Later that evening, at the hospital to see my mother and crying baby sister, I thought again of the shark. I began to cry once more. The day had been too exciting.

"I lost my dagger," I told my mother.

"But I promised to buy him another," my father hoarsely told her. Mumbling, he added, "When business gets better."

Later, when my mother and sister came home from the hospital, there was cash around, but the toy dagger was never replaced.

My father was thinking about other things. So, I suppose, was I.

-2-
The Depression

IT'S SUPPERTIME IN FLORIDA IN THE 1930s. A sunburned, slender man—my father—and the young woman with the bobbed hair—my mother—were transfixed by a voice on the radio. The speaker was the new president. Tears ran down my father's cheek as he listened. The speech over, my father invoked the name of a local banker who loaned him money to rent a house when he and my mother first came to Florida.

"Saw Mr. Hitchings today," my father says. "He has a job again. He's a timekeeper on a street crew."

Talk such as this wasn't unusual in those days, as my parents often discussed politics at home. The WPA, PWA, NRA, SEC, CCC, TVA—those New Deal alphabet programs, one of which likely hired Mr. Hitchings—were the conversational spice at meals. Muff and Al were newspaper readers, the *Sarasota Herald* in the afternoon and *The Tampa Tribune* in the morning, and they eagerly searched for headlines that affirmed their faith in Franklin D. Roosevelt. Although my father's parents in Nashville had their doubts about *Mrs.* Roosevelt, they, too, admired the president, impressed by the promised benefits of the Tennessee Valley Authority.

Three of my uncles, however, had different inclinations. My mother's brother, Robin Mace, was a stockbroker who manned a Detroit outpost of Goldman Sachs, one of FDR's Wall Street enemies. Then there were my other two uncles: McGregor, who lived in New Orleans and was my father's brother, and Malcolm "Lad" Williams, who lived in Nashville and was Dad and McGregor's brother-in-law. Those two had roomed together at the University of

Tennessee, and Lad went on to marry McGregor's sister, Eudora "Dollie" Smith. McGregor and Lad were both frontline fighters against Roosevelt's public power programs, which they scorned as socialism.

Although I grew to cherish these uncles, each of them affectionate and generous to me, even as a child I was immune to their rants against Roosevelt. No rhetoric from the right has ever prevailed over the courage I remember in that voice on the radio and its effect on my father, who had seen a broken banker on the street. President Roosevelt, a new national leader who promised to help everybody, and Mr. Hitchings, an old local leader who could no longer help anybody, became the iconic frame for my perspective on politics. I didn't acquire my "liberal" social conscience from books. My parents gave it to me in the Depression.

MEANWHILE, IN THE EARLY 1930s, relatives and friends filled The Acacias as if we owned the place. A Nashville mayor, Hillary Howse, came down to catch grouper and red snapper, bringing with him a man with a pistol whom my father referred to as the mayor's bodyguard. When my Smith grandparents, Rutledge and Graeme, visited, they were so excited by their tarpon catch that my grandfather was persuaded to co-sign a note for a boat deal with the laconic guide who'd helped them catch the fish, Ben Seale, one of Dad's closest pals. Ben traded in his old boat for two new ones that he christened "The Rutledge" and "The Graeme." He promised free fishing trips for our family until the loans were repaid.

Ben, a paunchy, squint-eyed Dutchman who was a top guide in those days, had a police dog named Ruffles. Ruffles entertained his master's clients at the pier with round-trip strolls to fetch his lunch from the butcher three blocks up the street. Ben would put a dime in an envelope, and Ruffles would take the envelope in his teeth and scamper to the store. The butcher replaced the dime with a morsel of meat, then handed the envelope back to Ruffles. When Ruffles got back to the pier, Ben rewarded him with the meat.

It was Ben who pulled my first loose "baby" tooth. One day Dad and Ben had snared a monster sea bass at Midnight Pass, using a rope and hook baited with a piece of chicken carcass. As they wrestled the fish—it was so big it rocked the boat—Ben turned to me and said, "Let's tie that tooth to this line and let the old fish be the dentist." I screamed. As I did, Ben reached a pudgy paw into my mouth and popped out the tooth.

"Guess we don't need Dr. Fish after all," he said. "Here's one of Ruffles' dimes for being brave."

When my mother's brother Robin came down from Michigan, their older sister Kate, who lived in South Carolina, came as well, bringing her beautiful daughter, Lilla. Dressed in identical white linen men's trousers and cotton shirts, Lilla and my mother were two modern young women, smoking, drinking and always smiling at "the boys" as they cast for the big fish. My Grandmother Ella baked extra pies, cakes, and cookies when her children visited, and my sister and I feasted on licks of frostings from pans and spatulas. When he was back in Detroit, Uncle Robin sent his old copies of *The New Yorker*, a cut above the several "mass" magazines to which my parents subscribed. (It was one such periodical to which I referred in what Mother proudly boasted was my first sentence—"Hand me *The Saturday Evening Post*, please"—reportedly uttered while I was sitting on the potty.)

Eventually, Uncle McGregor, the pipe-smoking young engineer in the seersucker suit and straw boater, came through Florida on business. McGregor was gruff and tough, yet given to edgy joking. He was quick to whip out a harmonica to charm a child or an investor with "Turkey in the Straw." He was already head of Louisiana Power and Light and boasted of his battles with Huey Long, and he assured us the Depression was just a prelude to another Florida boom.

As I played beside the columned front porch one day while Uncle McGregor visited, I overheard my mother complain to him in confidence about my dad. Mother talked about my father's behavior as if he were a child like me. I didn't understand what was wrong, but I heard her ask my uncle why my Grandmother Graeme, Dad's mother, couldn't make him change. My uncle's tone was harsh, but I heard the break in his voice as he replied, "She has always loved him more than me." This made me feel sorry for my uncle. I didn't know that parents loved one child more than another.

At that point in my life, Granny Graeme was the bossy old lady who lit into me for leaving a Christmas gift she had shipped from Tennessee outside in the rain. It was a large yellow toy car with pedals, in which I could sit and steer around on my own. The month after I ruined the gift, she arrived in Sarasota, apparently to heckle five-year-old me for the car's abuse. "Forgetting to protect your toys is a problem of character," she said. "It suggests lack of gratitude and a failure to understand the consequences of neglect."

She frowned at me and continued to interrogate me like a prosecutor in a courtroom.

"Do you understand what character is, young man?"

I clapped my hands to my head. "No ma'am!" I shouted.

Thus began my Grandmother Graeme's second chance to mold a boy named Albert. She was determined not to fail again.

MY FATHER'S BOND WITH HIS MOTHER is memorialized in a packet of letters they wrote to each other while he was in Europe during World War I. The many letters, kept in the family for years, have been featured along with other collections of letters from that period in magazine articles and a television documentary on the History Channel. They are now part of a collection at the Tennessee Historical Society.

The letters contain exhortations from my grandmother to live a "pure" and Christian life and promises from my father to return and to make his parents proud. My father's letters contain pleas for food packages and for more letters from my busy grandparents, who seem to have been distracted by home front tasks that my grandfather expansively described as "running the war effort in Tennessee." (Major Rutledge Smith, dressed in uniform, chaired the Tennessee Selective Service and other state defense projects in World War I.)

When the topic turned to combat, my father's letters home were graphic, credible, and poignant. They were written by an idealistic twenty-one-year-old who never rose above the rank of corporal, a figure who seemed so different from the father we knew that my sister says the author was "a man I never knew."

Rejecting officer training school, my father had been a scout for a field artillery battalion commanded by a cousin. Although he wasn't wounded, his emotional scars, which my mother described as "shell shock," were sufficient to earn him a disability pension. He returned from France so jumpy that before he left for college, he asked the night policeman, at Cookeville, Tennessee, to walk home with him anytime he was out very late. He was physically brave; I once saw him swim through storm waves with a rope to rescue a disabled boat. And later, when we lived on a farm in Tennessee, he grabbed a car crank and chased away an angry tenant, despite the fact he had a broken arm in a sling. But he was a haunted, restless sleeper, always afraid of the dark, who usually ended his nights dozing off in a chair while reading a magazine. Or he slept alone in another bedroom, the light left on.

Muff and Al met when she was a reporter for a weekly newspaper and he was a student in a nine-month law course at Cumberland, a little college in Lebanon whose graduates earned their licenses by "reading" law and working for a firm before taking the bar exam. They married when he was twenty-three and she was eighteen and moved to Marianna, Arkansas. Dad clerked there for two country lawyers, the Daggett brothers.

It might have been the arrival of a sickly baby who soon died, or the desire to strike it rich in the real estate boom. Whatever the reason, my parents left Arkansas in 1925 and moved on to Florida.

My father was popular in Sarasota, and my mother was glad to put some distance between herself and the other Smiths. At that time Sarasota was a beautiful little town of eight thousand, where palms, hibiscus, bougainvillea, and memorial oaks flanked Spanish Mission and Mediterranean-style homes and stores. More than I was aware at the time, my father was challenged by problems with money and booze when we moved there. But he and my mother were still in love, buoyed along by dreams of better days.

Life in Sarasota was glorious in those early days. John Ringling boosted civic spirits by moving his circus winter quarters there. Parades, pageants, baseball games, and fairs stirred the blood. Princess Cantacuzene orated to school children on the greatness of America and of her grandfather, Ulysses Grant. Will Rogers did rope tricks on the stage of the Edwards Theater; boxer Jim Braddock, only recently deposed as heavyweight champion of the world, gave me an autograph; and Dad and I saw fat old Babe Ruth waddle from first to second in an exhibition game with the Red Sox.

MY FIRST YEAR OF SCHOOL WAS A PARTY. Graduating from story hours with my mother and Grandmother Ella, I started reading on my own after a few weeks of Mrs. Clark's first-grade flash cards, the most useful exercise I would experience in a regular classroom until I went to cadre school at Fort Sill, Oklahoma.

In the spring of 1934, I finished first grade at Bay Haven School in triumph as leader of the class band. I could barely keep time, but I carried the evening in a red and white cape my mother made, waving an ivory baton given to me by our friend Merle Evans, conductor of the Ringling Circus band. Whether it was the cape, my curly blond hair, or my poise in public, I'm not certain, but when school reopened the next fall, the principal insisted that I skip the second grade in favor of the third-grade class that she taught. Confronted with incorrect assumptions about my skill in arithmetic and without a band to lead, I panicked. My parents' euphoria over the double promotion soon dissolved into a desperate attempt by my father to tutor a catch-up, but the harder he tried, the harder I cried. Finally one night, I told him how it was. "You just don't love me!" I wailed.

Next day, Dad came home early, and we drove out to the circus winter quarters. Slim Haley, the manager, and Johnny, the horse boss, were waiting. There was a surprise—a coal-black Shetland pony with a gorgeous full mane and a forelock almost to its nostrils. I don't know whether the horse was purchased that day for $50 or won the night before in a poker game. Whatever its provenance, the pony was mine, saddled and ready for action. He was a veteran of five years in the ring spent with a troupe of other ponies, circling under the big top for bareback riders, tumblers, clowns, and assorted whip-crackers. A peace offering from a distressed father to a troubled son, he was headed for early retirement at The Acacias.

"What's his name?" I asked timidly.

"We call him Tuffy," said Johnny.

"Why is that?" my father innocently inquired.

"Because of this here big tuft of hair," Johnny said, twisting the beast's forelock until he bared his teeth and shot his ears back. "Did you ever see such a tuft? Almost thick as his tail."

No, we hadn't seen such. Ignoring the twitching tail, I was encouraged to mount and steer the pony onto the road. Tuffy and I followed my father in his Essex out to the Tamiami Trail and then south a mile towards home.

As we turned into the gate at The Acacias, Tuffy changed his mind. Bucking twice, he tossed me into an oleander bush, whirled around, and galloped back to the circus. By suppertime, my father had walked Tuffy back to The Acacias as my mother drove the car slowly behind to keep them company. Dad tethered Tuffy on the front lawn for the fishermen in the bay to admire at sunset. My mother put iodine on my cuts. That night, we skipped the homework.

My skills with fractions, long division, and decimals improved, but there would be no détente with Tuffy. That horse had my number. He bit, kicked, and butted me, bucked whenever I took the reins, and made several escapes to the circus. He was the only chronic runaway pony in all of Sarasota.

The following summer, at age eight, I made a confidence-building trip to Tennessee on the train by myself. At the Nashville farm of my Aunt Dollie and Uncle Lad, I regained my nerve and began to ride gentler steeds.

By the time I went home to Florida, Dad had swapped Tuffy to some local dairy farmers, the Whitakers, for a three-month supply of milk.

There is a picture in a Sarasota history book of the noted equestrienne Marjorie Whitaker riding a horse in a Christmas parade. Thankfully, the photo does not show a younger Whitaker female, the one they called "City," who was about my age. City had waved to us as she rode by—on a coal-black Shetland pony.

-3-
Little Boy on a Train

MY TRIP ALONE ON THE TRAIN TO NASHVILLE the summer of 1935 was the most grown-up thing I had ever done, even more significant than drinking my first Coke. Roosevelt was still in his first term and I was still eight years old, but my world was changing.

Traveling first class in a Pullman sleeping car, I was in the charge of a smiling porter, who must have seen my father tuck a dollar bill in my pocket to award the man for my safe arrival in Atlanta. My protector escorted me to the dining car, where I proudly ordered dinner from the menu all by myself, making sure the dessert was pie *and* ice cream. Having feasted until I was satisfied, I thanked, paid, and tipped the waiter as my mother had instructed and found my way back to the sleeper, where the covers of a lower berth had been turned down, but no adult hovered to cut off the lamps.

I'd brought along a bag of books for the trip, enough to get me through summer months on the Nashville farms of my relatives—if I read them twice. *Black Beauty* and others from my Grandmother Ella's room, which I could now read for myself, were on the top of the bag. Hidden underneath was a stash of "Big Little Books," cartoon stories I purchased every Saturday at Kress from a quarter's allowance that also bought a picture show ticket and a candy bar to fight off any hunger I might experience while Tom Mix dispatched the bad guys. Since I suspected Granny Graeme would object that I was reading trash, the Big Little Books—about Dick Tracy, Terry and the Pirates, and Flash Gordon—were out of sight when the Tennessee welcoming party met me at Union Station.

My Smith grandparents, my Uncle Lad and Aunt Dollie, and a clutch of young cousins hugged me. Then, leading the way as if he owned the station (some of the children thought he did), my grandfather, who we referred to as "the Major," directed us into cars for the ride to the Williams' Mill Creek Farm. There we celebrated with fried chicken, corn on the cob, garden tomatoes, and freshly churned ice cream.

After supper, Aunt Dollie brought out a banjo, and we sat around the picnic tables singing her favorite campfire songs for kids: "The Blue Ridge Mountains of Virginia," "Coming Around the Mountain," and "My Old Kentucky Home" (a prophetic choice given where I ended up). Then my grandparents climbed into their big Packard and drove off to their own farm, Chateau Graeme, five miles away on the Cumberland River.

Later that night, lying on my cot beside my cousins out on the screen porch, I pulled up a blanket against the early evening chill. My heart was warm with love. I was in heaven with the angels, and no Florida problems would disturb my sleep.

I WAS STILL EIGHT WHEN THE DEPRESSION became very personal. My father, although lucky to have a job, took a pay cut. My sister spent several weeks in a Tampa hospital with a kidney infection. My mother, her voice hollow and depressed, took to her bed for days with a diagnosis of "anemia." While Mother tried to rally with a dollop of sherry and raw eggs, Dad began relying on a flask of "tonic" he kept in his glove compartment. I developed asthma, and tests showed I was allergic to everything I enjoyed—notably dogs, cats, chocolate pie, and fried chicken.

For help with my illness, Mother consulted the pharmacist at Badger's Drug Store, whom she called "Doctor." He treated me with a shot of castor oil mixed with orange juice. When that prescription failed to clear my lungs, Mother would take me to Brother Anderson for "an adjustment." The laying on of hands by the warmhearted chiropractor-preacher usually caused me to relax, throw up, and start breathing more easily.

Once I finally learned to swim, I trusted Brother Anderson enough to let him baptize me. My commitment to Jesus Christ as my personal savior took place on a Sunday afternoon near the Ringling Bridge. I was baptized in a part of Sarasota Bay that my father had pronounced polluted, but I survived the exposure, perhaps because of certain guarantees Brother Anderson and I made to our Heavenly Father.

That night, my mother froze a tray of pineapple sherbet, and my grandmother ironed on my shirt two Little Orphan Annie Club logos I had received by mailing a label from an Ovaltine can to Annie's radio announcer, Pierre Andre. I don't remember what I did with my secret ring and the decoder. But I do remember that when my father asked a special blessing for me at supper, I was wearing the shirt. It was like another bandleader cape or my Indian costume, but more mature.

Becoming a Christian was a comfort I needed after several confrontations with death. My uncle Marcellus Bush of South Carolina, who was married to my mother's sister Kate, died in a car crash, and my father took it hard. Dad got drunk as we packed for the funeral. Then he told my mother he was taking his pistol from the war; if it turned out that Uncle "Cell" was blameless, he could shoot the other party involved in the accident.

A.K. Foster, who was twelve years old, also died, drowning in the public pool at Lido Beach Pavilion unnoticed by lifeguards. The son of Mr. Foster at the post office, who was also my Sunday School teacher, A.K.'s death left me a legacy of guilt because I successfully pleaded I was too young to go to his funeral. I guess I also wondered why a loving God would let the son of a Sunday School teacher die.

Then God showed His benevolent hand. He spared the life of James, the yardman who took over when Ward and his family left The Acacias.

James had been shot by another man, and was running a fever and talking giddily when Dad and I visited him on his sickbed in a cabin north of town. My father said James was in the wrong, that he was a sinner who had coveted another man's wife. But God worked in mysterious ways; he raised James from near-death to organize the cleanup after the Hurricane of 1935 blew down a pile of tree limbs in our yard.

The day James and I raked at that brush, Mother called to me with two pieces of lemon meringue pie, "one for each of my heroes." James, almost blinded by sweat, reached for the pie, then dropped it—plop!—upside down in the dirt beside his rake. Gasping at the catastrophe, I handed him the other slice on a paper plate. "Here, James, take mine," I said. "I'll get another in the kitchen." Shortly thereafter, startled that I had committed an unselfish act, I ran crying to the house, where, I knew, there was no more lemon meringue pie.

As a prelude to repenting my sins in church, I had confessed to my parents what I knew about the mysterious disappearance of a little savings bank that Prince Mike had given me. It was a toy replica of the Palmer Bank, with a slot for coins at the top and a lock at the bottom to which I had no key. One day, disheartened by so many oppressive encounters with bad news and stricken by a craving for a Baby Ruth at the grocery near our home, I took an axe and smote the little bank asunder. Then I snuck away to the store and with my ill-gotten gain appeased my candy attack.

My parents weren't aware of the robbery until I became so nauseated at supper that I told them what happened, leading them to the hoard of leftover pennies I had hidden in a drawer. To my relief, they hugged and kissed me, perhaps sensing that my crime was what would be called in today's psychological jargon "a cry for help."

Nevertheless, Dad soon shifted responsibility for the crime. Remembering that I had played after school that week with some poor white kids, the oldest of whom was named Joe, Dad quickly rejected the obvious truth for a conspiracy theory: bad companions.

"It was Joe who put you up to it, wasn't it?" Dad asked.

"No," I said. "I just wanted some candy."

"Well, let's not play with Joe and his brothers anymore."

That was my father: At time of trial, find denial.

THE YEAR I TOOK THE TRAIN TO NASHVILLE was the first of three carefree summers I spent in Tennessee with my Smith relatives. My Aunt Dollie, my father's sister, was the queen of "let's pretend," so accomplished at cheering us through the Depression that she later owned and directed children's camps for fifty years.

Dollie, who had graduated from Vanderbilt as a state champion tennis player, had two daughters, Marion and Eudora, and a son, Malcolm. But motherhood hadn't slowed her down. She could still ride a horse, swim a river, beat most anyone in tennis, play the piano and guitar for sing-alongs, and organize each day from dawn to dusk with one goal in mind: making sure children had fun. She and my Uncle Lad, who with nail, hammer, and saw provided the infrastructure for Dollie's Peter Pan world of never-grow-old, turned their farm at Mill Creek in Nashville into a playground where I could forget life back in Florida.

Summers at Aunt Dollie's and Uncle Lad's were filled with storytelling, canoe races, croquet tournaments, and wild west rodeos. There were two clay tennis courts, a swimming hole, homemade swings and seesaws. There was a stable of docile ponies and horses and a barn with trunks of costumes for plays and games. There was even a sleeping porch lined with cots for the Williams children, their cousins, and any extra children who slept over after one of the potluck picnic suppers to which local families flocked with dozens of kids in tow.

Dollie was a leader like her mother, and had married a strong, stoical man like her father. Lad Williams, the son of a railroad engineer, had grown up in Chattanooga. He earned enough as an engineer with the Tennessee Utilities Commission in Nashville to keep a rocky hillside farm staffed with a cook and field help. What Uncle Lad loved was helping Dollie enchant the world for one child at a time.

Closer to Nashville than Aunt Dollie's house was the more formal home of my grandparents, Chateau Graeme. That farm was a picturesque stretch of bluegrass meadows and river-bottom cornfields that was also supported by income from other sources. At least once a week during those wonderful summers, I'd crowd into the Major's Packard with my cousins—eventually there were seven of us—and head out for a night on the town. The Major was a savvy freeloader of train tickets and show passes from his newspaper, railroad, and political connections. Whether it was vaudeville at the Princess Theatre or wrestling matches at the Hippodrome, these evenings were generally free.

MY NASHVILLE RELATIVES, as well as my Uncle McGregor's family, enjoyed a security we didn't know in Sarasota, where my own family grew increasingly troubled by Dad's emotional instability. At the end of the summer of 1937, when I was ten, I learned that we were leaving The Acacias. Because my father had been unable to arrange its sale, he had lost the contract that had allowed us to live there. We moved to a little house he had bought on an obscure drive in north Sarasota. Grandmother Ella had a tiny bedroom and bath adjoining the garage, and my sister and I shared a room. My parents moved into the only other bedroom, which meant my father had to end his sleepless nights in the living room.

The week after we moved from a mansion to the shabby cottage, I found a pint of Four Roses concealed in the sun visor of my father's Chrysler. When I asked my mother why it was there, she told me my father's drinking was out of control. Her answer filled me with as much shame and guilt as I'd felt the afternoon I broke into my toy bank.

Thus began a terrible year of waiting every night for my father to come home so that I could scrutinize, evaluate, and score his degree of sobriety. My mother was complicit in this game, but it left me wracked with feelings of disloyalty. I ended up resenting them both.

One night that winter, as my mother, my grandmother, my little sister, and I huddled in terror on the back steps of that wretched house, my crazed father stood out in the yard with a shotgun, muttering to himself. Suddenly he raised the gun, pointed at the sky and ... *Bam! Bam!* ... he squeezed off two shots. Then he walked into the house, put the gun away, and went to bed.

The next month, Uncle Robin sent a check to Sarasota for a train ticket to carry my grandmother to South Carolina. My Grandmother Ella had survived the Civil War and Reconstruction, two other wars, the deaths in infancy of three children, a traumatic injury to her husband, farm panics, bank busts, and a fire that destroyed everything she owned. But she was eighty-one. She deserved not to be frightened by her youngest child's husband, the man she had loved back when he led the singing at the Church of Christ.

Was it the war that made my father that way? How many German boys did my father kill, close up, and never forget? He never said, nor did he explain a German helmet with a hole in it he brought back from France. My grandparents' expectations for their first-born son may have been as much to blame—they were such strivers. Perhaps it was just the Four Roses. To this day, I do not know.

At the train station, Dad embraced Ella hard. He broke away and wiped his eyes, then tipped the porter, who promised to take good care of her. As the train moved out, we waved at the old lady, who waved back through the window.

Grandmother Ella lived eight more years, dying in 1945 after President Truman—a more decisive leader than James Buchanan—dropped the atom bomb. Eight more years, but we never saw her again.

-4-
"Just Write, Albért, Just Write"

I DON'T KNOW HOW MOTHER FOUND Marguerite Barthes—
known as "Maddy," short for "Mademoiselle"—and her Joan of Arc
School, where I spent my afternoons after "official" school ended
once my Grandmother Ella left us. I was bored by an austere sixth-
grade teacher, Mrs. Kickliter, about whose frosty style I complained
daily to Mother, and I needed something extra. Maddy provided it. At
her little school in her home on Hyde Park near Sarasota High School,
I would be out of my mother's hair, and perhaps would acquire some
skills in crafts, in which I had no interest, and in French, for which I
saw the potential but lacked the discipline.

Maddy was a short, stocky, square-jawed woman with a slight
mustache, olive skin, and long black hair plaited and roped around the
top of her head. If not ugly, she wasn't pretty, but she had a lovely
smile and an engaging habit of hugging even the most difficult kids.
Despite her obvious liking for me, we began poorly because we
started on the wrong end: with my hands instead of my head or my
heart. Mother had told her about the discarded Tinkertoys, the rusted
tool box, the hated picture puzzles, and the disastrous adventure with
Boy Scout knots. Maddy, accepting my ham-handed past as a
challenge, gave me a warm squeeze and some pieces of leather to
make a belt.

Even at ten, I knew that braiding leather belts was for inmates.
Besides, it was a waste of time—you could buy one at Kress. Maddy
soon learned that I was a stubborn case and reassigned me to
construct a desk. With another positive squeeze, she handed me off to
her partner, Miss Wealtha Bevier, a much-admired science teacher at
the high school. Ms. Bevier shared with Maddy the proprietorship of

the Joan of Arc School, a tiny stucco house with a porte-cochere for their Ford roadster, and a bedroom with one bed.

Miss Bevier was tall, blonde, buxom, and sturdy. In addition to her science classes, she coached the shot put, the high jump, and girls' track. Able to repair the car or unstop the toilet, she was the man of the house, so to speak.

Miss Bevier, who was of Alsatian descent, and Maddy, the daughter of a wealthy Parisian lawyer, were a curious bonding of German and French. They had met somewhere in the northern United States, but in earlier years, Maddy reportedly had been a tutor for the English royal family at Buckingham Palace.

Together the women had established a menagerie of chickens to lay eggs, goats to milk, and rabbits to skin for hats and food. Each of their creatures had a name, including a goat called Yvonne that they eventually gave to me as a Christmas present. Miss Bevier styled rabbit fur hats for the high school drum majors, and Maddy delivered the goat's milk to a circuit of Sarasota asthmatics. For awhile, I was privileged to collect eggs from the hen house, another repetitious trick to build my character.

I viewed the desk project with as much disdain as the belt. Miss Bevier, guessing my intentions to fail, finally gave in and assembled the pieces herself. Progress was made once we adopted a reward system—thirty minutes of badminton, quoits, or croquet for every half-hour I spent sanding the desk or memorizing French nouns and verbs. The afternoons' best moments came when, fortified with a cookie and a glass of Ovaltine, I stood behind Maddy at the piano, where we sang, *"My grandfather's clock was too large for the shelf, so it stood ninety years on the floor…"* and *"Oh the days of the Kerry dancing, oh the ring of the piper's tune, gone alas, like our love too soon…"* There were French songs too: "March of the Kings," "In My Wooden Shoes," "Frere Jacques," and the national anthem, "La Marseillaise." We sang at the top of our lungs until my father came to the door to fetch me home.

My afternoons with Maddy were wonderful, but that fall of 1938, I fell apart again. Transferred at age eleven to the seventh grade in Sarasota High School, I staged a tantrum every morning until Maddy finally called and suggested my parents send me to her full-time. So began the best year I ever had in any school anywhere.

By then I could ride a bike, and each morning I pedaled several miles along the bay front to Five Points and across town to the little house on Hyde Park, where Maddy always greeted me with a hearty "Bonjour, Albért," and a cup of hot chocolate. Then we sang songs in French and English to raise our spirits for the book lessons and blackboard to come.

Maddy taught me everything except math, which she saved for the unfortunate Miss Bevier in the afternoons, along with the desk, which by then was in need of varnish or shellac—I still can't tell the difference. I suppose I won out; the project eventually went to another pupil who could.

I had three classmates at Joan of Arc: a girl named Teddy and two boys named George. Teddy Hamlin was a bright, pretty redhead whose father was the creator of the cartoon strip *Alley Oop*. One George was George Roper, a polio victim who was in a wheelchair. George Roper's father manufactured stoves, but was divorced from George's mother, who had moved to Sarasota with George and a handsome chauffeur who served as George's personal attendant. I don't recall the surname of the second George, but I know he had enrolled with us to escape a world in which the other kids called him "Fatty."

Day after day, Maddy's instructions to me were the same. "Just write, Albért," she'd say, pronouncing my name "Al-bear" as she would in French. "Just write!"

And she meant it. This wasn't weaving a belt or feeding rabbits, and we didn't play around. Whether it was a book I read, a movie I saw, a radio program I heard, or a field trip we took in her roadster, Al-bear had to write a report.

When Princess Cantacuzene stood up to tell the children of Sarasota about the Civil War, I sat down to take notes and write a coherent story. I wrote about the state fair in Tampa, the orange groves and celery farms on the Palmer properties, a reptile zoo, the Indian middens, the mullet catch, the circus, the Ringling Museum, and movies, with Paul Muni as Louis Pasteur, Will Rogers and Irvin S. Cobb in *Steamboat Round the Bend*, and Charles Laughton as Captain Bligh. I read biographies—of Napoleon, Washington, Andrew Jackson, Emile Zola, Teddy Roosevelt, and the Louisiana pirate Jean Lafitte—then wrote reports about them that I read to the class.

As a gifted teacher, Maddy's requests were clear: "Tell me how things work. What do they mean? Write it all down, Albért. Write it all down."

LATE IN THE SUMMER OF 1939, my parents gave Robin and me some exciting news. We were leaving Sarasota and moving back to Tennessee to become farmers. My father's parents would help us acquire the land and pay off our debts in Sarasota. As they saw it, our problems were caused by "the war," and they felt an obligation to help their oldest son, who had fought so bravely for all of us in France.

We would say goodbye to Maddy and our other friends, sell our house in Sarasota, and spend the winter with my grandparents in Nashville, looking for a farm to buy the next year. Close to nature and God, we were promised, the farm life would be a fresh start for Dad. Away from the Gator Club and other Sarasota saloons, he would quit drinking.

This pledge, however, became difficult to keep after the Major's check arrived. Many of Dad's debts were recorded on bar tabs. As he made the rounds to pay the bills, his old companions grew sentimental and offered toasts to his future. It wasn't long before Dad wasn't fit to finish the details. Mother called his parents, and another check arrived, this one for an airplane ticket to Nashville. Dad's buddies gathered up their old friend and poured him onto a plane at Tampa.

In September, with everything loaded on the mover's van, Mother packed Robin and me into the Chrysler for the two-day drive to Tennessee. Al-Bear and his sister fought in the back seat nearly all the way.

-5-
Chateau Graeme

MUFF PRESSED THE HORN AND GUNNED THE CHRYSLER up the hill to my grandparents' house. The Major tugged the rope to ring the big bell on the back porch. My father came in from cutting hay, smelling of sweat, not whiskey, as he hugged us. Granny Graeme charged from the kitchen, a feast of chicken frying on the stove. It was a jubilee! My smiling father, dressed in a khaki shirt, riding breeches, and cavalry boots, looked more the farmer than the tipsy lawyer in a tropical suit he had been in Sarasota. My mother was glancing at him affectionately. The Major took Robin and me each by a hand as we walked to the dinner table. We were rescued.

As I lugged our suitcases up the stairs after supper that night, I believed Dad would stay sober here in Tennessee. Stronger sentinels than I were standing guard. A new World War was breaking out in Europe, but my grandparents had brought their soldier home for a second time by negotiating a truce between him and the bottle.

Chateau Graeme was the fondly pretentious name the Major had given to the Victorian house and two hundred acres he bought in 1921, when he and my Granny Graeme agreed they had outgrown their prospects in Cookeville. The sprawling frame house, with its high ceilings, angled rooms, and odd porches, resembled a sailing ship anchored among tall trees in an immense yard where six sheep and a dozen horses grazed. (The horses, which were spoiled for lack of riding, were kept "mostly for show," my grandfather admitted, perhaps to remind him of how far he had come from poverty in the mountains.)

Inside, the house was a wonder, another "show" put together with trophies from Graeme's tireless scavenging for furniture with a history. Nineteenth century bric-a-brac filled the front hall, parlor, library, and two dining rooms. Rifles from every war in America's past were suspended over a special fireplace. Each of the five bedrooms had its own wardrobe and fireplace, although a few tacked-in closets, a third bathroom, and a coal-fired furnace for steam heat were concessions to modern times. My grandfather contributed music: He owned and could play a piano, a trumpet, a mandolin, an accordion, and a pump organ.

The farm had been the Major's plaything until Dad's arrival put it to work. Dotted with barns, tenant cabins, and other outbuildings, two large fields lay between the house and a mile of fertile bottomland along the Cumberland River. Chateau Graeme fronted the Lebanon Road in Donelson, a Davidson County community five miles east of downtown Nashville. The area was named for John Donelson, my grandmother's great-great grandfather, who fought off Indian attacks as he led a party of settlers to Nashville in 1780. John Donelson was the father of Andrew Jackson's wife, Rachel. Jackson's Nashville home, the Hermitage, was near enough to Chateau Graeme to add a dash of credibility to my grandmother's boasts of being kin to Jackson through "our Donelson connections."

Remote though their connection might have been, "Old Hickory" was a presence in Granny Graeme's house, invoked by a horsehair sofa that she said came from the Hermitage; a "Jackson Press," or cabinet, in the kitchen; copies of paintings of "General" Jackson and Rachel in the front hall; and books about Jackson and the Hermitage in the library. A thick file of correspondence from my grandmother's campaign to commission a portrait of "Aunt Rachel" to hang in the White House also served to remind us all that we were related to a president, if not exactly kissing cousins.

Although Rachel Jackson, who died before Jackson's first inauguration, was never First Lady, my grandmother reasoned that she at least deserved to have her likeness in the White House, where her widower served two terms. So Granny Graeme commissioned the popular magazine illustrator Howard Chandler Christy to copy a portrait of Rachel. When a White House arts panel disqualified Christy, Graeme was enraged.

Although she knew little about art, my grandmother was a zestful combatant over historical issues. As state president of the Daughters of 1812 and head of the Ladies Hermitage Association, she argued that the art snobs had sullied Rachel's character. Though her accusations were a bit misguided—it was Christy's artistic talent that was questioned, not Rachel's importance—General Jackson himself, who killed a man in Kentucky in a duel over Rachel's honor, could not have been more indignant. Appealing to her friend Cordell Hull, the Secretary of State and a fellow Tennessean, she ultimately won a reversal, or so she said.

Granny Graeme was also a daughter of the Civil War. She raised my pulse as she dramatically told the story of her heroic uncle. A Yankee commander in Nashville had threatened to exile her Confederate mother, Eudora McGregor, to either Florida or Canada. Risking capture or death to save his sister, Uncle Paulding Anderson, a Confederate colonel, galloped his bay horse into Lebanon, where he breached Union Army lines by moonlight to call out the mayor, a Union loyalist. Shaking her fist, Graeme channeled Uncle Paulding as she repeated his threat to the mayor: *"If as much as one hair on my precious sister's head is harmed, by the Eternal, I will come back and kill you!"* In my grandmother's world, history was the story of courage. Heroes need not be famous to earn a chapter, just show some spunk.

Whenever I climbed the stairway to our second-story quarters, I passed a photograph of Graeme, a broad slash of ribbon across her bosom, gowned and pearled for action as state regent of the Tennessee Daughters of the American Revolution. In demand to orate at Fourth of July picnics or Memorial Days under the maples in the cemeteries, she was a firecracker who rendered aging veterans teary-eyed. With hats off and hands on their hearts, these men, who had braved enemy cannon in their youth, jumped to their feet as Graeme sat down and the band struck up. My admiring grandfather concealed his pride in her patriotism with a joke. "She is an old battle-ax," he said.

"The thought of peace disturbs her mind."

THE WEEK AFTER WE ARRIVED IN NASHVILLE, Mrs. Rutledge Smith bustled into the office of a startled headmaster at the prestigious Montgomery Bell Academy to plead for a last-minute scholarship for the abashed grandson at her side. Tested on the spot, I was deemed strong in English, weak in math, and rejected for anything less than paid tuition. Changing strategies, my grandmother accompanied my embarrassed mother to enroll my sister and me in a rural public school near her farm. It would soon be clear, she explained to the principal, Mrs. Allen, that "Albert, Jr." was gifted in "expression" and theatre and would most likely "make a lawyer" or an actor. Thus did she squeeze permission for me to leave school early each afternoon to ride the streetcar into the city to the Nashville Children's Theatre. That resourceful idea, as well as a successful audition, kept me occupied with rehearsals and plays all year. Mrs. Allen, who was also my eighth-grade teacher, was the new angel who unlocked the classroom to free my imagination.

But there would still be homework, this time in animal husbandry: an expensive surprise the Major hauled back from the Tennessee State Fair.

Never was a hog so awesome or ugly as the gigantic Duroc sow that waddled down the truck ramp, grunting and sniffing in extreme displeasure. She was wild-eyed and feverish; her belly, swollen with babies, was about to burst. "Albert, Jr.," the Major said solemnly, "this is the finest hog in Tennessee. Meet Gleeful Lady."

She was the Grand Champion of the fair, he explained, and now she was mine, a gift to build my character and welcome me into farm life. Within the hour, Gleeful Lady went into labor and delivered ten piglets—four of which she rolled upon and crushed and two of which she ate. The remaining four, which Gleeful Lady could not or would not nurse, were bundled in a blanket and taken to my grandparents' bedroom. Watching Graeme sitting by the fireplace as she fed the tiny squealers with a cloth "sugar teat" dipped in warmed cow's milk, I felt anxious and sad, as if thrown again from a bucking pony.

The daily slopping of my prize porker became a duty without a destination. Shackled again to a beast retired from show business, I was certain we were merely marking time until Gleeful Lady could botch another birth.

The care and feeding of Gleeful Lady, however, yielded an unaccustomed companionship with my father, who happily milked a dozen cows while I dealt with my hog. The cows were a legacy my Aunt Dollie and Uncle Lad left Dad when they sold their farm and moved to Louisiana. Their milk was to provide the cash flow Dad and the Major would need for the new home they were seeking for us somewhere in middle Tennessee.

Meanwhile, Dad's labors revived his memories of earlier chores back in Cookeville, where he milked, tended a garden, rode a pony, and drove a buggy to the train station on Friday nights to meet the Major. (My grandfather commuted weekly to Nashville while he was "running the railroad," living weekdays at the Tulane Hotel.)

In those days, the Tennessee Valley Authority (TVA) was transforming Tennessee with cheap electricity, flood control, navigation improvements, reforestation, and new tourism-boosting lakes created by the dams for hydroelectric power. Although my uncles Lad and McGregor loathed the TVA, we welcomed it at Chateau Graeme. My father said that once we acquired our own farm, we could look to TVA for inexpensive fertilizers, advice on soil-building methods, possibly even milking machines.

In the meantime, we observed a few of the old customs at Chateau Graeme. My father milked by hand. Granny Graeme and her farm helpers butchered hogs to make hams, bacon and sausage, souse, lard, and even lye soap. They killed chickens with an axe or by wringing their necks. On two kitchen stoves—one electric, one still fueled by coal—the women canned produce from the garden. My sister and I were tasked to churn milk into butter, the vilest I ever tasted because the cows ate wild onions.

The squirrel and rabbits that Dad shot provided delicious hash at breakfast for everyone, but the four of us also sometimes ate meals on our own that my mother had prepared on a little stove upstairs. Muff needed time-outs from too many hours downstairs with "the old battle-ax," who, she said, wore her to a frazzle.

IN THE AFTERNOONS, home from his office at the Tennessee Central, the Major donned boots to ride horses with my father. My grandfather's steed was a Tennessee Walking Horse named Red Allen. The Major was a sharp dresser and a handsome man—more than six feet tall and strong, with white hair and gray eyes—and a grand sight sitting erect in the saddle. With the confidence of the self-made, he had an air of command that stood out in town or country. Late in the day, he relaxed in a rocker on the front porch of his home, which sat on a bluff that overlooked the highway that led to the towns of his beginnings, Lebanon and Cookeville. My father whispered that Chateau Graeme had once been purchased by a mayor of Chattanooga for his mistress. For Rutledge Smith, however, it was a billboard that proclaimed his success against the odds.

The pro-TVA *Nashville Tennessean* had taken note of my grandfather's decision to decline the government's offer to move the graves of his paternal grandparents before a new lake in the Cumberlands flooded their hillside cemetery. The Major said he would endorse progress and spare TVA the expense of moving the graves because he believed Thomas Jefferson Smith and his wife, Mathilda Puckett Smith, would have been pleased by the prospect that the new lake would raise land values and improve the region's economy. Rutledge and Graeme gloried in industrialization. When a majority of the Ladies Hermitage Association protested that the new Nashville airport was planned for a location too close to the Hermitage, Graeme dissented. The risk of a plane crashing into Andrew Jackson's home, she told the papers, wasn't nearly as serious as a future without the airport.

My grandfather's paternal grandparents' remains weren't the only ones lost to change on the upper Cumberland plateau. My grandfather's parents, Walton Smith and Marion Black Smith, and Marion's mother, Margaret Black, were buried behind the fine brick house the Major had designed and built for his young family in Cookeville in the early 1900s. When my grandparents sold the house and moved to Nashville after World War I, the graves disappeared as the area was developed.

Like most of my ancestors, my grandfather's parents had lived colorful lives. Walton Smith had traveled from Cookeville to Arkansas to enlist in a Confederate quartermaster unit [1] and rose to the rank of captain. Shot through both legs at the Battle of Chickamauga, he was handed over to the care of Marion Black, a volunteer nurse. As he recovered, they fell in love, married in Milledgeville, Georgia, and went home to her mother in Charleston, South Carolina.

Five years after the war, Walton decided to return to Cookeville. With Marion and her mother, he traveled up the Cumberland River by steamboat from Nashville to Carthage, Tennessee. The ox-drawn wagon that transported their possessions on to Cookeville brought Marion's piano, the first in the town according to the Major. Marion and her mother missed sophisticated Charleston and disliked Cookeville, which they considered primitive. The two women were the only Catholics in town, so they attended the Presbyterian church with Walton. When a visiting revival preacher called the Catholic

---

[1] Cookeville, in Putnam County between Nashville and Knoxville, leaned Confederate. But there were also many Unionists in that politically volatile region, which supplied three generals to the federal armies.

Church "the whore of Rome," Marion and Margaret angrily walked out and never went back.

The Major, born in 1870, left school in the eighth grade to work as an apprentice surveyor for the new Tennessee Central Railroad. Four years later, he had saved enough to acquire the *Cookeville Press*, a weekly newspaper, in a trade involving $500 and a wagonload of hogs. He was eighteen, and, as he told me, "I had learned the value of a dollar."

My grandfather always neglected to mention the identity of the seller: his own father, Captain Walton Smith. Of course, the paper might have sold at a fair price. But if there were concessions made in the swap, the Major neglected to mention them; he liked to claim he had achieved everything in life on his own. He was generous with his family, but never failed to emphasize that he had not had the educational advantages he gave his children—boarding schools, fraternity dues, allowances. The first day of each month, when he slipped a $100 check under my grandmother's breakfast plate for household expenses, we all knew that no one had done that for his mother.

My grandfather was unsentimental about the past. He despised it, he would sometimes say abruptly. That was no doubt an exaggeration, perhaps uttered simply to annoy my grandmother, but his attitude toward his ancestors' graves showed that he felt far less attachment to history than did my Granny Graeme. "Some men write history," he'd say. "I'm for those who make it!"

BY NASHVILLE STANDARDS, the Major and Granny Graeme weren't rich: They were "comfortable." In the 1930s, those who had been too risk-averse the previous decade to speculate heavily on stocks or real estate were respected for their prudence. It was clear to me as a twelve-year-old that my grandfather's sterling reputation was based more on his integrity than his money, and he was appreciated for his competent leadership of the state's defense programs—the draft and such—in the previous war.

The Major was the keeper of his own flame. Our walks together around the farm were tutorials, a tad sententious, on how he had learned the value of a dollar. He repeated himself—how he became a registered civil engineer (despite his scant schooling), a congressional staffer, a promoter of the Cookeville region in his newspaper, a secretary of the state press association, an investor in rural banks, and the developer of the Putnam County Fair. By the time he mentioned he had "met the Wright brothers," I was too numb to ask how.

One Sunday morning in the winter of 1939, the Major and I were leaving church when we encountered a frail, elderly man whose uniformed chauffeur was helping him down the steps. "Good morning, Mr. Caldwell," said my grandfather. "Good day, Rutledge," the ancient said indifferently. This tough old lion of Nashville business was James E. Caldwell, a man once so feared that some people would step off the sidewalk when he approached. He had grown rich from more than a half-century of shrewd banking and insurance deals, but his brilliant son, Rogers Caldwell, grew many times richer.

Rogers Caldwell's bond business, Caldwell and Company, had evolved into a $650 million conglomerate of banks, insurance firms, newspapers, industries, mining, and mercantile enterprises by the time it began to collapse in November 1930. Then, as stocks tumbled and an attempted merger with James Brown's Banco Kentucky Company failed, Rogers Caldwell—once called "the J.P. Morgan of the South"—crashed, ultimately taking down one hundred thirty banks across the South. With $7 million of state funds on deposit in banks that Caldwell and Company controlled, the governor of Tennessee asked a federal judge to appoint a receiver to represent the aggrieved citizens of Tennessee. The judge named Rutledge Smith.

On the church steps that Sunday, I recognized the name "Caldwell" as one frequently heard in family conversations. Rogers

Caldwell had become the most hated man in Tennessee, because he had been the richest before he made so many others poor.

I wouldn't have known James E. from Rogers, but I realized that this flinty old man was wary of my grandfather. Everyone in Tennessee business circles had watched to see if James E. could save Rogers and wondered if the Major might be duped by father and son, as he picked up the pieces and assessed the blame. Although neither Rogers Caldwell (nor James Brown,[2] who also crashed) went to prison, and Rogers survived comfortably with the help of a "spendthrift trust" that creditors couldn't reach, my grandfather emerged from the Caldwell workout undeceived and unscathed in the turbulence.

Just as James E. had fought to save his son, the Major was determined to rescue his, and the $50,000 receivership fee he received for settling the Caldwell mess would help him do it.

---

[2] James Buckner Brown was born in 1872. A Louisville banker, politician, and newspaper publisher, he dominated Kentucky banking in the 1920s. He went bankrupt after the merger with Caldwell & Company failed.

-6-
Gone with the Wind

WHEN *GONE WITH THE WIND* CAME to the local Loews Theatre, Mother and I went, packing a cold lunch for the matinee intermission—chicken, deviled eggs, and two Milky Way candy bars. As promised, she treated me to Cokes during the show.

Of course we loved the movie—everyone did—but it was also a day to enjoy each other. My sister, who was recovering from scarlet fever, was sufficiently strong to be trusted with Granny Graeme who, in perpetual denial of illness, was incompetent to nurse sick people of any age but had graciously volunteered to at least keep Robin safe from harm.

After the movie, we speculated over ice cream at Candyland, a local sweet shop, as to whether Rhett and Scarlett would get back together. We agreed that the Hays Office had made the right call in letting Clark Gable say goodbye to Vivian Leigh just as he had in the book: "Frankly my dear, I don't give a damn."

As for the Civil War and slavery, Mother shuddered over the burning of Atlanta and bemoaned the sufferings of Scarlett's family during Reconstruction. Nonetheless, she observed that the South brought ruin upon itself by resisting emancipation. Jefferson Davis had clouded the truth for future generations in the region by defending the conflict as a "War Between the States" over states' rights, but my mother was clear that it was not. "Albert," she said, "the issue was slavery."

Mother had an up-and-down personality—vivacious and interested one day, sad and anxious another. Remembering her severe depressions back at The Acacias, I was grateful to Margaret Mitchell for giving us a book and a movie that engaged our thoughts about our

Southern heritage. After seeing tough Scarlett get on with life, Muff and I were having delicious grown-up talk that was not about ourselves or our family members. I was thrilled to be expressing myself in an adult way while on "a date" with the dearest person in my world. It was doubly exhilarating that she was listening to me seriously.

Mother was bright, well-read in a general way, devoid of prejudice, and idealistic. She believed that government could and should improve the lot of its disadvantaged citizens. She accepted the fundamental tenets of her Church of Christ upbringing, but seemed not to have found any rules in the Bible against drinking, smoking, playing cards, and dancing, all of which she enjoyed.

Sometimes when we talked, she would vent her fears that the promised farm would not materialize, but otherwise our conversational topics were politics, books, and the news from the radio and the papers. She was curious about the lives of writers and the political convictions of newspaper owners. In Nashville she and my father enjoyed the rivalry between publisher Silliman Evans' pro-Roosevelt *Tennessean* and James G. Stahlman's reactionary *Banner*. Mother's happy memories of working on *The Lebanon Democrat* as a teenager and Dad's family stories of *The Cookeville Press* instilled in me a romantic view of journalism. So romantic that I began writing letters to the editor in elementary school.

THE CIVIL WAR WAS STILL TALKED ABOUT at home in my childhood. I heard that "Pappy Nick"—my Grandmother Ella's father—hid for a spell in a cave on the Cumberland River after the Yankee authorities suspected he was helping the Confederacy. ("Doctoring on both sides of the line" was the way I believe it was described.) I was also told that Pappy Nick's wife, Elvira Lassiter Mace, my great-grandmother, had freed the slaves she inherited from her family before Lincoln's Emancipation Proclamation.

In the summer of 1936, when I was nine, my Aunt Dollie took me and two of my cousins, Marion and McGregor, on a car trip through North Carolina and Virginia to see Civil War battlefields and other historic sites. At the Confederate Veterans Home in Richmond, I shook hands with a bewhiskered Methuselah who might have been a drummer boy in Lee's Army of Virginia. We emerged from that visit clutching a packet of small photographs of paintings of Confederate generals that inspired many games back at Dollie's farm. My cousin McGregor and I took turns as Union or Confederate commanders, just as we alternated playing cowboys and Indians while riding Aunt Dollie's horses.

The rise and fall of the Confederacy, however, was not an obsession in my family. The saga of that conflict had to compete with stories our elders passed down: tales of Indian attacks on John Donelson's flotilla to Nashville; stories about the exploits of Revolutionary War ancestors named Puckett and Martin and of Andrew Jackson and Green Babb Cook at the Battle of New Orleans (the last battle of the War of 1812); and accounts of the Tennessean Davy Crockett's battle at the Alamo.

The issue of civil rights was not my family's primary concern in the 1930s, nor were we really very conscious of what blacks might claim those rights to be. But each of the women closest to me helped those on the other side of the color line. The men also probably treated black people well, but it was the women whose demeanor influenced us. Mother, Granny Graeme, and Aunt Dollie treated black people with courtesy and were sympathetic to the hardships of their everyday lives.

When Graeme was driving her car and saw a black woman walking along the highway or a black man whom she recognized, she stopped and offered a ride just as she would with whites. She filled her Model A Ford with sacks of canned vegetables from the cellar and meat from the smokehouse and drove them over to Fisk University as a gift for Mrs. Johnson, the voice teacher who coached the school's famous Jubilee Singers. Aunt Dollie and Uncle Lad took in a teenage "colored" girl from the streets during the Depression, making room for her in their home in exchange for her assisting the cook. And back in Florida, when James, our yardman, was laid up after being shot, Mother sent my father over with meals for him.

Still, when the Daughters of the American Revolution refused to let Marian Anderson sing at Constitution Hall (and Mrs. Roosevelt irked Southerners by arranging for the concert to be given on the steps of the Lincoln Memorial), I don't recall that Graeme, the DAR regent, criticized the organization, even when the president's wife resigned from it.

GRANNY GRAEME AND THE MAJOR were loyal to the ideals of Jackson and the Democratic Party as exemplified by the leadership of Woodrow Wilson and Franklin D. Roosevelt, and my parents stood with them. In every way, all four were what used to be called "New Departure Democrats"—those who believed in leaving the Civil War behind to build a new South and get on with the business of business.

In the spring of 1940, as France and the Lowlands (Belgium and Holland) fell to the Nazi armies and England braced for an invasion, there were no isolationists at Chateau Graeme. It was Winston Churchill's resolute speeches and FDR's call for preparedness that inspired our support, not Charles Lindbergh's America First movement. When Roosevelt and Congress brought back the draft, Governor Prentice Cooper asked my grandfather to organize the Selective Service program in Tennessee for a second time.

Meanwhile, my grandmother had decided I should also help defy the Axis powers, at least in Nashville. Commanding me to pick up her flag, so to speak, she made me memorize a patriotic essay we pulled from a book called—what else?—*The Spirit of the American Flag* for a countywide eighth-grade speech contest. In May 1940, at age thirteen, I "pulled out all the stops" as she had coached me and won the contest. As a county judge presented me with a little gold-plated cup, my grandmother hastened towards the stage to share the spotlight and the credit.

Here We Are Farm

IN LATE SUMMER, 1940, I RETURNED TO TENNESSEE from a visit with my cousins in Miami—McGregor, Jr., then fourteen, and his brother, Wilson, twelve—to learn that the search for a place of our own had ended. We were moving to Hendersonville, a crossroads community about twenty miles northeast of Nashville.

For a purchase price of $6,500, my grandfather and father had settled on a three hundred-acre farm on a gravel road three miles off the main highway between Nashville and Gallatin, the Sumner County seat. Our new home was no plantation; with scanty grass and second-growth scrub timber covering its mostly rocky hills, it was decidedly run down, with a mere twenty acres of tillable cropland. At most, it might sustain some milk cows, a few beef cattle, and a little tobacco for cash.

We would have to do without electricity or running water until the TVA discovered us and ran a line over the gullies. We would live in a weatherboarded log house that had been there since Civil War days. The barbed wire fences needed mending, the sagging gates had to be dragged open, the barn and stable slanted downhill, and the peach trees had gone barren.

But the old owners were leaving the beehives, as well as a tenant family named Dyer with whom we would share the profits of the harvest. We would also share the house and an outdoor privy with the Dyers until we built a tenant house.

When I visited my Florida cousins at their home in Coral Gables, we had spent our time swimming in the pool of their new home. We played tennis at their country club, built a skiff in their backyard, got milkshakes at a Howard Johnson's, saw movies at downtown theatres, and sailed on my uncle's company yacht past Al Capone's retirement mansion and into the waters of Biscayne Bay, where the best fish abounded.

The waters at my new home gurgled up in a springhouse and filled a pond that we bulldozed late that summer. The winter rains ran down the ravines to overflow a creek, across which my sister and I jumped—from rock to log to rock to the mailbox—to meet the school bus that would take Robin to the second grade at her school in Hendersonville and me twenty miles further to a high school in Gallatin.

Compared to The Acacias or Chateau Graeme or Coral Gables, ours was a primitive life, but it was a fresh start. My parents were so excited that they wanted to give the new place on the Center Point Road a special name. I suggested "Here We Are Farm," and that was what they painted on the mailbox.

The transfer of our possessions from Chateau Graeme to Here We Are Farm required a journey of about fifteen miles. We moved to our little farm only seventy-five years after Appomattox. A mile beyond our sagging fences lived Old Man Johnson, a neighbor who claimed to recall seeing a line of Union cavalry processing in single file to battle. Our farm lay in the heart of the heart of old Sumner County, near the eighteenth-century station from whence Casper Mansker and other long hunters explored all the way north to the Green River country before that area became part of Kentucky.

Even if it was mostly rock, ridges and ditches, we had our own land, at last. We would think of ourselves as pioneers, as settlers, the autumn nights pleasant enough, at least until the first frosts that made us fear winter in a drafty old house with no running water.

Accompanying us to Here We Are Farm were Aunt Dollie's cows, my gelding horse Silver Spot (a gift from the Major, and the first animal sufficiently docile to earn my trust), some spare pieces of Graeme's antique furniture, and leftovers from Florida for our half of the house we would initially share with the Dyers. The cargo included the indestructible but still irascible (and perennially pregnant) Gleeful Lady and a Belgian mare named Pearl.

Nowhere in the consignment was either a truck or a tractor. For the heavy lifting and hauling, the plowing and mowing, we would use Pearl and a pair of mules that showed up somehow (by then the Major's checkbook had snapped shut). Our rolling stock consisted of a horse-drawn mower to which we could attach discs and harrows for breaking up the sod, a wagon with iron-rimmed wheels, and the old Chrysler. The car had made it up from Florida, but was spending its last days on a hillside where there dwelled not a single man or boy with the slightest talent for repairing a busted hose or a leaky oil pan.

The Dyers, who had a son my age named June, welcomed us, and Dad and I helped them cut the hay, tobacco, and corn. They in turn helped us, milking some of our cows and cranking the separator for the cream that we poured into ten-gallon cans and loaded on a wooden sled. Pearl pulled the sled a mile down to Center Point Road, where a truck stopped every morning to collect our cream and take it to the cheese plant at Gallatin, twenty miles away.

June and I brought buckets of water up from the springhouse for cooking, drinking, and bathing. An icebox sat on the back porch, but most of the time we had no ice and kept perishable food in the springhouse. At this time, fewer than half the farms in Tennessee were electrified.

My mother had never lived in such primitive conditions. But she remembered the farm skills she'd cultivated in Lebanon as a girl. Thankful to be out of earshot of my grandmother, Mother happily set about canning the vegetables we scrounged from the late-summer garden and helping Robin and me adjust to reading by the light of kerosene lamps, bathing in tin tubs filled with water heated on a wood-burning stove, and making moonlight dashes to the backyard privy (or peeing in slop jars when it was too cold for the trip).

Like Scarlett O'Hara, Muff was getting on with life.

-8-
The Rural Experience

AS IF MR. ROOSEVELT HIMSELF KNEW we deserved better, soon after we arrived at Here We Are, a WPA crew showed up to replace our smelly old three-holer with a more sanitary privy, leaving a bag of lime as a gift from the New Deal. My grateful mother planted some vines around the new amenity and asked my father to make a sign that said "The President's Office," but Dad had little time for scatological humor. He was busy dealing with Nestor Silvey, a crazy neighbor who turned up in our lives just as school began.

Nestor was six feet tall, bearded, brawny and, until winter set in, usually shoeless. He dressed in a pair of overalls with neither the customary shirt nor underwear. Nestor lived with his widowed mother, but in good weather preferred to sleep outdoors in a brush pile.

Once school began, he started waiting in the afternoons on a hillside for the bus to deliver my sister and me to the mailbox near our gate. Nestor never came close or spoke. He just stood still and stared at us as we walked away, glancing back occasionally over our shoulders to see if he was following.

Nestor was scary.

None of the other neighbors was anxious to make trouble over Nestor. In fact, they told us, he hadn't done anything harmful since he threw a rock at Mr. Walter Freed and broke his leg—and that was three years ago.

But my father was the only lawyer on Center Point Road. He went to Gallatin and filed a petition asking a reluctant county judge to commit Nestor to a safe place. When Nestor and his mother showed up in the judge's office, Mr. Freed was the only person willing to testify against Nestor besides my father.

Nestor arrived at court clean-shaven and in a white shirt, dress pants, and shoes. We heard it had taken two cousins to wrestle Nestor down for a shave, a bath, and the outfit, but the judge didn't know it, and the Silveys seemed likely to prevail until the judge called a recess. It was then that Nestor reached over to the basket of fresh eggs his mother had brought to town to sell and popped two into his mouth. When the hearing resumed, Nestor's poor mother was still pleading with him to spit out the eggs, but he adamantly refused.

We never saw Nestor again, and Dad, the newcomer, became an instant hero along Center Point Road.

Our other neighbors were "just the best," my parents said. My parents were sincere and generous with their compliments. Those traits quickly won them acceptance into the community and its customs: sharing work, taking meals to the sick, or just "sitting a spell" to visit.

Carl and Hartwell Choate, bachelor brothers who lived with their mother and stepfather, Charlie Rice, worked at the rayon plant at Old Hickory, but they also farmed a little with Mr. Rice. On Saturday nights, the brothers would pull out their fiddle and banjo, Mrs. Rice would invite us down for ice cream and cake, and the boys and Charlie would entertain us with country songs on their front porch. We could hear the Grand Ole Opry on a battery-operated radio, of course, but Mother told the Choate brothers they were as good as Roy Acuff.

For help with planting, harvesting or cutting wood, my father and I also could count on Babe and John Dillard, who lived in a log cabin down the road. Also bachelor brothers, the Dillards were not very bright. But they were kind and willing to help in most any way we needed.

And John Freed, Walter's son, provided us transportation when our old Chrysler broke down. John, who owned a tiny store and a gas pump on the Gallatin Highway (old-timers called it "the Pike"), would drive all the way back to our place and risk breaking a spring on our rocky driveway to take us to church on Sunday.

John's father and mother, Walter and Ella Lee Freed, were special friends from my mother's youth. Muff's and Ella Lee's mothers were so close back in Lebanon at the turn of the century that Ella Lee DeBow Freed was named for my Grandmother Ella Mace, and my mother was named for Ella Lee's mother, Elvira DeBow. By coincidence, the farm my grandfather and father found for us was only three miles from the Freeds.

Walter Freed, who was older than my father, was small and stooped from too many years of milking. His was a much better farm than ours, and his dairy operation, although heavily mortgaged, was electrified. That meant that machines, not human hands, squeezed milk from the Freed cows' udders. The Freeds also had a tractor and a telephone. When our Chrysler broke down, we "borrowed" their phone to summon a mechanic or ask my grandparents to drive out with supplies from Nashville.

FIVE MILES FROM OUR FARM, Hendersonville became our community center. It had a post office, an elementary school, two grocery stores, a barbershop, and a Church of Christ. With Hendersonville's new high school still under construction, I rode the school bus to Gallatin with DeBow Freed, John's much younger brother, who was a year ahead of me. To emphasize my solidarity with my parents in their new life, I signed up for a ninth-grade agriculture class and joined the Future Farmers of America.

The kindly Ag teacher, Mr. Robbins, explained several facts of reproductive life about which I was hazy. ("We breed mares when they are in heat, Albert, not when the moon is full.") Clearly believing I was better suited to public speaking than to charting the fertility of Madame Gleeful Lady, he pointed me to an upcoming FFA state speech contest.

At lunchtime that first semester, I was welcomed to high school by a sophomore boy, Walter Durham. A red-haired "A" student whose father owned a lumber yard, Walter was mature beyond his years and a member of an old Gallatin family. He was also DeBow Freed's best friend. He had more time than DeBow to talk to me and help me feel accepted in this new school, perhaps because he didn't have to milk twenty cows twice a day, nor try to get into a military academy to pay for college.

Walter's after-school job was more to my interest than cows. At 15, he was the county correspondent for *The Nashville Banner* and a friend of Tom and Marybelle Bancroft, the young couple who had recently purchased the *Gallatin Examiner*, one of two weeklies in town. Walter introduced me to the Bancrofts, both former reporters for daily newspapers, and they suggested I write some news from Hendersonville.

At church, I met another redhead, this one a girl named Jackie Comer. Her father, Monte, and uncle, Guy, were cash-laden and land-rich. The Comers had started out in southern Kentucky as drummers—traveling salesmen—then crossed the border into Tennessee and prospered, in part because they didn't hesitate to exploit their devotion to the Church of Christ, which was strong in the region. The Comers owned Washington Manufacturing Company in Nashville, which made Dee Cee overalls, and also operated a chain of retail clothing stores across Tennessee.

Guy, the president of Washington, and Monte, the vice-president, lived in colonial-style mansions, with horse and cattle barns to match. Their white-fenced, sleekly polished bluegrass farms sat a few miles apart on the highway between Hendersonville and Gallatin.

On Sundays, Monte—a small, soft-spoken gentleman who dressed seven days a week in dark blue suits, white dress shirts, conservative ties, and shiny high-top leather shoes—led the a capella singing at our church. With his soft white hair parted neatly in the middle and his fat pink cheeks puffing like a chipmunk's, he would slap a tuning fork against the hymnal and launch us into one of the great old hymns I had first heard as a little boy in Sarasota. *"My faith looks up to Thee, Thou lamb of Calvary, Savior Divine; now hear me while I pray, take all my guilt away, oh let me from this day be wholly Thine ..."*

"Wholly Thine" to the Comers were thousands of acres of prime agricultural land spreading out from Nashville toward Lebanon and Gallatin. Among their holdings was Clover Bottom at Donelson, once owned by Andrew Jackson and the site of a racetrack on which Jackson pitted his horses against the best in middle Tennessee.

At Hendersonville, our scrubby little farm set back several miles from "Monte Haven," Monte Comer's spread, but Monte and his wife, Marie, had taken a liking to us. The extremely wealthy but unaffected folks did not seem troubled by our lack of money. Certainly we weren't the only family of respectable background who was poor in those days. My parents never appeared to feel either inferior or superior to anyone who was reasonably civil. Perhaps that social ease helped them to gain acceptance at any rung of the ladder from all but snobs or folks with a grudge.

AS WE SETTLED IN THAT WINTER OF 1940, Jackie, who was a student at the private Ward-Belmont school for girls in Nashville, invited me to take her to a dance at my high school in Gallatin. Cowed by all the novelties and obstacles—among them the facts that I had never had a date, that I couldn't dance, that I couldn't drive, and that if my parents drove, our car might not make it to Gallatin and back—I was prepared to decline.

But Mother quickly accepted for me. It soon became clear that Jackie and I had been "fixed up" by our mothers. As their plan had it, the Comers would send their chauffeur in the Lincoln for me and then drive us to the dance. I was so mortified that I prayed for an illness, or that the Comer limousine would break down on the nearly impassable half-mile of rutted driveway from our front gate up to our house. But the chauffeur had his orders. He found me, cowering on the front porch at Here We Are Farm. I don't remember a thing about that awful dance, but I do remember this: I never had another date in high school.

The TVA turned on our lights in late 1940. We wired our kerosene lamps and bought a new radio and a stove, but because we could not afford the pump and pipes to bring water from the spring to our house, a bathroom had to wait. Modernization was not without other costs, however. Before the linemen arrived, a heavy rain fell, and two of Gleeful Lady's newest litter drowned in the water-filled post holes that an earlier crew had dug. Other mishaps claimed a couple more of her piglets. But my teacher Mr. Robbins told me to quit worrying about the livestock and concentrate instead on a new speech I had composed for the FFA oratorical competition.

Lifting a few lines from William Jennings Bryan, I became an advocate for the rural experience. My grandmother boasted that my speaking evoked the rhythms of the "Cross of Gold" speech the Great Commoner had delivered at the 1896 Democratic National Convention.

The reality, however, was that I was beginning to find the going a bit bumpy again. There were still enjoyable days on the farm: hunting with Dad, gossiping together at supper, listening to our new radio. But when the rough times set in during the winter—a snowstorm that kept us housebound, a disappointing milk check, the disabled car—Mother became depressed. Dad forgot his promises and began to turn to his familiar medicine, a pint of Four Roses. All four of us were beginning to feel the old despair.

Unlike our days in Florida, however, Dad was inhibited from prolonged drinking by his daily routines with the cows. Then, one terrible spring morning when Mr. Freed was sick, Dad went over to help DeBow milk the old man's herd. When he came home, he found three of our cows toppled over on their sides, bloated and dying from eating young sorghum cane. My frantic father found a knife and stuck each cow in the ribs to release the gas, but it was too late. Suddenly, we had lost them, a quarter of a year's income gone for a good deed.

A few weeks later, at the state FFA convention at the Peabody Hotel in Memphis, I delivered my optimistic speech about the joys of rural life so eloquently that I was certain I had won. But the judges felt differently and awarded me second place. Stunned, I disgraced myself by bursting into tears before a thousand teenage boys as the winner was announced.

The Dyers had sensibly left Here We Are in the fall of 1940 as soon as the tobacco sold, and the following summer the Fetherton family came to replace them. My grandfather brought out a crew of carpenters and supervised the building of a tenant house for the Feathertons, so we finally could have a house to ourselves. Dad and Tom Fetherton soon fell into constant bickering over the details of their deal to make the once-barren fields fertile, but Oliver, the middle son in the enormous Fetherton brood, became my friend. Barely a year older than I but already a dropout, Oliver had just laughed the day I plowed up a half-acre of corn shoots, having mistaken them for Johnson grass.

As winter drew on, Oliver proved wise in the ways of the woods. He trapped animals to peddle for their pelts and gathered nuts and roots that could be sold in town. One moonlit night when he had taken me on a hunt, we built a fire to warm ourselves while we listened to his two baying hounds chase a fox somewhere on the back of our farm. It was time to talk about dreams.

Oliver said the military coat he was wearing had been passed along to him by a cousin who had worn it in the Civilian Conservation Corps. The coat, or perhaps it was just Oliver, smelled slightly of skunk. But it didn't matter: He would soon get a new coat, he confided, because he was headed for the CCC himself. He would join up when he turned sixteen, or could look it. He would get away from his father and mine, and never come back to this farm.

"What about you?" Oliver asked me.

By that time I had made another grown-up friend, Harold Roney, a cashier at the Bank of Hendersonville. Mr. Roney had a Speed Graphic camera and a car, I told Oliver, and we had decided to become partners in the news business. The new Hendersonville High School had a football team, and Mr. Roney and I thought the community (and we) would benefit if we could get some publicity about sports at the new school into the Nashville papers.

We had pitched our idea to the state editor of *The Tennessean*, and he had signed us on as the paper's official Hendersonville correspondents, or "stringers." I would write or phone in the stories, Mr. Roney would take the pictures, and we would be paid 50 cents an inch for everything of ours the paper printed. At the end of the month we would paste our clippings together in a string, count the inches, and mail them to the paper as an invoice.

"So maybe I'll become a newspaper reporter," I said to Oliver.

By then, the German armies were advancing towards Moscow, and the Nazis submarines were sinking English merchant ships in the Atlantic faster than they could be replaced. Twenty-five hundred Royal Air Force flyers, some of them not much older than Oliver and I, had won the Battle of Britain in the skies over England, discouraging Hitler from an invasion after the collapse of France. But as we heard after Dunkirk, Winston Churchill was still waiting for the New World to come to the rescue of the Old.

Millions of human beings would likely perish before this conflict ended, but we were just two teenage boys eager to leave the farm. I found an old plank to rake over and smother the fire, and Oliver called his dogs off the chase.

Shivering, we started towards home under the clouded, uncertain moon.

-9-
For This We Fight

A FEW SUNDAYS AFTER MY FOX HUNT WITH OLIVER, the Japanese attacked Pearl Harbor.

The news itself settled around us that afternoon like a sudden unfamiliar illness, an enveloping presence that choked off conversation as we tried to process its meaning and listened in silence for what would come next.

Finally, near dusk, my father put on his jacket and went out to the woodpile in the backyard. A week's supply of logs and kindling had already been cut, but he needed to strike at something. Seizing an ax, he began chopping the fire logs in half. He was sober, but I could see the tears on his cheeks as I walked towards the barn to feed the cows, and when I closed the gate and turned away, I could hear him crying.

Next day, Graeme telephoned Mr. Hawkins, the principal at Hendersonville High School, to request that arrangements be made for the students to hear President Roosevelt ask a joint session of Congress for a declaration of war against Japan. Mr. Hawkins assured my grandmother that he had already secured a radio for that very purpose.

By Christmas, with the news grimmer and Germany also in the war, Graeme had mobilized me to write a speech and enter a new national oratorical contest for high school students sponsored by the American Legion. The subject was the U.S. Constitution, about which I was reading in books she brought out to the farm from the Nashville Public Library. The first prize would be a $4,000 college scholarship, worth nearly $60,000 in today's inflation-adjusted dollars.

Soon after I turned fifteen in January 1942, a month after Pearl Harbor, I had finished the speech, an analysis of the guarantees and mandates of the Constitution. The speech began with a recitation of the Preamble:

We the people of the United States, in Order to form a more perfect Union, establish Justice, insure domestic Tranquility, provide for the common defence, promote the general Welfare, and secure the Blessings of Liberty to ourselves and our Posterity, do ordain and establish this Constitution for the United States of America.

The rest was a short summary of the document's articles and amendments, followed by a rousing evocation of historical events in which our country and Constitution had been defended, including the dark days after Pearl Harbor. I ended each example with the refrain "For this we fight."

I was already too much the rebellious adolescent to allow my grandmother one sentence of authorship. Besides, the contest mandated an original speech. To help assure independent work, the rules required that each contestant give an extemporaneous reply to a random question from the judges about the Constitution.

There were no restrictions, of course, on coaching about delivery, and I had in my grandmother perhaps the best public speaker in Tennessee to help me. But Graeme herself decided we needed an evaluation from an expert who might be even better than she.

Though immodest about most of her talent—"Albert, Jr., your grandmother is a remarkable woman," she often said, with a merry, self-satisfied air as well as a twinkle in her eye that suggested the faintest note of irony—the prize at stake merited the gamble that a Mrs. Weems of Dickson, Tennessee, would note some need for a correction that my grandmother might have overlooked.

A professional speech and debate coach who journeyed weekly to Nashville to give private lessons in a suite at the Maxwell House Hotel, Mrs. Weems was the state's premier teacher of "elocution."

She was an aunt and mentor of young Frank Goad Clement, who became a popular, Bible-quoting, hard-drinking Tennessee governor after the war.

Highly esteemed for silver-tongued platitudes from the stump, Clement once gave the keynote speech at a national political convention, about which the columnist Red Smith wrote: "The Democratic delegates were slain last night by the jawbone of an ass."

At the Maxwell House, Graeme wound me up like a talking doll, and I orated on command. Mrs. Weems listened intently, then declared she could find no fault in me. "This lad will go far," she said, taking a deep breath. "Miss Graeme, he is certainly *your* grandson."

By mid-April, I had won three rounds of the contest—in Nashville, Lynchburg, Virginia, and Indianapolis—and my grandmother and I were once again together in a Pullman on a suspenseful train ride, this time to the national finals in Milwaukee.

In the men's lounge on the first lap of our journey, I recognized Nashville Congressman Percy Priest, an ex-newspaperman who was one of my political heroes, and introduced myself to him. Stubbing out his cigarette, he accompanied me back to our seats to greet my grandmother, who was intently thumbing through our travel copy of the United States Constitution.

"Congressman, tell me," said my grandmother. "Do you understand what it means here that Congress is entitled 'to grant letters of marque and reprisal'?"

"No," replied Mr. Priest. "But I will find out and get word to you at your hotel in Milwaukee."

Late the next afternoon, the hotel bellboy brought us a telegram from Priest, in which he explained that letters of marque and reprisal were congressional authorizations that allowed American merchant vessels to engage in combat against maritime interests of countries hostile to the United States.

The next day, when the four of us finalists from across the country had finished our speeches, "marque and reprisal" was the question I drew and glibly answered.

Whether it was her school teacher thoroughness about preparation or her Scottish intuition, Graeme's improvised collaboration with the congressman produced the bullet for the final shot.

I had won the contest that had drawn more than 100,000 entrants.

The judges' announcement was met with cheers and applause from an auditorium full of students and teachers at the largest high school in Milwaukee.

Suddenly, to my dismay, my jubilant grandmother seized the moment. Standing up in the middle of the auditorium, she announced in a thundering voice, "Albert is the grandson of Major and Mrs. Rutledge Smith and the son of Mr. and Mrs. Albert Smith Sr. of Tennessee, and I am proud to have been the coach who trained him for this awesome victory."

I was embarrassed and angry. But this time I did not cry.

ON THE TRAIN BACK TO NASHVILLE, I read a copy of *Time* that Graeme had bought me as a treat and enjoyed listening to her gloat about the value of the scholarship we had just won. Truthfully, I couldn't comprehend that much money, but I was glad it earned me another treat in the dining car. My grandmother, regaling strangers with reports of our triumph, didn't notice I had elevated my dessert order to pie *and* ice cream, just as I had when I traveled alone as a young boy.

Back in Tennessee, the major and my parents had saved the newspaper write-ups that called me a national champion. The *Gallatin Examiner* reprinted my full speech. The *Milwaukee Sentinel* headline read, "Youth from Dixie Talks Judges Out of $4,000." The teachers and students at Hendersonville High, still in its first year of operation, were amazed and pleased over the publicity. They proudly talked about it for a few days, then got on to other things.

Hendersonville was the third school I had attended in the three years since we moved back to Tennessee. Although the teachers were competent—with fewer opportunities for smart women outside the classroom back then, many bright females became teachers—I don't recall learning much in class. The most interesting and informative adults in my life were in my family.

But the teachers I encountered in the rural schools in Tennessee were all kind to me, and lenient about bending the rules for my extracurricular pursuits. Whether for acting in the children's theater in Nashville, chasing down newspaper stories in Hendersonville, or even leaving early to hitchhike to Nashville to meet my grandparents or go to the public library, I was never denied permission to leave school. There was always someone who, like Maddy, encouraged me to find my own way.

I wished I had a girlfriend, but I didn't. Although I was elected president of my classes at Hendersonville, I was always the youngest in my grade and too immature to convert my popularity into a seduction. I envied a male classmate who was so sexy he seemed to drive one of our teachers wild, but while other teenagers in our class began to pair off, I was left to admire old *Life* magazine pictures of Rita Hayworth in secret.

Although I was always outspoken in classes and accepted as a show-off, I didn't give anyone cause to say I had become stuck-up or "different." As more of the stories and photos that Mr. Roney and I produced appeared in *The Tennessean*, the school valued my efforts to include everybody in the spotlight.

That year the male teachers began to leave for the service or find defense jobs to defer them from active service. Rationing was underway for sugar, coffee, meat, cars, farm machinery, tires, and gas. Women and older farm laborers signed up for defense work, and one day Oliver Featherton was gone, accepted at last in the CCC. I never saw him again.

THAT SUMMER, I learned there were other rewards for winning the oratorical contest. A man named Homer Chaillaux, who directed the patriotic efforts of the American Legion's "Americanism" committee, took charge of my public life. He arranged several trips for me to promote the contest and to charm donors for their financial support.

This time I rode the trains alone, first to New York City for a luncheon with the executive committee of the National Association of Manufacturers. The NAM, I learned, had provided funding for the contest's scholarships from an initial commitment by the famous comedian Eddie Cantor, who was returning to Broadway with a new hit called *You're in the Army Now*.

My lunch appearance was a hit, Chaillaux told me, and earned me both an invitation to come back for the national NAM convention in the fall and a promise that the contest support would continue. In the new brown suit and McGregor plaid tie my grandparents had bought for me, I was only two days' journey from Here We Are, where our old Chrysler had finally croaked in a pothole by the front gate. But I might as well have flown to Mars.

That afternoon, Chaillaux took me to a cocktail party in a posh suite at the Waldorf Astoria honoring the country's newest wartime hero, Brigadier General Jimmy Doolittle, who had just led sixteen B-25s, launched from an aircraft carrier, on a surprise bombing raid on Tokyo.

Doolittle gave me a wide grin and a handshake, and then Chaillaux lined me up to meet other aviation stars in the room, including presidents of several airlines and the fabled Eddie Rickenbacker, the World War I ace who would soon become famous all over again by surviving a plane crash in the Pacific.

Amid the party's high-altitude excitement, Rickenbacker was telling me he knew my Uncle Greg in Miami when suddenly the doors swung open. Two middle-age jokesters rushed towards Doolittle, yelling and whooping, then fell to their knees, pulled out pocket handkerchiefs from their coat fronts, and began polishing his shoes.

These were Ole Olsen and Chick Johnson, old-time vaudevillians who, as the comedy team Olsen and Johnson, were making visitors to New York laugh again with *Hellzapoppin'*, a sellout Broadway revival of every wheezy stunt and gag they had learned in burlesque.

That night, Chaillaux and I had free seats for the show, courtesy of Olsen, who promised me backstage that when I returned in the fall he would take me to a nightclub and dinner. (He kept that promise, taking me to the Stork Club with a tall blonde chorus girl from his show.)

Another night we went to the Lambs Club, a dinner club for actors, to a "roast" of movie star Pat O'Brien, where I sat with Navy Lieutenant Douglas Fairbanks, Jr. Uncertain whether Mary Pickford was his mother—she wasn't—I talked about mine.

Before this first junket ended, Chaillaux and I took in a Yankees game, in a good box which he didn't pay for, and were guests at the national radio show that Fred Waring and his "Pennsylvanians" produced on weeknights for Chesterfield cigarettes

Chaillaux was a short, smiling, olive-skinned man of French ancestry, full of pep and savvy, especially about having his way with celebrities. Being boss of "Americanism" for the American Legion was no small thing in a country at war again, where many leaders of high military or political rank were veterans of the First World War.

In addition to his gift for easy small talk with the rich and influential personalities we were meeting, Chaillaux was also given to dropping references, at strategic moments, about enemies to be feared—not the Japanese or Nazis, but "the Commies" here at home. I didn't hear much about those folks back in Tennessee. But Homer

Chaillaux knew who they were, and he told me he often compared notes about them with his great friend J. Edgar Hoover.

Throughout 1942, Chaillaux's largesse with his expense account kept me riding the rails across the country to inspire anyone who would listen, from aging patriots at an American Legion national convention in Kansas City, Missouri, to New York City again. There, I had a brief chat with a distracted Henry J. Kaiser, who had just learned that one of his liberty ships had cracked apart and sunk, with no enemy submarine to blame. After he said "Hello," I'm not sure he knew I was there.

This was a crucial year of the war. General Douglas MacArthur had begun slogging his way back to his lost command in the Philippines, and Admiral Chester Nimitz's amphibious forces were leapfrogging across the Pacific islands. The disasters the American forces had suffered at Pearl Harbor and on Bataan gnawed at the country's pride until the Japanese lost their first major battle of the war to Nimitz and Admiral Halsey at Midway Island.

General Dwight D. Eisenhower's American GIs joined British forces in the campaign in North Africa, finally seizing control of the skies over the Mediterranean. At year's end, a massive counterstrike by the Russian Army at Stalingrad had destroyed more than 200,000 German troops, and it seemed as if Hitler was losing the war in the East.

In the United States, FDR had yielded to anti-Japanese paranoia and removed more than 100,000 Japanese Americans to internment camps out west.

But what I remember most about that time is a sense of America stirring again. Everyone was going somewhere. Buses and trains were crammed with passengers, some standing from depot to destination. The soldiers and sailors, too young to stay awake and worry, slept on their duffel bags in the aisles, and the haggard rural folks squeezed in the coaches, eating greasy biscuits from box lunches as they headed north for jobs in the new defense plants.

The days and nights at home began and ended with "the news" on the radio:

"Eight-fifty-five Eastern Standard Time, and Elmer Davis and the news ..."

"And now, H.V. Kaltenborn and the news ..."

"This is London, and I'm Edward R. Murrow."

Newspapers were different in those days. They could surprise us with something we hadn't heard—"ROOSEVELT IN NASHVILLE," the headline read. It turned out the President had been at Fort Campbell, but he was gone before we even knew he was coming. There were secrets to be kept. Hitler was listening, and "loose lips sink ships."

On each of my two visits to New York that year, I spent some of Chaillaux's expense money in the hotel lobby buying every newspaper the city had to offer—many more than it now has, among them *The Sun-Telegram*, *The Herald-Tribune*, *The Mirror*, *The Journal-American*, and *PM*. Then I would splurge again and buy the papers from Washington.

Upstairs in my room, I would pull down the shades, as hotel guests were instructed, to darken the skyline and make it harder for enemy subs to see our convoys offshore.

I would spread the papers across the bed. And then, beginning with the tabloids, I would read until I fell asleep on top of them.

–10–
School Dazed

BY THE FALL OF 1943, I was enrolled for my senior year in a third high school, Castle Heights Military Academy. My work that summer on two issues of a special newspaper at the American Legion's Boys State program had earned me an interview with the president of the school, which was in Lebanon, the birthplace of my mother and both grandmothers. He offered me a half-scholarship, including room and board, with the understanding that I would try to win a speech award for Castle Heights and pay $500 from my Legion college funds to match the school's contribution.

I assumed a year at Castle Heights would prepare me for the rigorous academic work of a university like Vanderbilt and give me opportunities I otherwise might not have had. At my previous high schools, I had taken few of the requirements for admission to a top-ranked college: little math or science and no foreign or classical languages. The year I spent on the road, speaking across the country after winning the American Legion contest, left no time for chemistry, physics or even geometry. My travel schedule allowed me to do what I liked to do—and gave me good reason to avoid subjects I despised.

Castle Heights was a cultural surprise. Enrolling at age sixteen, I was an academic upperclassman but a freshman ROTC cadet, and I didn't fit in very well at first. The other seniors and juniors who were cadet officers began to scorn me as a brown-noser on scholarship, too eager to please "the enemy," also known as the faculty. I had to endure hazing, even carrying laundry for younger cadets who ranked above me in the ROTC.

For the first time in high school I felt isolated from my classmates, even my roommate. Arthur Shemwell, who was my age but a junior, had been a cadet at Castle Heights since the sixth grade. Arthur was very bright, but he had been there so long he was cynical about the place and scornful of my efforts to get along and be accepted.

By Thanksgiving, however, I had hit upon a strategy to ease the "difference" between me and the other boys. I started smoking, which was against the rules. And at the apartment of a permissive English teacher and his wife, Frank and Peggy Cutwright, I abandoned all inhibitions, smothered painful memories of my father's problems, and took my first sips of whiskey.

CUTWRIGHT WAS THE SCHOOL'S speech and drama coach, so the other cadets he favored with invitations to Peggy's "teas" or dinners had interests beyond sports and were friendly with me. These evenings, where we talked of politics and questioned religion, gave me a place to belong. J.B. Leftwich, another, more straight-laced teacher who was faculty adviser for the school paper and yearbook, took me into a tiny circle of student writers who became the buddies I needed to get through those first months.

Our student newspaper, *The Cavalier*, became my other off-campus retreat. The weekly *Lebanon Democrat* printed the Castle Heights paper, so I could easily get a pass to leave school, walk downtown to the *Democrat* office with *Cavalier* copy, then linger for a Coke and a chat with Frank Burns, the editor.

On Sundays, when we were marched from campus to the churches of our parents' choice, I would enter the Lebanon Church of Christ by the front door, quickly exit through a side door, and slip down the street to the newspaper office. Rapping on a side widow, I roused Bob, an alcoholic Linotype operator who slept off his Saturday drunks on a cot in the print shop. Once admitted through the window,

I would light a cigarette, sit down at Burns's typewriter, and pound out my editorials for *The Cavalier*.

All I needed to become the complete professional journalist was a slug of Bob's whiskey, but I couldn't risk the smell on my breath— not yet.

THAT WINTER, AS THE SCHOOL PRESIDENT HAD HOPED, I won the Mid-South Oratorical Contest with a new speech I wrote about the war. For Cutwright, I acted in several plays; for Leftwich, I edited the yearbook; and for myself, I wrote an editorial attacking the Jim Crow laws that forced Negro soldiers to stand beside empty seats in the white sections of buses. (Leftwich had the guts to print it ten years before *Brown v. Board of Education*.)

Just after my birthday in January, I enlisted in the Army Reserve, beguiled by a new specialized training program for seventeen-year-olds that would place me in college in uniform. In May, I graduated at the top of my class with three other seniors.

When the greatest military armada in history crossed the English Channel on D-Day, I was wearing the uniform of my country. But I feared I had made an awful mistake by enlisting.

I wasn't nearly as worried about the enemy "over there" as I was about the consequences of letting the Army think I was qualified to be "over here" where it sent me—at Vanderbilt University's School of Engineering. Less than a month after leaving Castle Heights, I was in a company of other teenage volunteers, many of whom, unlike me, had studied math and science and had an interest in engineering. *Engineering*: me?

Under the command of an active duty officer and several sergeants, my fellow students and I lived in a dormitory. The required English and history courses were so simple I could have passed their tests without attending a class or opening a book.

We took classes in chemistry, physics, and trigonometry, none of which I had previously studied. The complexities of the math and science put me in a funk. I couldn't comprehend the initial lectures, and I was too agitated to do the lab work. In no time I learned that the only medicine that calmed my anxiety was several beers at a campus bar.

BY MID-AUGUST 1944, my first attempt at college had ended. In Europe, the Allies were moving forward, but at Vanderbilt, my grades unacceptable, I couldn't establish a beachhead. The university and the Army collaborated in a letter of regret from the Provost, Philip Davidson,[3] discharging me from any obligation to either.

I had arrived in college after a spectacular climb from the peculiar circumstances that had taken me from a mansion on a Gulf Coast estate to a log house on a backwoods Tennessee farm. Why was the landing at Vanderbilt so bumpy?

Whether I could have mastered the challenges of engineering with more determination and less beer is impossible to know. Looking back, I can see that my lack of college prep courses had doomed me.

But was that my only problem? Was I developing a habit of rejecting goals that I did not pick for myself? Or is it possible that I was already becoming addicted to alcohol, seeking solace for my anxieties as my father had for his?

Dismayed by my failure in Nashville, Aunt Dollie sent word from New Orleans that there was still time for me to enroll in the fall semester at Tulane. I could live with her family in Algiers, where Uncle Lad was now a vice president at Louisiana Power and Light. Dollie and Lad's three children were not yet in college, but there was an extra room where I could sleep. I accepted the offer.

---

[3] Among the few positive memories from this fiasco is Davidson himself. I didn't meet him personally that summer, but his gracious welcome to his new students foretold the warmth I would find in this fine man when we became good friends thirty years later in Kentucky.

Waiting to greet me were two friends from my happy summers on Williams' Nashville farm. Claude and Nell Simmons, who had worked for Lad and Dollie in Tennessee, now lived in an apartment in the spacious backyard, where Claude and my uncle were building a swimming pool and tennis courts and converting an old barn to a play area for Dollie's new camp for children.

As president of the New Orleans YWCA and head of the area Girl Scouts, Dollie had replicated the same leadership roles she'd filled in Nashville. Nell was her housekeeper and cook, and Claude earned extra money working at the Todd-Johnson shipyards in Algiers.

The Williams home was a large plantation-style cottage on a gravel road that skirted the Mississippi River levee. When Dollie's children rode their horses, they could see across the river to the spires of the St. Louis Cathedral in the French Quarter.

It's possible that Lad and Dollie suspected I had developed a smoking and drinking habit at Castle Heights, but I didn't hang around the house to help them figure it out.

Every morning, rising in the dark, I walked to a bus stop near the Immigration Services office, rode to the Algiers Ferry, and then crossed the river to the foot of Canal Street, where I caught the first of two streetcars that took me to Tulane's campus uptown in the Garden District.

In the afternoons, I rode the streetcar back to Canal and then walked down in the Quarter to Jackson Square. In good weather, I would study on a bench by the statue of Andrew Jackson on his rearing horse, a duplicate of the ones in Nashville and Washington, D.C. On rainy or chilly afternoons, I studied at the Café Du Monde, warmed by a cup of chicory coffee au lait and a beignet.

My academic standing at Tulane was never in question. In a university where young males were in short supply, I soon was skimming along with classes in the liberal arts, earning As and reading one of the most influential books of my life, *The Autobiography of Lincoln Steffens*.

A muckraking magazine editor of the early twentieth century, Steffens was the mentor of many great journalists, such as Ida Tarbell and Walter Lippman. Steffens investigated corporate and political corruption. He shaped his findings and his outrage into stories that shook the nation and confronted governments with demands for reform.

Steffens was important to me because he put his idealism to work. I wasn't sure, but perhaps Steffens's was the career I wanted.

Returning to my aunt's home in the late evening, I had no one to talk to about ideas, books, or even my classes. My young cousins were busy with homework. Their parents were helping them or pursuing their own projects. They tried to make me feel welcome and loved, but I felt like a stranger around my own kin.

My most comfortable companions were Nell and Claude, who laughed when I sneaked over to their apartment for a cigarette or admitted I was too tipsy to go into Dollie's house until everyone else had gone to bed.

AFTER TWO MONTHS AT TULANE, I became acquainted with two gay students, Maurice and Jack, an odd couple I met on a streetcar. Maurice, a good-looking, slender English boy, had "jumped" a British merchant ship after he was befriended by a kindly widow in New Orleans, the mother of a Navy buddy of his. He could have passed for straight. Jack, in his mid-twenties, had grown up in a blue-collar Catholic family in New Orleans. He was extremely effeminate and got by on campus by saying very little.

On the streetcar, however, Jack talked. He invariably drew the attention of other passengers with his loud accounts of sailors he met cruising bars near the river. He made Maurice laugh at me by suggesting that I was so impassive and aloof from their world they should rename me and the novel I was reading *I'm-Moby Dick*.

Despite the joke at my expense, Maurice and Jack accepted me as a straight Tennessee boy with no friends. That is how they introduced me to their friend, Dr. Pierce Patrick, one of the more unforgettable figures I came across that winter.

Slender and blond with a thin face and gray eyes, the well-dressed Dr. Patrick gave me a limp handshake and a strong smile when we met at the Monteleone Hotel bar. The "Doctor" was for a Ph.D. in English Patrick had earned at the University of Chicago while in his early twenties.

Still not yet thirty, Patrick was the executive assistant to a prominent—and straight—businessman who didn't care what Patrick was as long as he did his work. Dr. Patrick had tried to join the Army, but the Draft Board physician had good-naturedly inquired, "Where on earth would we put you?" and sent him home.

"Home" for Dr. Patrick was a bungalow on Canal Boulevard, where I was soon invited to a party. The occasion celebrated the arrival in port of Joe Marshall, the son of Maurice's benefactor. As a Brit deserter, Maurice would win no decorations for serving the Allied cause.

Marshall, whom Maurice referred to as his "foster brother," had earned a chest full of ribbons and was a chief petty officer in the U.S. Navy. Dark-haired and reserved, with a dry wit, Marshall had the good looks to get lots of girls, but like Maurice, he was a gay guy who acted straight.

Meeting Joe, I remembered a short story by Ernest Hemingway in which a weary officer who has come off the battle line suggestively asks a younger man, "Are you corrupt?" But Joe didn't try anything with me in that direction. There were women at the party, but I was confused about who they were with, if anybody. I suppose it didn't occur to me they were with each other.

I was a long way from Here We Are Farm. Patrick played Leider music on the phonograph and sang along in German. By the time he finished to everyone's applause, I had drunk so much whiskey I got sick. The only thing I remember of the rest of the night is that Chief Petty Officer Marshall held my head as I threw up.

I left Tulane at Christmas break and did not go back. The Army had sent me a notice to report, this time for active duty.

I was due at Fort Oglethorpe in Georgia on January 8, 1945, my eighteenth birthday.

-11-
Over Hill, Over Dale

HAD IT NOT BEEN FOR MY GRANDMOTHER'S OBSESSIVE interest in Andrew Jackson, I could have had one more day of civilian life in early 1945.

My birthday, and thus the day I was to report, was actually January 9, according to my mother. And shouldn't she have been trusted to know? Graeme, however, insisted that mother's memory was foggy. She had brainwashed me as a little boy to believe I'd been born a few minutes before midnight on January 8, which happened to be the date on which Andrew Jackson had whipped the British at the Battle of New Orleans in 1815.

"It was an omen, Albert, Jr.," my grandmother said. "You were born on a great day in our country's history, and it should inspire you to do great things for your country."

And so, despite my mother's gentle protest that the Army was taking me twenty-four hours too soon, I showed up at Nashville's Union Station on a dark, cold, and smoky January 8 and presented my transportation orders to the train conductor.

My parents, grandparents, and sister were on hand for a tearful farewell. The Major, who had drafted thousands of Tennessee boys during two wars, seemed proud that, like my father before me, I had volunteered. He nodded approvingly as Graeme presented me with a small travel Bible that they had inscribed to a grandson "who has bravely left hearth and home … *TO FIGHT!*"

THE NEXT AFTERNOON AT FORT OGLETHORPE in Georgia, I passed a physical exam, drew uniforms, and was sworn into active duty. I was in barracks with some fifty other new soldiers, learning to make beds the Army way, when a sergeant called my name and ordered me outside and into the presence of a waiting officer.

"I'm Colonel Craig." the officer said. "I hear you want to be in the field artillery because your father was an artilleryman in France in the last war."

"That's right," I said. "But how did you know that?"

"Because your father told my brother, and my brother phoned me. Your dad was our friend when we were boys back in Tennessee."

The colonel's brother turned out to be Francis Craig, the bandleader at the Hermitage Hotel in Nashville. It would be a couple of years before Francis Craig's song, *Near You,* became a popular hit. But it was only two days before I was on a troop train bound for the Field Artillery Replacement Training Center at Fort Sill in Lawton, Oklahoma. The Army assigned me to seventeen weeks of basic training in fire control and surveying.

The plan was to transform me into a mapmaker and a calculator of whatever settings were necessary to blast hell with shell upon the Axis forces, wherever they might be. Meanwhile, I would also receive some elementary instruction in soldiering, including how to operate the vehicles and cannons, or howitzers, essential to the field artillery's mission. Like the song said, over hill, over dale, I would hit the dusty trail, as those caissons went rolling along—just as my father had.

At rifle practice that first month, we lay in snow on frozen ground as the wind sliced across the range at us. It was a miserable exercise, but one immeasurably safer than the ordeal faced that winter by the Allied troops who were beating back Hitler's desperate counterattacks in the Battle of the Bulge.

After all, behind us were heated barracks awaiting our return each night. And some of us, myself included, warmed our bellies with brandy that off-duty cooks had smuggled up from Texas. Over the loud speakers, between rounds of target shooting, our instructors played Fats Waller's "Two Sleepy People" and "Your Feet's Too Big."

"... Mad at you cause your feet's too big; I really hate you, cause your feet's too big ..."

It wasn't the worst of times. I made sharpshooter, despite the brandy, and became buddies with several older soldiers who'd been drafted in hometown panics over the last Hitler offensive in Europe.

My best new friend was David Douglas, who, at thirty-eight, was twenty years older than I. A freckled, blue-eyed, stocky fellow, Douglas had been a welder in civilian life and followed jobs on the road during the Depression and the war's early years. During a one-day stop in West Virginia, Douglas had registered for the draft in a county in which he never lived. After Pearl Harbor, he'd worked in defense plants for three years, accumulating enough money to buy a farm.

When he returned to West Virginia in December 1944 to inform the draft board that he was ready for a rest and was taking a vacation, the draft board exercised its prerogative and snatched him into the service. (Douglas claimed the board drafted him so that a popular local boy could stay home.) His dismayed wife and twelve-year-old son were left stranded in Morgantown.

Douglas was no stranger to adversity. He claimed he'd begun his welding career as a teenage safecracker in his home state of Arkansas. The youngest in a ring of Ozark burglars, he was small enough to be hoisted through transoms until one night he tripped an alarm that ended his crime spree and also, unfortunately, his formal schooling.

He took to the road in the eighth grade—the only member of the gang to escape—and grew sufficiently skilled to work on the big power dams being constructed in the United States and Canada. He and his family were living a vagabond life in a trailer when he was drafted. But now, here he was—an over-aged private bundled up and squinting at targets in the snow between shots of the booze I shared from my canteen.

Douglas was fourteen when he quit school a jump ahead of the law, the same age the Major had been when he left school to become a surveyor for the Tennessee Central. There were other similarities. David could repair and make things, had a gift for mathematics, read a newspaper every day to keep up with the world, admired Franklin D. Roosevelt, and was not intimidated by surprises. Within the first month of our basic training, he had sent for his wife and son, found a place to park the trailer, and charmed a first sergeant into letting him spend his nights off base.

By pooling our talents, Douglas and I began to ease through basic training as partners. In a month he had taught me enough of the practical trigonometry he knew from welding to allow me to keep up in surveying and fire control classes. From my experience in ROTC at Castle Heights, I coached him through the elements of drill and military discipline that he found confusing.

Despite his age, Douglas was a match for any march or physical test and was quicker than most of us teenagers to master the weapons, from machine-guns to howitzers. Like a generous older brother, he turned back to help me catch up with what I didn't understand from the instructors.

On the frozen plains and hills of Fort Sill, it soon was time to take a test I knew I could not pass—the one proving that I had mastered the operation of the two-and-a-half ton truck that towed the 105-millimeter howitzers. The Army had shown us a film to inform us "by the numbers" what was expected, but the movie and a few hours of simulated driving were certainly inadequate to prepare a novice to steer one of those big trucks up, down, and around a curvy obstacle course known as "the Burma Road."

Fortunately, most of the trainees already knew how to drive. Unfortunately, I was not one of them.

I tried to explain that I was not up to this challenge, but the scowling young second lieutenant sitting beside me in the cab of a truck parked on the snow-covered summit of the Burma Road was not persuaded. Behind us on benches in the canvas-covered bed of the truck were a half-dozen other trainees shivering in the near-zero cold as they waited their turn. The lieutenant's expression turned testy.

"Take the wheel, Smith," he said impatiently. "Let's get going."

Resigned that we would die on that hill, I shoved the gearshift into what proved to be Neutral. The truck began to roll down the slope.

"Now what?" I asked the officer.

"Put it in low!" he yelled.

I shot him a pleading look. "Which one is that?"

As we picked up speed, cries of alarm sounded from the back of the truck. I am not certain how many jumped before the frantic lieutenant elbowed me aside and halted the skidding vehicle.

"See what I mean?" I said.

WHEN WE FINISHED BASIC, my problem with trucks was taken into account, I suppose. I was posted to Fort Riley, Kansas, as a forward observer for a mule-pack battalion. They were going to the jungles of Burma where I would never have to drive a truck.

The cannoneers were strapping six-footers, or more, weighing at least two hundred pounds. They drove, tugged or even, it was rumored, toted their mules into combat. The mules in turn bore the pieces of seventy-five millimeter howitzers, which could be assembled and fired from positions no truck could reach.

My job would be to crawl out in front of these fellows and beasts, advancing far enough to spot the enemy and send back coordinates for firing their guns.

Franklin Roosevelt, the only living President I could remember, had died and Germany had surrendered as I was completing my training. But the war in the Pacific went on. Pat Parker, a Castle Heights football hero who was on the honor list with me before he joined the Marines, was killed on Okinawa that summer. But I was spared, at the last minute, from the mission to Burma.

THE INTERVENER WAS A SERGEANT NAMED GASKINS, who had seen so much combat time in the Pacific that he had been rotated back to Fort Sill as an instructor. Spying my name on the transfer to Fort Riley, he protested to a colonel that I would be of more use to my country as an instructor. "The little bastard sure can talk," he told me he had told the colonel. "Why waste him on them mules?"

To become an instructor, I attended Cadre School. The training I received was excellent. The lecturers taught us to speak distinctly, use a pointer effectively, maintain eye contact with students, use humor, and make everything simple. This was the best training I'd had since the first grade with Mrs. Clark's flashcards.

Sergeant Gaskins also had recommended Douglas for the program, so together the two of us gave new cycles of inductees the same drill in field artillery basics, surveying, and fire control that we had received that winter and spring.

Because many of the senior non-commissioned officers like Gaskins had been discharged as a reward for long combat service, we privates were acting as corporals and sergeants. In my pocket was an Army driver's license issued on graduation from cadre school by a clerk who obviously had not been in the truck on the Burma Road.

Back in the old barracks, I had the privilege of a private room, which allowed me to hide from my new wards the fact that I was pouring nightly over books on the care and maintenance of trucks and howitzers, and, with coaching from Douglas, learning to strip down machine guns and rifles. Thanks also to Douglas, I had mastered the math I needed to lead a mapmaking survey party through the woods without losing them.

Douglas and I had become favorites of our first sergeant by midsummer. Sergeant Barnes, a wheezy, chain-smoking, beer-bellied old man with a red face and bloodshot eyes, had joined the Army for its promise of regular meals during the Depression. Barnes liked me because he enjoyed my platform lectures on military life, my desperate jokes, and my skill at motivating trainees. He also appreciated that I kept Douglas acting like a soldier. He liked Douglas because Douglas was competent, and because he knew Douglas kept me from wrecking the guns and trucks.

We were on maneuvers among the buffaloes in a national park in the Wichita mountains ("don't fuck with the furlidge [foliage]," Sergeant Barnes cautioned us) when we heard, with wonderment and relief, about the atom bombs and the surrender of Japan.

In the national clamor to bring the troops home by Christmas, the Army struggled to train replacements. Over a two-month period, I was promoted from buck private to corporal to sergeant, then staff and finally tech sergeant.

As I was sewing on stripes, so was Douglas, who had been promoted to staff sergeant. Meanwhile, I had acquired two patrons in the officer ranks: a Mormon captain named Stephenson with a chest full of medals, and an elderly colonel who had served in both world wars. Stephenson was impressed by my impersonation of a drill instructor, if not my driving skills (when we were in a jeep together, he drove). He convinced the colonel that I deserved a higher role in the peacetime Army.

At Thanksgiving the colonel called me into regimental headquarters and announced that he wanted to recommend me for an appointment to West Point, his alma mater.

After politely requesting a week to think it over, I declined the offer. I told the colonel I wanted to be a civilian and a journalist. He didn't throw up, but as I saluted and turned to leave, he seemed to look at me with a mixture of disappointment and nausea.

The Christmas leave of 1945 was an unforgettable journey I shared with millions of other men and women in uniform who were going home after a long time away.

I stood on a packed bus all the way from Lawton through Oklahoma City to St. Louis. After sleeping on the station floor, I sat on my duffel bag in the aisle of a train from St. Louis to Memphis.

Two more bus rides, and I was home on Center Point Road by Christmas Eve.

My duffel bag, lost between Memphis and Nashville, was returned to me in Nashville a week later, the day I boarded a train back to Oklahoma. My seat was next to a pretty young woman who was headed to Oklahoma City to meet her officer husband. She was reading that year's racy bestseller, *Forever Amber*; I was reading Hemingway's *A Farewell to Arms*. By nightfall, we had exchanged a few literary comments and introduced ourselves. After supper together in the diner, we snuggled closer, and, between hugs and kisses, somehow groped our way through the night.

BY FEBRUARY 1946, Sergeant Barnes and I were in charge of two coaches full of other noncoms headed to Fort Knox, Kentucky. Our mission was to prepare a new Field Artillery Replacement Center by reopening some barracks and classrooms that had been shut down for a year.

The deserted buildings were a wreck—windows broken, furniture missing, kitchens stripped, plumbing uncertain. It was a job to awaken the dormant talents of Sergeant David Douglas. Surveying the scene, he requisitioned a small truck from Sergeant Barnes and, with me by his side, resumed his career as a thief.

Beginning with a break-in at a warehouse, we stole slicing and mixing machines and pots and pans for the kitchen, then moved on to typewriters, lamps, and desks. (The refrigeration units we swiped required a larger truck and thus a second trip.) We progressed to drums of paint, lawn care equipment, heaters, and several truckloads of bathroom fixtures. We had no choice, really. Had we requisitioned the stuff through the proper channels, we would never have been prepared by the deadline to receive our first cycle of trainees. By Derby Day, we were back in the training business.

To celebrate, Douglas took me to a bookie joint in Louisville to learn how to read a racing form and bet the horses. The chosen venue, a basement several steps down from the sidewalk, was under the protection of a uniformed policeman who cheerfully greeted the clients as they pushed past him on their way down to the action.

Not long after—emboldened by the freedom of the fort, so to speak—I checked out one of those two-and-a-half ton trucks, filled it with six other noncoms and a designated driver, and headed to Churchill Downs for an afternoon of racing and an evening concert in the paddock.

By August, I had earned an Army Commendation Medal, and so many three-day passes for exceptional teaching that Sergeant Barnes asked the inspectors to stay out of my class. But as our time to leave the Army neared, Douglas and I were growing dissolute.

Two years of heavy drinking were taking their toll on me. Well-paid, by Army standards, I spent everything I made on booze between paydays. Douglas was no alcoholic, but after towing his trailer to Michigan and leaving his wife and son there to await his discharge, he was ready for some extra fun. One night at Fontaine Ferry Park in Louisville, the two of us picked up a girl there. After a quarrel over whose date she might be, we left her and drove back to the barracks, irritated with each other.

The next morning, as he and I packed to leave the Army, we hardly spoke. I knew he was going to settle down and build a greenhouse business on some land he had bought in Michigan. He knew I was going back to Vanderbilt, this time to enroll in a liberal arts program.

As we boarded the truck that would take us to the trains for different separation centers, we shook hands with Sergeant Barnes and Captain Stephenson. All of us promised to write and stay in touch.

These men were some of the best, most generous friends I ever had. But I never wrote nor saw nor heard from any of them again.

-13-
The Jack Daniels Seminars

I WAS ONE OF THE MANY VETERANS swarming Vanderbilt's campus in September 1946, a year after the end of World War II.

I took French alongside a twenty-seven-year-old former lieutenant colonel who had been a combat fighter pilot. I studied in the library with a bright young Wisconsin man who had served with the OSS in China and was now a smiling fraternity guy dressed in expensive sweaters. (When I saw the fellow on TV forty years later, he was an anxious-looking ambassador defending a bad U.S. policy in Central America, and he was no longer smiling.) I hung out at the Student Union with several men who had been in Army Specialized Training Programs at Vanderbilt at war's end and remained as civilian students, living in temporary barracks the military had turned over to the university.

My high school friend Walter Durham, also a veteran, was studying political science at Vanderbilt, but we saw little of each other. Walter was focused on his studies. I was focused on students, cultivating those who were English or theater majors over coffee or beer in any venue except the classroom. In my pathetic need for constant excitement, I found a class the most boring place on campus.

Not all of my friends were World War II veterans, however. I developed a homey relationship with the folks who rented me a spare room in their basement close to campus. I suppose Jimmy Riddle, a Nashville coal dealer, was responsible for a lot of the infamous smog that clogged our lungs and eyes in winter. But he generously invited me to breakfasts he cooked for wife Betty and their young daughters on Sundays, and urged me to borrow their second car, a tiny Crossley, anytime I needed transportation for dates.

Genial Joe Wright, my first faculty friend, was a tall, thin speech and drama professor who encouraged me to consider a career in the theater. He invited me home for supper with his pretty blonde wife, then gave me the lead role in Maxwell Anderson's *Winterset* and an "A" for a paper I wrote on the poet W.H. Auden.

And I drank beer at the Pimlico Diner with Russell Anderson, an underpaid adjunct theater instructor. Anderson was a slight fellow with a baritone voice of such range and emotional affect that, whether he was giving stage directions or quoting Shakespeare, I marveled he had taken the bus to Nashville instead of Broadway. He was envious of his Northwestern University classmate Patricia Neal's early success in Lillian Hellman's *The Little Foxes*, but his gossip about her inspired my hopes for a similar opportunity.

AT VANDERBILT, ACTING WAS MY CHANCE to make friends and be noticed. Perhaps it was a gene I inherited from Graeme—maybe even the Major. Whatever the reason, I always needed a stage. That was probably why I did so poorly as a student. If I couldn't be in front of the class as the teacher, why bother?

My fascination with acting faded, however, as another new acquaintance insisted that writing plays was superior to reciting them. Three years older than I, Walter Sullivan was a former Marine lieutenant and a senior English major who was back at Vanderbilt to finish a required freshman chemistry course. That class was the only thing he lacked for admission to the Master of Fine Arts program at the Iowa Writers' Workshop.

One of Sullivan's short stories already had been included in a collection of works by some of the English Department's notable teachers and graduates, some of whom were known as the Fugitive Agrarians[4] for their association in the 1920s with a Vanderbilt poetry

---

[4] In 1930, twelve of the Agrarians—six of them current or former members of the Vanderbilt faculty and four former students, including Robert Penn Warren—published an anthology of essays that was called a "manifesto" against the destruction of Southern culture. *I'll Take My*

magazine called *The Fugitive*. Walter had found his muse as a writer and teacher in the works of Fugitives such as Donald Davidson, John Crowe Ransom, Andrew Lytle, and Allen Tate.

Aside from their sizeable literary talents, the writers and poets of the Fugitive Agrarians achieved national attention as critics of the industrializing New South. They believed that the values of the rural Old South were being undercut by the effect of financial capital and mechanization on cities. They charged that factory assembly lines transformed the dignity of labor into robotic work and broke down the security and civility of an agrarian society where each had known his place. They blamed the loss of faith and order and the unchecked growth of capitalism on Northern economic imperialism.

My new buddy-turned-mentor was a tall, imposing man— graceful, with a large head, piercing eyes, arching eyebrows, and a Mephistophelian smile. As our friendship evolved from coffee breaks at the Student Union to Saturday night double dates at a lounge at the Andrew Jackson Hotel, I found him a compelling conversationalist. I was now a liberal arts major who sporadically attended classes and whose participation in the ones I made it to was undistinguished. An evening with Walter, however, was different. His Saturday night ruminations over Jack Daniels were the highlight of my time at Vanderbilt.

Warmed by the whiskey, which we brought in a brown bag to pour over setups of ice and soda, Walter made those winter nights glow. In a soft drawl, he spun out stories from the Bible, Bullfinch,

---

Stand: The South and the Agrarian Tradition became a historic polemic. Although the writers did not all share the same views on race issues—they ranged from conciliatory moderates to stand-pat segregationists—they were united in a call for the region's people to go back to the soil. Granny Graeme was not a fan of the Fugitive Agrarians. "They're not much," she said dismissively. "When they gave a reading for my book club, they smoked cigarettes in my parlor." But more thoughtful contemporaries leveled more serious criticism against these writers. Some believed the Agrarians' economic prescriptions were too weak to revive an impoverished countryside in steep decline, that they were trying to roll back progress in urban areas, and that their quirky pose as "unreconstructed" Southerners ignored inequalities that were supposed to have been resolved at Appomattox. There were no black Agrarians.

and Milton, woven into a backdrop of William Faulkner's version of Hubris and Nemesis[5] in Yoknapatawpha County. It was comedy, tragedy, Adam and Eve and the Fall. It was the genesis of a superlative professor, and I was present at the creation. He was the best teacher I ever had in college.

Walter was in love with a Nashville girl named Jane Harrison. On their first date, Walter took Jane to see me in a play. Jane was writing a master's thesis on Robert Penn Warren, and by the time she and Walter were engaged, we were discussing Warren's novel of that year, *All the King's Men*.

My date on those evenings at the Andrew Jackson Lounge was an interestingly haughty girl, Amanda Ames. She lived in Nashville's fashionable Belle Meade and kept a stable of horses, including a champion jumper. Although I was crazy about her, she was cautious. The flicker of our romance faded—she decided she liked her horses better than me, I suppose—but she remained a friend of Walter and Jane for the rest of her life.

I was with Walter and Jane the night they stayed out to wait for the Sunday paper that announced their engagement. When they married that summer in a Methodist church, Walter had passed freshman chemistry and they were headed to Iowa.

ON THE DAY OF WALTER AND JANE'S MARRIAGE, I was emotionally drained. My dearest friends were leaving, and a dean's letter in my pocket confirmed that I had been expelled from Vanderbilt again. This time I had cut so many classes I'd failed my courses.

I was the member of the wedding party most uncertain of his future. And of all those gathered in the church, I have no doubt I was

---

[5] The two concepts, originating in ancient Greece often acted out in Greek tragedies. Hubris was the term used to describe actions that humiliated a victim or defied the gods that resulted in the fall of the protagonist or retribution, called Nemesis.

the only one convinced that he was completely, irreversibly Godforsaken.

When the wedding was over, I made the rounds of the local bars with another groomsman, Revel Ransom. We ended the evening staggering up the stairs at Chateau Graeme to sleep in the same rooms where my parents, sister, and I spent our first winter in Tennessee after Dad drank us out of Florida.

Leaving my grandparents' house before noon, I spared them the news that I had been expelled from college a second time. That conversation could wait until I arranged some financial support by registering for the "52-20 Club," a GI Bill unemployment benefit that provided as much as a year of weekly $20-dollar checks for single veterans in search of work.

The unemployment office was in the same block as the Andrew Jackson Hotel, but I brushed away memories of those happy Saturday nights with Walter, Jane, and Amanda to sign myself up as a newspaperman in search of a newspaper. Then, with a few of my remaining dollars, I bought a ticket at the Greyhound station and took the next bus back to Hendersonville and Here We Are Farm.

There was still no telephone at the farm, so my arrival surprised my father. He was out there alone with his little herd of beef cattle. My mother and sister had left him in January.

In 1947, my mother was forty-five, my sister was fifteen, and my father was fifty years old. Telling my father they were going to visit a relative in a nearby county, my mother and sister had instead taken a bus to Nashville. Muff had called the Major from the bus station there and announced she would no longer expose my sister to the same family tensions that had motivated me to leave home in high school. She asked him to buy train tickets for her and Robin to go to Springfield, Illinois, where they would stay with a sister of hers who had offered her shelter until she could find a job.

Muff's plan was that she and Robin would come home when my father had straightened up, found legal work to supplement his meager farm income, and made our farm home more livable.

This was only the second time Dad and I had been together since the separation. The first had been the previous Easter, when I set aside my resentments and wrote a letter asking for a hundred bucks for what I said were unexpected college expenses. (In reality, I had liquor bills to pay.) Dad had come to Nashville then to give me the money. This time, Dad was glad to see me, even when I told him I would be there until I decided what to do next.

So that summer, there were *two* wretchedly lonely men on the farm of our dreams, drinking whiskey together at night. We were roommates in a womanless old log house, not much better than the one where the kind-but-dim Dillard brothers lived at the foot of our hill.

DAD RETURNED FROM A TRIP TO NASHVILLE one day that August with startling news. I had been reinstated at Vanderbilt for the fall semester. He had gone to see the dean and blamed himself for my academic troubles. The breakup with my mother was his fault, Dad had told the man. Coming so soon after my return to civilian life, he explained, it was more than I could cope with.

"But what about those plays?" the dean asked.

"That was Albert, Jr.'s way of escaping real life," my father said, in words truer than he knew. "Albert might be depressed, but like his mother, he can still put on a show for a public occasion."

The dean bought this mostly bogus story, but Dad had omitted the problem he and I shared: our alcoholism. Getting counseling for my alcohol abuse wasn't a condition the dean set for my readmission. Staying off the stage, the only school activity in which I excelled, was. The dean also insisted that I catch up with the school's math, science, and language requirements and live with my grandparents because of the "supportive environment" they would provide.

Back on campus that fall, I spent two months dissecting eels in Biology 101. I had another go at French nouns and verbs and tried to remember enough trigonometry from the Army classes I had taught to pass the same course as a student. When I encountered Amanda, we smiled at each other and passed on. I was even more miserable than before.

As the evenings with Graeme and the Major invariably turned to discussion of my parents' problems, I knew that it was time for me to go.

There would be no turning back.

My mother Muff, at
eighteen, when she
married my father.

Dad, who faced the
bullets and was gassed, a
genuine hero. His letters
tell some of the story.

With my lovely mother, the "flapper"—the hat tells it all.

At the wheel in Sarasota.

With sister Robin,
who shared much,
gave much, and
put up with me.

The Acacias, a Sarasota landmark
where we lived and dreamed.

Tuffy the Terrible,
my run-away pony.

Graeme McGregor
Smith: teacher,
editor, and family
force, born in 1875.

My grandfather, Rutledge Smith, "the Major," with WWI hero, Alvin York, in 1927, the year I was born.

Florida fish catch: Granny Graeme and the Major with me on the dock at Sarasota.

Happy days in Sarasota: from left, my parents Muff and Al, Grandmother
Ella Mace, born in 1857, Uncle Robin Mace, and me.

Six cousins on a pony
at Aunt Dollie's farm:
from left, Malcolm,
Eudora, McGregor,
Al, Wilson, and
Marion (missing,
my sister Robin).

Photo from *Milwaukee Sentinel* in 1942 when at fifteen, I won the American Legion National High School Oratorical Contest, defeating three seniors.

Triumphant Granny Graeme with me at Nashville train station, returning from victory in Milwaukee.

WATCH YOUR TEP

Cadet Editor Al Smith at Castle Heights Military Academy, in Lebanon, Tennessee, in 1943.

With my stripes, Tech Sergeant Smith on leave from Fort Sill, Oklahoma, at Christmas 1945.

-13-
Copyboy

THAT MELANCHOLY AUTUMN OF 1947, I had moped at Ireland's, a Vanderbilt campus bar, listening to Bunny Berrigan's "I Can't Get Started" on the jukebox and fantasizing about starting over in New Orleans. Like Paris for American expatriates in the 1920s, might not New Orleans be just the place for me to write, drink, find a new love, and forget Tennessee?

Ward Allen, my best friend still at Vanderbilt, encouraged me to quit college. "Do it, Albert!" he told me. A brilliant graduate student who was accomplished in Greek and Latin, Ward traded antiques to pay for the education that would make him a scholar and teacher for the rest of his life.

Ward was a devout but witty Episcopalian with a romantic view of institutional order in the Old South. He relished the eccentricities of other nonconformists like me, whose skepticism about academic requirements and refusal to join a fraternity he admired.

Ward pushed me along the road he had not taken. "You're a writer who is not writing," he told me. "College is defeating you. In New Orleans, you'll be free to write on your own terms."

I'm still not certain whether his advice was the best I ever received or the worst. But that November 1947, when I was twenty, I accepted it. New Orleans it was.

WHEN I TOLD THE DEAN THAT I WAS DROPPING OUT to go to New Orleans and become a writer, he had asked, "Do they know you're coming?"

They didn't, of course. Nor did the Major and Granny Graeme. Just a few years earlier I was their star—the Albert with whom they'd succeeded. But I was now a very different boy than the one they'd adored.

My father, depressed and desolate on the farm, pleaded with me to stay in college. But I was not to be persuaded that there was a tolerable future for me in school or in Tennessee.

After scribbling a goodbye note to my grandparents, I headed for the Greyhound station with one suitcase and a book bag in which I'd stashed the Viking *Portable William Faulkner*, a writing tablet, and a pint of Early Times. Of course I was scared—after buying the bus ticket, I had only $100 to launch this adventure—but an hour south of Nashville, the desperate feelings eased. Toward dark, the whiskey and the Faulkner began to warm the lonely ride to the Gulf Coast. When I awoke, it was a cool day, but the sun was shining on Canal Street.

WHEN I GOT TO NEW ORLEANS, I mailed postcards to my parents and grandparents to tell them where I was. Then I set out to build my new life.

With a few drinks that first night, I acquired a new friend, Owen Brennan. A stocky, convivial Irishman who was proprietor of the Old Absinthe House, Brennan presided at a bar decorated with autographed dollar bills that wartime customers had posted for good luck. Instead of strippers, the back room of that Bourbon Street joint featured entertainment by black singers and piano players.

After my third drink—the fourth was on the house—Brennan was calling me "Al" and sharing his plan to open a restaurant across the street. The following night, I watched Ethel Waters sing about "A Cabin in the Sky." When I adjourned to the bar for another drink with Brennan, he grumbled that the segregated city's accommodations for black entertainers were so shabby that he'd built a "cabin in the sky" for Miss Waters—an apartment upstairs over the lounge.

By week's end, my cash slipping away, I replied to an ad and was hired by *The Times-Picayune* as a copyboy at $22 a week. It was a bottom-of-the-barrel job, but the paper couldn't be convinced it needed another would-be reporter who thought he was Faulkner. I also had rented a seedy, second-floor room in a shabby building on Dauphine Street at the edge of the Quarter.

Not long afterwards, I answered a knock at my door.

There was my father. Standing beside him was my Uncle Lad.

"Come home, please," my father pleaded, his voice anguished. "Please come home."

"No," I said. "Maybe later. But not now."

My dad, with whom there'd been so few happy days, began to cry. My beloved uncle, who had given me so many, said nothing. But he, too, looked teary.

"I've got a job at a newspaper," I told them. "I start Monday."

"I'll be all right."

I'm not sure, but I think my father hugged me before he turned to leave.

What I remember for certain, though, is that after the door closed, I could hear my father's muffled groans as Lad took him down the steps for the bus ride back to Tennessee.

DESPITE THE FACT THAT MY FIRST JOB was a humble one, I grasped that I might get somewhere at the *Picayune* if I made a good impression on my new bosses. I also still vaguely hoped to write a book.

What I didn't plan on was a decade of increasingly heavy drinking that would finish me off in New Orleans as I finished learning the newspaper trade.

Though I would have denied it back then, I was already an alcoholic when I stepped off that Greyhound bus. I had abandoned a once-promising future, the American Legion scholarship, and G.I. Bill benefits for nights in the French Quarter and days at the beck and call of every hack at a New Orleans newspaper. But I was sipping absinthe frappes with the founder of Brennan's restaurants, and I was where I thought I wanted to be.

"CUT OUT THAT GODDAMN WHISTLING!"

That command came from the man in the "slot," the assistant news editor with the green eyeshade who sat in the interior apex of the V-shaped Copy Desk on the fourth floor of *The Times-Picayune*.

I wasn't the whistler. The offender was Vernon, the senior copyboy who, like most of us, hoped to become something else: in his case, a photographer. Also like several of us, Vernon was not a "boy," but another veteran who was hoping for a break by coming in the back door.

Why should I whistle, for God's sake? Vernon, who lived with his family, might whistle in a moment of absent-minded pleasure, perhaps thinking of the PoBoy sandwich, chips, and praline his mother had packed for him before he left home for the newspaper. But this was my second week on the job, and I was always hungry. I was rationing myself to Krystal hamburgers or doughnuts one day so I'd have enough coins for beer the next, and wondering if I would have $7 for rent on Saturday.

The dark-haired, bushy-browed man in the green eyeshade, French cuffs rolled back, sleeves pulled up and fastened with rubber bands, took the unlit cigar from his mouth, the better to chew me instead. But Vernon apologized.

"Beg your pardon, Mr. Head," Vernon said. "It wasn't Smitty whistling. It was me. I wasn't thinking."

"Not thinking is for publishers," Harry Head, the assistant news editor, said sharply. "We expect better of copyboys." Grinning at his own wit, he nodded at me. "Sorry, kid."

Thus began my first friendship with a boss on the Copy Desk. It was mid-afternoon and the work hummed as the other old guys, arriving on a staggered schedule, swung into action.

Vernon and I had assembled the artillery at each chair along the rim: sharpened soft lead pencils to black out errant prose in wire and local stories; trimmed pads of scrap newsprint on which to craft the next morning's headlines; and scissors, paste pots, and brushes at the ready so that the finished copy could be reconnected before it was passed along to the slot man for final approval.

Of the dozen desk men—there were no women on the rim back then—most were middle-aged former reporters. Few were college graduates, but all were widely read and politically informed. Skilled enough to spell, punctuate, and correct faulty grammar, they transformed bad writing into not-so-bad writing. Several of them were "radical," Vernon volunteered. In fact, the paper's managers considered the Copy Desk a nest of sedition, perhaps with good reason.

Disgruntled over wartime wage controls that left them earning less than workers at the local Higgins shipyards, the eyeshades had petitioned for, and then lost, an election for a Newspaper Guild union contract. They blamed a domineering managing editor, George W. Healy Jr., who they believed had cowed the city desk reporters and other newsroom minions into voting against the union. Still working a forty-eight-hour week in a building without air conditioning, most of the copy editors were sympathetic to almost any claim of injustice that surfaced in the stories they edited—especially those concerning race, labor relations, and Democratic Party politics.

Healy was in his mid-forties. His rise from reporter to city editor and then managing editor was hastened by national publicity over his astonishing month-long coverage of the Mississippi River flood of 1927, which included a daring swim to reach the only phone in a river town so he could report the details to *The Times-Picayune*.

Ruggedly handsome, tall, and robust, Healy had always lived near the Mississippi River. As a young reporter, he joined the Yacht Club in New Orleans, the better to sail small craft (and, his enemies said, to hang out near the publisher). Ferocious over story errors and blustering with subordinates, he was friendly, if slightly condescending, toward ordinary folk. For people of prominence who visited the paper, however, Healy reserved a welcome that was equal parts thigh-slapping enthusiasm and hearty deference. "Come aboard!" he would say, strutting and bowing at the same time.

As a student at the University of Mississippi, Healy had a tenuous friendship with William Faulkner, then the campus postmaster. When the future Nobel Laureate wound up on a binge in New Orleans, it was Healy who rescued him, dried him out in a hospital, and then packed him on a train to Oxford with a farewell gift for shaky nerves—a bottle of beer wrapped to resemble a fifth of whiskey.

While Healy courageously attacked conventional targets such as thieving politicians, he seemed uninterested in the growing agitation for social change across the South. Like many Southern editors of his generation, his capacity to imagine equal justice had been blunted by ancestral memories of losing the Civil War. And his ingrained gift for toadying to the publisher limited his push for improved benefits for employees.

Neither a change to a forty-hour work week (for the same wages) in early 1948, nor a promise to air condition the building, appeased the eyeshades. With no hope for pensions or certainty about paid sick leave, they lost respect for the old publisher, Leonard K. Nicholson, a New Orleans Bourbon, and they resented his serving man Healy.

LIKE EVERYONE ELSE, I WAS AWED BY HEALY. But News Editor John McClure, for whom Harry Head was merely the warm-up act, was different.

A romantic personality of modest renown in New Orleans literary circles, McClure, who was born in the Oklahoma territory, had lived in Paris before the First World War. He was a poet and critic who had turned to journalism to earn a living.

As news editor, McClure was the top supervisor of the Copy Desk. He had even served as acting managing editor during Healy's patriotic stint in Washington at the Office of War Information. His titles, however, daunted no one. He was more a figure of affection and respect than authority.

McClure wore the dark suit, starched white shirt, vest, and blue tie of an executive, but his flowing white hair, soft handshake, gray eyes, and milky-pale face suggested a prophet and a dreamer. His was a Scotch-Irish spirit that had signed up for a Cajun charade. His artistic imaginations locked up for nine hours, he reported at 4 p.m. each day with the first fortifying toddy of the day on his breath, ready to organize a new narrative about the triumphs and tragedies of the twentieth century.

We were putting out the paper of record in the greatest city of the South. Head had prepared the way, slashing and spiking at the copy that told of floods, famines, distant wars, disturbances in the capitals, and the poverty of ideas in our public life. Then it was time for the gentle but stubbornly idealistic McClure to wrap up our news in a final package and send it out on deadline to destinations across three states in successive editions known as the Pup, the Pup Replate, the Widow, the Widow Replate, the Late Mail, the Late Mail Replate, and, as grand finale, the City.

Getting out those seven editions while tolerating Healy's nagging rules was a vexing challenge for McClure. He could read Latin, Greek, and French, and might have been happier at home in the Quarter writing blank verse.

But, as with the rest of us in the newsroom, journalism was a way to survive in New Orleans, to pay the rent or mortgage, and to savor the gumbo, all the while dreaming of a book to write, a small paper to own, or a long shot horse to come in first in the last race at the Fairgrounds track.

–14–
A Stick of Pied Type

ACROSS THE NEWSROOM FROM THE COPY DESK sat another
of my new masters: Buddy Felts, the city editor. Felts was a former
sportswriter whose climb to management, it was said, had been
facilitated by a wartime exemption from the draft and an absolute
loyalty to Healy. A jittery fellow, given to jumping whenever Healy
coughed, Felts shared command over a platoon of reporters with the
handsome night city editor, Alex Waller, an ex-Army captain who
was cool in a crisis and seemed unburdened by any dissatisfaction
with the Delta's whites-on-top, blacks-on-bottom social order.
Waller's rise from the ranks was enhanced by the good luck of having
haled from Mississippi, like Healy, and having worked on the
Hattiesburg American, a small daily Healy favored as a sort of farm
club.

Only two years after the end of World War II, reporters typed
their stories for newspapers still produced with Linotypes, pots of
molten lead, engraved asbestos mats, curved metal plates, and rotary
presses. It was a cumbersome process that hadn't changed much since
Mark Twain's day.

As reporters rushed to finish writing before deadline, I listened
for "Copy!"—my signal to pick up the pages and pile them at the city
editor's elbow for the first editing. The reappearance of those pages,
now marked-up, was my prompt to carry the story briskly to the slot
man at the Copy Desk, who would assign it to an editor sitting along
"the rim," the outer edge of the big, horseshoe-shaped desk. The
chosen copy editor would read the story again for errors, then pencil a
headline on a separate sheet and return both to me. I would stuff the
story and headline into a pneumatic tube, then pop the tube into a

pressurized air shaft that sucked the story to the composing room above us. Later, galley proofs from the Linotype operators would slide down the same shaft for the eyeshade guys to check over again. And so it went, on into the early evening, when the Page One proofs were brought to the newsroom by the elderly and respected composition editor, Arthur Stone.

Mr. Stone wore a putty-like prosthesis for his lower nose; his real nose had been severed long ago in an accident involving a runaway horse and wagon. He was a kindly old man, bent from many years of stooping over page forms on their way to the engravers. Yet one grunt from him amid the hellish din of clacking Linotypes, and production stopped. His was power *over* the press.

Power over me belonged to anyone who wasn't a copy boy. It originated primarily from the Copy Desk, out of which a handwritten note emerged one night. "*Mr. Smith,*" the note said, "*please go to the composing room and fetch a stick of pied type.*"

Inside the noisy composing room, I showed the note to Mr. Stone's assistant, Dick Seither. Shaking his head, Seither pointed to a young printer in a blue denim shirt who was locking galleys of type into a page form. I took the note to the printer, who also shook his head and then pointed across the aisle to a Linotype operator. This man squinted at the message, stood up, and waved me toward a bearded compositor, who angrily gestured at his ear, seized my arm and marched me back to Stone's assistant.

Then all the men smiled. Unbeknownst to me, "pied type" was the name for an accident, when sticks of words set in lead became scrambled, out of order, when a galley of them fell to the floor. Sending me on a hunt for pied type—something to fix, not fetch—the copy editors and Dick Seither were hazing me, in partnership with three printers who were deaf and mute. (Many deaf, mute men worked in such jobs since the loud noise didn't bother them.) Laughing with the others, it was my happiest moment since Owen

Brennan treated me to a drink in his own bar. Did this mean I was now one of them?

Seither was a stocky, barrel-chested ex-Marine. Dick worked at night and went to law school by day. He was the excitable opposite of his calm old boss Stone, given to outbursts of yelling over the slightest hint of a problem between news and composition. He had been in the Pacific long enough to seem a little combat nutty, but not so goofy that he wasn't doing better with the GI Bill than I, by using it to climb into the middle class. After my hazing, we were instant friends. Equally important, he became one of my financial angels, lending me money every week so I could make it till payday.

AROUND THANKSGIVING OF THAT YEAR, McClure had begun inviting me at quitting time—1:30 in the morning—to walk with him, often in the fog, from LaFayette Square down St. Charles to the Old Gem on Royal near the corner of Canal for a nightcap and a chat about books and politics. A romantic figure in black and white with a dark raincoat slung over his shoulder, he suggested one night that I ride the rest of the way home with him on the Desire streetcar, which looped from Royal onto Canal Street and back into the French Quarter. "Mr. Mac," as I then called him, and his wife lived on two floors of a four-story house they owned in Orleans Alley next to St. Louis Cathedral.

His wife, Joyce, had been a young woman making her way in the city in the 1920s, when John was still married to his first wife, Grace, with whom John had run a bookstore until her death. Joyce had become friends with John and Grace after she rented a tiny apartment in another tall, balconied house next door to theirs. The other renter, where Joyce lived in the building next to the McClures, was a friend of John's, a young Mississippi writer by the name of William Faulkner. Joyce and Faulkner's landlord in those Bohemian days between the wars, a Tulane architecture professor named William Spratlin, also lived in the house, and provided Joyce and Faulkner breakfast in his apartment as a "lagniappe," or something extra. The morning he offered them cold eggplant and orange juice, however, the arrangement collapsed, and they went back to corn flakes in their own quarters.

Joyce told me that story at 2:30 one morning, when her husband had brought me home for a nightcap. For her it was the cocktail hour. She was waiting for us in a bright colored dress, a flower in her hair, ready to mix the drinks and talk until dawn. The McClures rented out their first two floors. Their living room was on the third floor, a steep climb up the stairs.

In 1947, Joyce, who by then was in her late forties, was a popular professional tour guide of the Quarter, or Vieux Carre, pointing out the best restaurants and spicing her repertoire with racy gossip about their owners, chefs, and notable patrons. The incomparable knowledge of the Crescent City that she later sold to tourists she generously gave away to visitors like me in her picturesque apartment overlooking the garden of the St. Louis Cathedral.

Little over a month after my lonely ride from Nashville to New Orleans, I was nearly destitute, but my gamble on a lowly job at the newspaper had won me entree to the McClures' unique memories of the world of American letters. I was hungry, but this generous, childless couple fed my soul as they recalled their years on this narrow alley, where they had lived as friends with the great author of the stories I had read on the bus from Tennessee, and where a century earlier, the cathedral bells had pealed in celebration of Andrew Jackson's victory.

From my Army days at Fort Sill, I was familiar with enough Western history to respond to John McClure's account of growing up as a child of Methodists among the Indians in Oklahoma. His wife, who called me "chère" after her second drink, hailed from a more exotic culture. A "cradle Catholic" from Opelousas in St. Landry parish in southwestern Louisiana, where her nephew was a Jesuit priest, Joyce was either a Cajun or a Creole—she called herself both—of German and French extraction. She said she accepted the occasional efficacy of voodoo to fix a romance or sicken an enemy, and nodded approvingly when John confided that he admired the Church's tolerance for ghosts, the prevalence of which in Louisiana was evident to almost everyone.

John McClure attracted aspiring writers. As an editor and founder of a little literary magazine called the "Double Dealer" in the 1920s, he had published early works by Faulkner and Ernest Hemingway. Some of the best-known writers of the 1920s and 1930s—among them Sherwood Anderson, Sinclair Lewis, and Thomas Wolfe—sought John out on visits to New Orleans. The year before my arrival in New Orleans, John and Joyce had hosted another midnight visitor. They said little about Truman Capote, except that he liked the cookies Joyce baked at least as much as their whiskey.

After publishing his own poems in a small volume called *The Stag's Horn Book,* McClure told me that he had confided in "Bill" Faulkner that he didn't expect to be famous. "'We can't all be Shakespeares,' I told him," John said. But he recalled that Faulkner wasn't so accepting.

"I don't know about you, John," he quoted Faulkner, "but I'm not so bad myself!"

How good was McClure? Well, H.L. Mencken, in a tirade against the South as "the Sahara of the Bozart," wrote that "once John McClure (an Oklahoman) and Robert Loveman (an Ohioan) were counted, you will not find a single Southern poet above the rank of a neighborhood rhymester." Of course he exaggerated, as McClure would note, but Mencken's praise sustained his reputation long after he stopped publishing poems.

McClure's transition from man of letters to journalism was classic. The bookstore having failed, the magazine unprofitable, he needed a job. In his first years at *The Times-Picayune*, he was the book editor, often filling an entire newspaper page with his own review essays which he wrote in long hand.

The newspaper's hospitality to writing about literature may have reflected the interests of Eliza Poitevant Nicholson, mother of Leonard and Yorke Nicholson, the publisher and vice president, who wrote her own poetry under the pen name "Pearl Rivers." Mrs. Nicholson acquired a major interest in *The Times-Picayune* through inheritance from a second marriage to an owner named Holbrook. Mrs. Nicholson's primary contribution to American journalism history was her friendship with a young Kentucky-born woman who wanted to be a writer. Elizabeth Meriwether Gilmer, a native of Todd County, was unhappily married to an alcoholic invalid. Hoping to improve his health, she had taken her husband to the Mississippi Gulf Coast where she met Mrs. Nicholson, who, like many affluent New Orleanians, had a second home on the Coast.

The meeting between two women with "minds of their own" and common interests led to a beginning reporting job for Mrs. Gilmer with *The Times-Picayune*, which became the springboard for success in New York. As "Dorothy Dix," writing about murderers and fallen women, Mrs. Gilmer became the queen of the New York tabloids in the 1920s. But when I started reading newspapers, she had pioneered a new genre of journalism with a popular, nationally syndicated "advice" column for the lovelorn. By the time I hired on at the paper, she was an old lady living in a Garden District mansion, where two secretaries helped her get out the column. She was an honored figure in society and dear to the hearts of the Nicholson brothers, who called her "sister," and to a real-life relative on the Copy Desk, Reuben Killebrew of Clarksville, Tennessee, who called Dorothy Dix "Cousin Lizzie."

I wondered … should I call her Mrs. Gilmer or Mrs. Dix? I had started reading her columns in the *Nashville Banner* at twelve, dreaming not of the juicy prose in her tabloid past but rather hoping for more explicit guidance about girls than she gave. But in New

Orleans, when my need for sex was more insistent than ever, I blew my one chance for a personal consultation with this cultural icon.

I glimpsed the *grande dame* one day as she entered the elevator when I was leaving the office on an errand. I felt like I'd seen one of McClure's apparitions. There she was, Dorothy Dix, a gray ghost that had sprung right off the pages of the *Nashville Banner* folded on my grandparents' reading table. But this woman wasn't Dorothy Dix; she was too old to be anyone named Dorothy. *This* was Mrs. Gilmer, who smiled at Carnival Ball debutantes, Creole beauties who would never stab their lovers with a kitchen knife. She may have kept her husband locked in a basement. She may have been the spiritual grandmother of every sob sister who wrote about Lindbergh's baby. But she would never smile at me; we would never even speak. When the elevator door closed behind her, that was it. Out on the street, I ventured a timid "hello" to her waiting chauffeur, a black man who had parked her limousine at the front door in a no-parking zone. He just looked away.

-15-
Pistols Killed Huey

AS MY FIRST CHRISTMAS IN NEW ORLEANS NEARED, my situation at the paper became desperate. I simply couldn't afford the job.

After Friday's payday, when I routinely returned the two- and three-dollar loans I had sheepishly cadged from Dick Seither and the old copy guys during the week, I was out of money again by Monday.

It wasn't that I was a spendthrift; when the errands that sent me out of the building justified a streetcar ride, I pocketed the 14 to 28 cents the editors had handed me for fare and raced around the business district on foot so that I could save the change for food.

For 30 cents or so, I could buy a lunch at the Virginia Kitchen, a PoBoy stand behind Maison Blanche Department Store. A canvas strip from the sidewalk to the counter segregated the customers as required by law, but once we'd bought our oyster loaves or roast beefs and RC colas, we sat side by side along the curb to eat, black and white, united in our hunger.

The week before Christmas, I opened a gift my father had sent from Tennessee. The box held a handsome gray wool suit from Loveman's in Nashville. The gift meant that my farming father had sold his tobacco and, despite the heartaches we had given each other, was spending some of the money to show he loved me.

I examined the suit more closely, and marveled that it was finer than any I had ever owned. Then I sadly wrapped it back in the box and walked to Rampart Street, where I showed it to a sour-faced man in a pawn shop. He gave me $15 and a claim ticket, and I gave him the suit.

I never reclaimed it.

On Christmas Day, I ate my holiday meal alone at Gluck's on St. Charles and Poydras. There were two Gluck's in town, and the pressmen had dubbed this one, which was near the newspaper, "Dirty" Gluck's. As I ate, I scanned the classifieds looking for a better job, perhaps one that would pay for dinner at "Clean" Gluck's, the pricier place in the French Quarter where they served the bread when it was freshly baked.

By the end of the week, I had begun a correspondence with the Institute of Living, a Connecticut sanitarium that was advertising nationally for attendants. The Institute was offering an attractive salary of $125 a month, free room and board with the facility's inmates, and, presumably, plenty of off-duty time to write novels.

But on New Year's Day, at the newspaper's entrance, I came face to face with the publisher, Mr. Nicholson, and his famous Sugar Bowl guest. Remembering my shyness with Mrs. Gilmer, I mustered my courage.

"Good morning, General Marshall!" I crowed.

"Good morning, son."

George Catlett Marshall and Leonard Nicholson had been roommates at Virginia Military Institute. Whatever else these old men had in common was enough to have brought them and me together on the first day of January 1948. Was there a signal in this encounter? Watching them disappear into a waiting car, I marveled that Tech Sergeant Albert Smith ("serial number 141-577-71, sir") had just spoken—smartly, pleasantly, and with enthusiasm—to the general who had commanded fourteen million of us in uniform. And the general had replied agreeably, perhaps even approvingly.

I reconsidered the job application I had sent to Connecticut. Was the security of room and board in an institution for mentally disturbed Yankees worth abandoning the random delights of daily living down here in the Delta? And just how annoyed with me were the folks I'd been borrowing from every week? No one had yet called me a pest; in fact, they still were showing me the ropes as if I belonged there.

Maybe I *did* belong. These people—the reporters, the editors, the bartenders—were standing in for the family I had lost.

Had he paused to inquire of my situation, no doubt General Marshall would have said, "Buck up!" Maybe, I thought, I *should* hang on to my perch in the window on the world at *The Times-Picayune*, come hell or high water.

And so, one week before my twenty-first birthday, two months on the job, refortified in my commitment to American journalism, I shook off doubt and made my way to the fifth-floor newsroom, where I shared with Reuben Killebrew, my fellow Tennessean, my amazement that anyone as intelligent as General Marshall would be all that attached to our publisher. I must have been learning the business, because questioning the worth of a publisher is a sure sign of self-confidence.

"Mr. Leonard is the brighter of the brothers," said "Killey." "His brother Yorke is really shy a brick. Years ago when Yorke tried to edit the Sunday Rotogravure, he had a hole across the bottom of a Page One layout. To fill it, he sent a photographer over to the Audubon Zoo to take a picture of a snake."

Killebrew had a clipped gray mustache and the voice and demeanor of a middle Tennessee squire. His family was prominent in the politics of education and agriculture back home. But he had left college to go to sea in the 1930s and wound up in port at New Orleans, where Cousin Lizzie helped him get a newspaper job. He was good every week for a $2 loan, as was another former seaman on the Copy Desk named Bob Barnes.

In his mid-twenties and still a student at Tulane, Barnes was a generation younger than most of the other copy editors. Stocky and broad shouldered, a skeptical grin fixed on his open face, Bob was the son of a prosperous Wisconsin family. As a boy he had learned to sail on the Great Lakes, then as a teenager joined the wartime merchant marine and was injured in the Normandy invasion. He wound up catching the eye of George Healy when Healy gave a guest lecture in a journalism class. Barnes was more radical than even Killebrew, who was just a Roosevelt New Dealer with a union card, but Healy, who had never met a Lafollette Progressive, missed the political signs. He was impressed by Barnes' prowess as a yachtsman, so he hired him on the night shift.

The other young copy editor who had begun buying a few beers with me—sometimes for me—after work was Alfred Maund, a tall, intense graduate student and ex-Navy lieutenant who worked on the night sports desk. He and Dorothy, his fiery, older fiancée, were keen on boxing and betting the horses. But Al was also a political lefty and perhaps the most brilliant intellect in the building.

I VIEWED MY FIRST MARDI GRAS DAY from the bed of a newspaper truck on Canal while sharing a flask of whiskey with a friendly reporter named Cope Ruth. Until Cope spotted me, standing near the truck, and pulled me up, I was the loneliest young man in a crowd of a million people.

Somewhere out there, Louis Armstrong was leading the Zulu parade for black New Orleans, and it was *his* face, not the white socialite Kings of Rex or Comus, on the cover of that week's issue of *Time*. At the office, I had shared the laughs of the guys on the Copy Desk at the embarrassment of the young reporters trying to write about Armstrong's recognition without stretching the paper's biased rules about black achievement. Armstrong might have made the cover of *Time*, but Page One of *The Times-Picayune*?

The next week I moved from my grubby garret on Dauphine into a cleaner room on the back courtyard of an apartment building on Chartres near the river. My new home was close to both Jackson Square and the McClures. It was also only a few doors down from the Pink Elephant Bar, which soon became my saloon of choice because it was open twenty four hours. And I could charge drinks.

The Pink Elephant was favored by seamen in port between trips who rented sleeping rooms upstairs. They trusted the proprietor, Nat

Robinson, to keep their money safe behind his cash register. Nat was Jewish, a large fleshy man of fifty who had seen better days as a gangster in New York and a nightclub owner on Bourbon Street during the war. He and his wife, Gerri, and his bachelor brother, Sammy, were easy to know and welcomed me into their lives. Soon I was bringing in the dawn by offering up the latest *Picayune* gossip to them as a bedtime story.

By February, when a letter of encouragement arrived from the Institute for Living, one could have made the case that I was already working amid lunacy. All of Louisiana had gone crazy over the governor's race, in which a Long was running.

Huey Long, the demagogic "Kingfish," had been a U.S. senator and governor when he was gunned down in 1935 at the state capitol in Baton Rouge. (Back then the owners of *The Times-Picayune*, the voice of the Bourbon class that Huey reviled, had hired armed guards to protect the paper from possible rioters.)

The official version had it that Huey was killed by a single bullet fired by an obscure Baton Rouge doctor who was enraged at Long for slandering his father-in-law. Another version claimed a larger bullet had hit Long as his panicky bodyguards slaughtered the doctor in a barrage. The autopsy revealed no evidence of a second wound in Long, but conspiracy theorists strained to link a treacherous bodyguard, hired by Long's many enemies, to the murder. Inept medical treatment also may have contributed to the fallen senator's end.

That first winter I spent in New Orleans, despite the passage of a world war, the death of Franklin D. Roosevelt, and the dropping of atom bombs, conversation in all the bars, bayous, cane fields, and courthouses in Louisiana was still rife with the same questions: Who really killed Huey? Was the Kingfish a saint or a sinner? Could he have become president?

A series of scandals among Huey's cronies had jailed a governor, the president of Louisiana State University, and a New

Orleans hotel operator to whom Huey had entrusted a lockbox that reportedly held millions in political dollars. But neither those outrages nor the ministrations of two reform governors had assuaged the state's thirst for another fizzy drink of Longism. If Russell Long, the heir apparent, was still too green to prime the pump, his sly and manic old uncle, Earl Kemp Long, had the juice for the job.

Earl had ascended briefly from lieutenant governor to governor during the earlier scandals, when a Huey legatee named Richard Leche was driven out of the governor's office and into prison. Ten years later, Earl was an agitated stump speaker promising to reincarnate his brother's populist programs—free roads, free bridges, better schools, veterans' bonuses, and old age pensions. He promised something for everybody, and all of it would be free. *Free*—paid for by the oil and gas industry and the other "big interests" who had squeezed the po' folks from the red clay to the bayous to New Orleans' back wards.

On election night, February 24, 1948, *The Times-Picayune* was reporting a landslide victory for Earl Long. He had captured all but two of the state's parishes, elected 75 percent of the candidates he'd endorsed for the legislature and local office, and even swept New Orleans. With a popular mandate that exceeded any Huey himself had ever won, Earl had buried the paper's candidate, a reformer Earl had dubbed "Sweet-Smelling Sam Jones." As we prepared the account of Earl's victory, we were writing our own candidate's political obituary.

When the tipsy winner's inevitable gloating phone call came, Healy, the managing editor, who by then had imbibed a few himself, answered in the newsroom so that we could hear his replies to Long's tongue-lashing.

"Yes, Earl," Healy said. "You whipped us aplenty ... That's right, Earl. Jones didn't go anywhere with that claim ... No, Jimmy Davis (the incumbent governor) didn't help him ..."

Healy was quiet a moment. Then: "How do you say we told the biggest lies, Earl? ... Over bodyguards? That you would bring back the bodyguards and gun thugs of Huey's day? ... Not so, you say?

"But those were editorials, Earl," Healy went on. "I don't write editorials. That's not my fault …

"You say you never carried a pistol? That pistols and bodyguards killed Huey? Well, they certainly did. That's one thing we agree on.

"Thank you, Earl … That's right, you beat the hell out of us. We have to go print that in the paper right now …

"Good night, governor. And good luck."

When Healy hung up, there was a hush across the whole floor. All the reporters and editors had been listening.

"I wish my uncle had heard that," I said.

I was standing beside Buddy Felts, the city editor, waiting to run another page of election copy. Felts was next to Healy, waiting for the call to end.

Healy turned to look at me. "What uncle?" he asked.

"McGregor Smith, who used to live in Louisiana," I replied. "He said Huey Long gave him his first ulcer."

I had been there four months, but Healy seemed to notice me for the first time.

"Mac Smith is *your* uncle? Why didn't you tell me?"

"I guess you didn't ask me," I said, emboldened by both the moment and a few snorts of election night firewater.

Uncle McGregor, who by then was the chief executive of Florida Power and Light Company, had been president of Louisiana Power and Light in Huey's era, when the utilities were whipping targets for the Kingfish. My uncle told me that Huey once summoned him to his suite in the Roosevelt Hotel, where the governor dictated a new reduced rate structure for the power company while sitting on the toilet.

"Mac and I started out in New Orleans together," Healy said. "We're still friends. He's chairman of the Orange Bowl and swaps me tickets for the Sugar Bowl. He's a helluva guy."

Two weeks later, there was a shift of assignments at the paper. Ed Brooks, the photo editor, became amusements critic. Harold Rubin, the assistant state editor, replaced Brooks.

And the new assistant state editor was Albert P. Smith Jr. With the change in title came a salary increase, from $22.50 to $52.50 a week, on a percentage basis the largest raise I would ever receive. With the raise had come an important lesson about business.

Connections trump merit nearly every time.

-16-
The Times-Picayune

THAT MARCH OF 1948, Fred Corwin, my new boss on *The Times Picayune* State Desk, muttered by the water cooler that he was the loser in George Healy's trifecta. Harold Rubin, Corwin's previous assistant, had a master's degree and taught part time in Tulane's journalism program. Corwin wasn't surprised that Rubin had been promoted, but he was bitter that Healy had dumped a vagrant youth on him as a replacement—one who didn't know a pica from an "em" or New Iberia from New Roads. The previous week, this kid Smith had been sharpening pencils and filling paste pots. Who was Al Smith, anyway?

Because Healy liked me, Corwin didn't. My first week as his assistant, Corwin—a tiny fellow with a pinched, worried face, and a wispy mustache—would glance up periodically, his eyes darting around the newsroom like a mouse contemplating an exit. But Corwin was used to bad news. Bullied at the office by Healy and bossed at home by a wife twice his size, Corwin had grown so accustomed to being mistreated that, in retrospect, his dismay that I was his new helper was a bit of an act. Corwin understood what my promotion was about. Granted, Healy might have seen potential in this tramp copyboy, but he'd promoted me to win favor with an old friend. It hadn't hurt that making me Corwin's assistant was also a means of inflicting pain on Corwin as punishment for his desperate act of courage: a vote in favor of unionizing the paper.

Still, green as I was, I was no dunce. My mother, the Major and Granny Graeme had all worked in journalism, as had I back in high school. Journalism was in my genes, printer's ink in my veins. Soon, thanks to coaching from co-workers, I began to catch on.

An obsessive-compulsive detail guy with an ulcerating fear of libel suits, Corwin scrutinized every headline and story I handled, anticipating mistakes before I made them. But he was a realist, so he began to help me learn the job. And Harry Head, the afternoon copy chief, decided I had talent. Over suppers at the Morrison's near the paper, he confided that success in playing the stock market with his wife's inherited money was about to liberate him from *The Times-Picayune* for early retirement in Texas. Until then, he was generous with instruction back at the office. Between Corwin and Head, I was a student in a master class in copy editing.

The busy Corwin left it to Harry and other old-timers to school me in management's unwritten rules: Keep Negroes in their place, and out of the paper, if possible. Never quote a crowd estimate, lest it encourage support for a candidate we didn't like. Shun any writing that seemed to "glorify" criminals, and never describe an attorney as "prominent," even if well-known. That was free advertising.

In *The Times-Picayune,* the conflict of the previous century was "the War Between the States." (A Civil War was what they fought in Spain.) "Mrs." and "Miss" were distinctions reserved for white ladies; African-American women didn't warrant such courtesies. A black preacher was "Reverend," but a white minister was "*The* Reverend." Except in rare cases of celebrity, photos of blacks were restricted to the sports pages. When Ralph Bunche came to town, we published his picture. But it wasn't on Page One, and rumor had it that it had taken a vote of the paper's board to drop our customary style, which would have been to write, "A key to the city was presented yesterday by Mayor DeLesseps Story Morrison to Ralph Bunche, 51, Negro, New York City, Under-Secretary General of the United Nations."

One of my new duties was editing the Reverend H.H. Dunn's miserably written submissions about black churches and schools for the "Colored Notes" column. Reverend Dunn, a middle-aged, copper-colored fellow with a head like an Indian chief, always shuffled into the newsroom after sundown, bowing and scraping. The story was that Yorke Nicholson, the paper's vice president, had fired Reverend Dunn late one afternoon when he found the preacher composing a hunt-and-peck story at a vacant desk in the Society department. Dunn's offense? "Using a white lady's typewriter." The next day Yorke's brother, Leonard, rehired Reverend Dunn but warned him not to show his face at the paper until after 6:00 p.m. By that time each night, Yorke would be certain to have left for the Boston Club, the ultra-exclusive gathering spot for white males, and the coast would be clear.

"Colored Notes" was fenced off in an obscure corner of the paper, segregated like the rest of black life in New Orleans. There were separate taxicabs for the races, shabby black schools that few whites had ever seen, and different unions for white and black longshoremen. A nasty worm of a City Hall clerk even obsessively checked the birth records of professional boxers to guarantee that no man with a drop of Negro blood climbed into the ring with a white.

Unlike the South's more liberal major dailies—*The Courier-Journal* in Louisville, the *Constitution* in Atlanta, *The Tennessean* in Nashville, even New Orleans's *Item*—the ultra-conservative *Times-Picayune* stood on the ramparts of resistance to civil rights for Negroes along with papers in Charleston, South Carolina, Jackson, Mississippi, and Richmond, Virginia. Despite the Louisiana newspapers' complaints against the state's pervasive political corruption, the editorial pages in New Orleans and elsewhere were silent about the fundamental evil of those times—racism.

The Times-Picayune's voice thundered in support of the Bourbon planters but barely whispered in defense of the masses. Underneath the parades and festivals, the spicy food and drink, the good times rolling to the beat of the soulful music, life in Louisiana was still about class and the power of money. Though privilege was not as conspicuous as before the Civil War, when Louisiana was the South's richest state, in 1948 the silk stockings remained determined to keep most of what was left for themselves. The only exceptions, it seemed, were the wealthy Jews who supported Negro schools and endowed the arts.

The Times-Picayune had the largest circulation in Louisiana and shared rural Mississippi readership with its regional rival, the Memphis *Commercial-Appeal*. The *Picayune*'s news was authoritative and thorough, if somewhat dull and gray. (Its sister afternoon paper, the *States*, was more flamboyant, having to compete for street sales with an independent afternoon paper, the *Item*.) While the *Picayune's* stories were factual, its normally leaden editorials could get hot when the owners were aroused. The *Picayune* was not a paper to engage in interpretive journalism or offer commentary that differed from its own regressive view of social issues. There was no "op-ed" page in those days, and few letters to the editor protesting racially discriminatory laws. Admirably, the paper ignored attempts at coercion from advertisers. Still, it risked nothing in hewing to the line that politicians like the Longs and their allies, who appealed to the poorer voters, were anti-business and corrupt. Those who didn't were standard-bearers of "good government."

Corwin and I processed the state news, including dispatches from our capital bureaus in Baton Rouge and Jackson as well as Washington, from two scarred desks flanked by floor fans. Within arm's reach was the Copy Desk, McClure or Head in the center, and their crusty compatriots hunched along the rim. This was a fortunate proximity, because Corwin and I needed their manpower when the stream of state copy turned to a flood on deadline.

Corwin and I each had a typewriter, a rotary telephone, "in" and "out" boxes, and spikes. The spikes were where we parked pieces of stories we excised from the worst of the copy that our correspondents in parishes and counties across Louisiana and Mississippi had submitted.

Those state stories reached us in several ways. The news from the mail was modest. "Cabbages are coming up in Copiah County," read the humble report from Crystal Springs, Mississippi. Sometimes the news was that cabbages were *not* coming up in Copiah County because of bad weather or insects. Daily reports from southwest Louisiana—Cajun country—or the Mississippi Gulf Coast cities of Biloxi, Gulfport, and Pascagoula reached us by telegraph, helped along by a Western Union operator who accepted and relayed horse bets on the side.

Some stories were phoned in. The three Bienvenue brothers were part-time reporters covering a stretch of bayous, fishing ports and sugarcane that extended around the towns of Lafayette, New Iberia, and Abbeville, Louisiana. The Bienvenue brothers spoke with such seasoned Cajun accents I could barely interpret as I first took dictation and attempted rewrite on the State Desk. Bad phone lines didn't help. *"Say that again, Shorty? The Monsignor—*pissed*? ... Oh—the Monsignor* blessed *the shrimp boats!"*

I COULD UNDERSTAND THE BIENVENUES well enough by election night in August 1948 to realize that the recently elected governor, Earl Long, was stealing a seat in the U.S. Senate for his nephew, Russell. After his inauguration in May, Earl had gone on a tax-and-spend spree of social legislation that raised teachers' salaries, funded hot lunches and new buildings for school kids, created old-age pensions and other benefits, and gave bonuses to veterans. Earl was keeping campaign promises but making enemies. To pay for the promised programs, he had imposed taxes on beer, gas, and cigarettes, and sharply raised the severance levies on oil and gas, thus increasing the total tax burden by 50 percent.

Public opinion really began to turn against Long when it became obvious he had reopened the state's gates to organized crime. Gambling casinos and slot machines ran wide open in parishes around New Orleans, and prostitution flourished. Police were on the take for systematic graft, and knowledgeable citizens were convinced that the governor himself was the chief taker.

There are legendary stories about Earl's earthy contempt for political hypocrisy during those early days as governor. When a delegation showed up at the capital claiming he had promised them a road, Earl sent word: "Tell them I lied." Accused of buying legislators the way Huey had, he denied it. "I rent 'em," he said. "It's cheaper that way." Abolishing civil service, he purged enemies from public employment "for political halitosis." He coined the term "transom money" for the bundles of cash tossed over the door into his hotel suite as payoffs.

In the U.S. Senate election, it seemed clear that young Russell would pay for Uncle Earl's resurrection of spoils politics in Louisiana. The anti-Long forces, headed by the mayor of New Orleans, had united behind a rural candidate, Circuit Judge Robert Kennon of Minden. Kennon was so far ahead in New Orleans that Russell was ready to concede.

Angered by the returns, Earl told Russell to pull up his socks, get a grip, and buck up. Meanwhile, with 90 percent of the returns counted and Kennon ahead by three thousand votes, Earl went to work, calling his sheriff friends who supervised the local vote counts. Soon our Cajun correspondents were phoning us with corrections on late returns from selected parishes.

"My fren' Al," said one of the Bienvenues. "De sheriff say he make a big mistake on dat ree-port. He's pencil slip—you know what I mean? It was Russell Long on top, not Kee-non. I give it wrong to you. Can you fix?"

Then came the next Bienvenue. "Hi, Al. What *I* know about politics? Nuttin. I tell you last week, Kee-non will win this parish? Ha! We still love dem Longs. I was wrong. De vote go to Russell. Kee-non jes too much de Baptist, I guess."

Russell Long wound up winning the primary, but with less than 11,000 votes, about 2 percent of the total.

AROUND THE CORNER FROM THE PICAYUNE on Camp Street there was once a "newspaper row." The area had been a killing ground for editors and politicians who feuded after the Civil War. Dominick Call O'Malley, proprietor of the *Item*, sustained fourteen bullet wounds in gunfights there over twenty-five years, but died of natural causes. And in 1908 the inspector of police burst into the office of the *Morning World* and fired at the editor—but missed.

Forty years later, New Orleans had toned down. Our bull of the woods, George Healy, would return to the office after a few drinks and dinner to check a late edition. While waiting, he would walk around the building demonstrating his managerial ability by switching off lights to save on electricity. Healy was not universally admired, but no one we had savaged in print came after him with a weapon. The only newsroom employee who died under extraordinary circumstances while I was there was the food editor.

A frail little bird of a lady in a dark straw hat with a veil, Miss Charlotte Green generally slipped into the office towards dusk. She always dressed in black, as if she were a ghost mourning Dominick O'Malley. Once settled in a corner of the newsroom, Miss Green clutched a large magnifying glass in both hands as she pored over a notebook of recipes. After a period of intense scrutiny, Miss Green would select several appealing menus, copy them in longhand, and deposit them with Mr. McClure to be printed.

When I was still a copyboy, I'd find Miss Green slowly chewing on a brownish slice of stale apple each evening when I delivered her a fresh newspaper. Was that her supper? I suspected she was hungrier even than I.

A few weeks after my elevation to the State Desk, Miss Green failed to show up for work. Healy sent someone to her one-room apartment, who found her tiny body cold and lifeless in bed. The coroner said it was natural causes, but Harry Head speculated that the food editor had starved to death. He was being mordant, but I believed it.

On the Copy Desk, some of the green eyeshade guys ate their dinners from paper sacks or a lunch pail. Lee Moore, also known as "The Eel" (Lee spelled backward), brought his whiskey habit to work in a cough medicine bottle and sipped his way through an eight-hour shift. It was Lee who gave me the Copy Desk's special secret rule on Christian Science: Only two headlines were to be used. One was "Christian Science Lecture Slated." The other was "Christian Science Lecture Heard." Somewhere in New Orleans, Lee said, there was surely a scrapbook about the Christian Science faith, kept by the elf who mailed us the publicity notices. "Our game is to write the same monotonous headlines year after year to stabilize his scrapbook," Lee explained. "It's a serenity thing. In a troubled world, we provide the Christian Scientists with certainty."

One of The Eel's buddies, Bill Burgess, was also an alcoholic, but he didn't drink on the job. "Bucket" (short for "Bucket Head") Burgess was a stubby, ill-tempered, ex-sportswriter who made jokes at everyone else's expense. Shortly after The Eel died of cirrhosis, the Bucket was fired. Drunk on his day off, he entered the newsroom and flung a handful of condoms at his secret lover, a woman reporter from Texas who wanted to ditch him.

They both recovered—the reporter by moving to Houston for a better job on the *Chronicle*, and Bucket by becoming a press agent for State Senator Dudley LeBlanc's Hadacol Goodwill Caravan, a traveling medicine show that sold a tonic that was 12 percent alcohol. LeBlanc, who famously campaigned in French and English on Cajun country radio stations, made an early fortune selling burial insurance plans, which Earl Long called "Dudley's nigger coffin clubs." When Groucho Marx asked LeBlanc on national radio what Hadacol was good for, LeBlanc replied, "For me, $5 million."

One of the most experienced copy editors, Len Hogan, wore a brown cardigan in winter and a short-sleeved dress shirt and bowtie in summer. In all seasons, he was a cigar-smoking New Dealer and a liberal Catholic. While editing copy, he would raise his arm to slowly pat his bald pate, as if to tamp down a wrath of migrainous dimensions provoked by whatever he was reading. McClure told a story of a tipsy Hogan taking his poodle on the train to Bay St. Louis for his brother-in-law's wake. Wobbling up to the casket, Hogan lifted the poodle for a better view.

"Look at him, Poochie," Hogan said. "Son of a bitch living, son of a bitch dead!"

As a former state editor, Hogan had worked many twelve-hour shifts on major stories before he was felled by a heart attack and gave up whiskey and the search for scoops. Sober and recovering his energy under McClure's easy pace, Hogan found inspiration in the Catholic labor movement and organized the campaign to win a Newspaper Guild contract for the newsroom. He was committed to the path of liberation theology before we knew the term. There were laws protecting Hogan from firing after the union lost, but even stronger protection came from Leonard Nicholson's appreciation of the years Hogan had traveled on behalf of the paper, making friends and battling enemies.

Nicholson's patience was also strained when another veteran employee, George Justice Martin, failed to file a story from a Louisiana Bar Association state convention, where Esmond Phelps, the paper's attorney, had just been elected president. When the vanished Martin was finally found, he was in the Shreveport jail, charged with disorderly conduct and booked as "Esmond Phelps." Healy immediately fired Martin, but as with Hogan and Reverend Dunn, Nicholson hired him back the next day.

DURING THE 1948 NATIONAL DEMOCRATIC CONVENTION, it was Len Hogan who drafted a telegram on behalf of the Copy Desk to Hubert Humphrey, congratulating him for his noble denunciation of racial injustice. Humphrey had told the nation, "It is time for this country to come out from under the clouds of segregation and walk in the sunshine of integration." But that wasn't how our paper saw it.

The Times-Picayune quickly threw its support behind the breakaway States Rights presidential ticket: Strom Thurmond of South Carolina and Fielding Wright of Mississippi. Popularly known as the Dixiecrats, Thurmond and Wright sided with the coastal states in their dispute with the Justice Department over valuable tidelands oil royalties. That dispute was one of the two most important issues for Louisiana Bourbons, the other being the protection of segregation.

While 1948 was the year President Truman proposed civil rights legislation and decided to integrate the armed services, that was also the sad year that Southern politicians rejected a future with equal rights for blacks. W.F. (Bill) Minor, *The Times-Picayune*'s idealistic young reporter in Jackson, wrote several articles about the efforts of the Mississippi Bureau of Investigation (MBI) to thwart civil rights activity. Minor's stories caught the eye of *The New Yorker*'s "Wayward Press" staff writer, A.J. Leibling, who praised Minor for exposing the Gestapo-like efforts of the MBI and its sinister masters on the Mississippi Sovereignty Commission. I was thrilled to have edited Minor's copy for *The Times-Picayune*, but crestfallen over the managing editor's chilly response when I showed him *The New Yorker*. "Be careful with these stories," Healy told me.

As summer turned to fall, Governor Long got into a battle over the Dixiecrat presidential campaign with his erstwhile ally, Leander Perez, the longtime political boss of Plaquemines and St. Bernard parishes. Perez had grown fabulously rich with corrupt oil deals involving public lands and was now using his power to keep the Harry Truman-Alben Barkley ticket off the Louisiana Democratic ballot. Defying the governor, a Truman loyalist, Perez advanced a phony argument about "interposition" of states' rights over federal law at a Democratic Party meeting until Long interrupted him with a derisive comment that has echoed through the history of the Civil Rights era. "Hey Leander," Long said. "The Feds have got the atom bomb!"

The national ticket stayed on the ballot, thanks to Long. But when Len Hogan and some union friends went to the New Orleans airport to greet Senator Barkley on a campaign swing, the welcome committee was a thin representation of the city's out-of-power "Old Regular" Democratic organization and a few Longites.

In Springfield, Illinois, on the other hand, my mother was optimistic about Truman's chances. She had written me about her trip to the train station to see President Truman on a whistle-stop tour. The largest crowd of her life had cheered while the President gave his foes hell. "Don't give up on him, Albert," she wrote. But the leading newspapers, *Time* and *Life*, the radio commentators, and the pollsters all said it was over: Thomas Dewey was the next president. What did my mother, working in a ladies dress shop, know about this election that they didn't?

"Ten dollars, even, says your mother's right," my friend Nat, owner of the Pink Elephant, said. I took the bet.

As the Nicholson brothers hosted a few friends to await returns over drinks in the paper's boardroom that November night, the evening began to sour. It didn't help that John McClure told the copy editors to "write the headlines on the story—don't project." All through the evening, as the presses stopped to re-plate for new editions, the old Bourbons who tottered into the newsroom read the same story—Truman was ahead, and Dewey wasn't catching up. They could hear Hogan indiscreetly cackling to McClure, "I believe the little man is going to win!"

As I finally left the building at 3:00 in the morning, the trash can near the guard's desk downstairs was littered with green States Rights buttons. Walking down Chartres through a heavy fog, I saw Nat Robinson under a streetlight in front of his bar, smoking a cigarette and waiting for me. I had cast the first vote of my life that morning, and lost my first election bet because my candidate had won. I handed him a ten dollar bill.

Nat laughed. "You news guys missed the story, didn't you? A lot of people didn't like Dewey." He tucked the bill in my pocket.

"Come on, kid," he said. "Let's celebrate. I'll buy you a drink."

-17-
Good Times, Bad Times

TIME AND AGAIN DURING MY NEW ORLEANS YEARS, the friends I made weren't merely companions. Those friendships opened doors for me to a wider world than I'd ever dreamed of back in Tennessee.

Bob Kelso is a good example. A new *Times-Picayune* reporter from Kentucky, Bob was the person who really schooled me in the music of New Orleans. He had edited the paper at the University of Louisville and been a national leader of Students for a Democratic Society before the communists had squeezed him out. Left cynical and apolitical, Bob had turned his focus to art and jazz. He and I hung out in the French Quarter listening to music.

While Bob and I were cultivating a taste for bop in the clubs, his wife Sylvia was cultivating a lover, "G," who came around to the Kelsos' apartment after she had put their four-year-old son to bed. The marriage was breaking up, but Kelso didn't seem to care.

Bob taught me to appreciate Dizzy Gillespie and Charlie Parker. I learned to love the music so much that, despite the fact that I was not yet a reporter, I wrote an article about it and made my first sale to a national publication. *Newsweek* led its Music section with my piece about the revival of Dixieland music in its New Orleans birthplace and the efforts of the New Orleans Jazz Club to promote the new careers on Bourbon Street of elderly black jazzmen Oscar "Papa" Celestin, Alphonse Picou, and George Lewis. The article also reported the growing popularity of the young white musicians Al Hirt and Pete Fountain, and the comeback of a white old-timer, the trumpeter Sharkey Bonano, whose band, the Kings of Dixieland, was packing in the crowds at Hyp Guinle's Famous Door.

Newsweek sent me a generous check, more than twice my weekly salary. But the money barely covered my "expenses": the drinks I consumed in what I jokingly called "research."

I have no doubt I would have found my way to bars even if I'd lived like a hermit in New Orleans, but there was no question that heavy drinking was as much a part of my new friendships as was cultural exposure. At twenty-two, everything I did after work involved drinking.

When I left the newspaper about midnight, I'd stop off at two or three bars on my way home. My first stop was always the newsstand on Royal and Canal, where I bought the latest issues of my favorite magazines: *The New Yorker, Time, Newsweek, The Nation,* and *The New Republic*. Outside the newsstand, on the corner of Canal, I always spoke to the unshaven old man who sat in a chair behind a box holding a stack of our newspapers—a dirty, red-checked shawl over his shoulders and an unlit cigar clamped between his teeth. All through the night he sat there, shielded by a store awning, sometimes dozing, sometimes sipping a glass of cheap wine to fend off the chill. It was good luck to say hello to him, I believed. He sold what I made. I wished us both well.

Then I'd stop in at the Old Gem, next door to the newsstand, where I'd read my magazines and drink until Mr. McClure showed up. The Old Gem was a half block down Royal from the Monteleone, William Faulkner's favorite hotel. Liberace and Rosemary Clooney performed at the Monteleone when they were as young as I. I'd once spied Ernest Hemingway dressed in a safari shirt and khaki shorts, peering at jewelry in the window of an antique shop just a few doors down from the Old Gem.

McClure would join me for a couple of whiskeys before he caught the bus home. Once he'd gone, I'd walk deeper into the Quarter, careful to stay at the curb to avoid muggers who might be lurking in the Cathedral shadows. I was mindful that somewhere out there in the dark was a famous thug named Peter Ysasi, who roamed the night streets with a baseball bat, ready for any rough encounter.

I'd decided that if I ever met up with Ysasi, I would interview him so I could write his life story. It might glorify a criminal, but it would damn sure distract him from whatever robbery he'd planned.

As it was, Ysasi never showed, nor did any other hoodlum ever bother me when I lived in New Orleans. I always made it safely to the Pink Elephant, my last stop before I fell asleep in my bachelor apartment on Chartres Street shortly before dawn.

Maybe my safety was earned by speaking every night to the old newspaper vendor, posted like a sentinel at the gateway to the Vieux Carre.

FOR AWHILE IN 1948, Mr. McClure and I would have a drink or two and then walk down Royal and over a few blocks to visit his friend, the writer Roark Bradford. We'd find him awake and alone at 1:30 in the morning in his art-filled house on Toulouse, waiting to die. His wife, who apparently found his sleepless vigil depressing, was usually absent, out drinking with friends. Sometimes she drifted home just as we departed, but she had little to say.

In 1928, Bradford enjoyed a great success with a book of short stories about Southern blacks and their vision of a genial God. *Ol' Man Adam and His Chillun* was adapted by playwright Marc Connelly into the Biblical fantasy *The Green Pastures*, a Pulitzer Prize-winning Broadway hit. By the 1930s, Bradford was one of the highest-paid fiction writers in America. He volunteered during the Second World War, contracting an intestinal illness in Africa and developing an aneurysm. He came home to a nation where his writings were dismissed as sentimental and racist and his popularity was waning. By the time I met him, the aneurysm and the African bug were in a race to finish him off.

McClure and Bradford were both members of the inner circle of the New Orleans literary set. "We are all internationally famous,

trying to put the make on my husband!" she screamed. The husband in question was descended from an early Louisiana governor; the accused was the playwright Tennessee Williams. Was this not an improvement over college classrooms and chemistry labs? Didn't alcohol make it even better?

ALL THE REPORTERS AT *THE TIMES-PICAYUNE* were fairly competent, a few even above average. The best was the relentlessly energetic Ken Gormin, who mentored me before he left the paper for a career in advertising. Gormin's departure meant that the sharpest and fastest writers in the newspaper building were the guys in the Associated Press bureau a few yards down the hall from my desk. Theirs was the work I admired most. And though I was not yet a reporter at that time, I learned a great deal about how to write by editing their stories about the region for our state editions.

On Saturday nights, I'd occasionally take a pint of whiskey out to the suburb of Metairie for a rare treat—a home-cooked meal with Keith Fuller and his wife. This young reporter from Texas was already on the star track, and after an eye-catching success with a book on John F. Kennedy's assassination released soon after the death, Keith went on to eventually become president of the AP.

Clem Broussard and Roy Steinfort of the AP wrote stories from the front lines of the civil rights struggle. Broussard became a colorful bureau chief in Detroit, as well as the only AP reporter in the country, it was said, who drove a Cadillac to work. Steinfort, a Kentucky native, went on to direct and expand AP's radio division so well that he was inducted into the University of Kentucky's Journalism Hall of Fame.

Not all of the AP guys were squarely on the right side of the civil rights issue. On weekends, without a wife or girlfriend waiting, I sometimes loitered after hours to listen as Rod Sparrow, a veteran of too many Southern courthouse stump speeches, reminisced about Delta politicians.

A particular favorite of Sparrow's was Theodore "The Man" Bilbo, a nasty white supremacist who was twice governor of Mississippi. Sparrow almost, but not quite, seemed to approve of white bigots like Bilbo. He would tug from a flask he kept in his desk while reminding me that during his tenure as a U.S. Senator, Bilbo had written "an important" book on civil rights. Its title? *Take Your Choice: Separation or Mongrelization.*

THE FOLLOWING SUMMER, I MET NOEL DILLARD of Birmingham.

Noel was the only daughter of a politically connected man who had given up the security of teaching school for the excitement of wartime duty with the OSS in China. In peacetime, still craving a scrap, he had become a Federal "revenuer," charging around in the Alabama woods with a pistol to break up stills and bust the heads of the moonshiners who ran them.

When we met, Noel had just graduated from Sophie Newcomb, Tulane's women's college. We shared a mutual friend, Vic Gold, a precocious student columnist for the *Tulane Hullabaloo*. Noel and Vic[6] were campus activists who campaigned for Henry Wallace for president on the Progressive Party ticket.

Meeting Noel was the beginning of a new chapter in my life. Noel was a petite, shapely brunette, sharply honed at the edges to argue radical politics. She was sufficiently realistic, however, to hold her tongue in a social work job which paid enough, she soon concluded, that we could afford to get married. One dark night on a romantic stroll along the levee uptown, we pledged our love and set the date for our wedding.

---

[6] Very funny and very liberal, Vic ultimately evolved from Tulane student radical to legendary conservative Washington journalist and champion of prominent Republican politicians Barry Goldwater and George H. W. Bush. His is one of the most curious career transformations of any of my early friends.

In August I set out on the bus to Tennessee to become reacquainted with my family and announce that Noel and I would marry at the beginning of Carnival season in February 1950. Before I got to Nashville, however, my homecoming turned tragic. Granny Graeme died in an automobile accident near Chattanooga. The Major seldom lost control of anything except his temper, but he had hit an oil slick and skidded off a mountain road, throwing her out of the car.

I was a pallbearer along with Graeme's three other grandsons. The funeral, held on the grounds at Chateau Graeme, was something of a state event, with the Tennessee governor, the Nashville mayor, and so many prominent friends that the undertaker ran out of chairs.

Until the accident shut her down at seventy-five, I don't recall my grandmother ever being sick, except for a bout of colitis and occasional gall bladder attacks, both of which she self-treated by smoking fine Cuban cigars Uncle McGregor sent her. (She never had much faith in doctors.)

There was another kind of sickness between me and my grandmother: one of the heart. She had been unable to forgive me for leaving Tennessee and her dreams for me. When I was a child, she had pushed me to the top and—at least as she saw it—made me a star. So why had I run away? I had hoped my engagement news might help to heal the pain between us, but her death meant neither of us would ever know, and I grieved that.

Graeme's funeral was also the occasion of a grim reunion with my parents and sister. My father was overcome with grief. My mother gritted her teeth until she could take the train back to Illinois and escape the tension with the Smiths, who resented her decision to leave Dad.

The funeral had been delayed for a few days after my arrival, and when it was time to return to New Orleans, I had exhausted my travel money. Just hours after the society preacher had prayed for comfort for Graeme's family, I telephoned my friend Nat at the Pink Elephant and asked for money. Within a few hours, a loan of $100 arrived by Western Union.

In the midst of all those affluent friends and kin, I had called on a New York gangster-turned-French Quarter saloon proprietor. Why did I ask Nat for help instead of my family?

Like the merchant seamen who gave Nat their money for safekeeping behind the cash register and slept upstairs over the bar, I trusted him. More than family, he had become my confidante. And his smoky, ill-lit bar, where the jukebox music never stopped, was my social center, and my refuge from all trouble.

-18-

My Life in Crime

BY ELECTION DAY 1952, MY DUTIES AT THE PAPER had changed. I had asked Healy to release me from the State Desk so I could become a reporter who wrote my own stories rather than an editor improving someone else's. Now, instead of going to the *Picayune* office in the afternoons to edit copy, I took the streetcar in the mornings to the Criminal Justice Building at Tulane and Broad so I could cover the New Orleans police.

Above the Tulane Avenue entrance to the building was carved the presumed mission of all who entered: "A Government of Laws, Not Men." Those words sounded noble enough, but old-timers in the press corps quickly made sure I didn't get the wrong impression.

They told me the perhaps apocryphal story of a notice posted long ago on the bulletin board at police headquarters, cautioning all majors and captains that if they did not pick up their paychecks within thirty days of issuance, "same will be forfeited and returned, without recourse, to the City Treasury." The suggestion, of course, was that police salaries were peanuts compared to the graft payoffs.

Frank Hay, the dean of the New Orleans *Item*'s police reporters, told a similar story. When Hay was assigned during the Depression to cover the cops at $5 a week, he protested to his editor that he couldn't survive on such skimpy wages. His editor was unmoved. "Live off the rackets, like everybody else out there!" he'd told Hay.[7]

---

[7] Frank, who was always kind to me, had modestly prospered by writing true-crime stories for the pulp magazines. It was also rumored that he and a policeman were partners in a handbook. If true, perhaps that business venture originated during Frank's five-dollar days.

AS *THE TIMES-PICAYUNE*'S DAYTIME POLICE REPORTER, I was expected to chase the police while they chased the bad guys, covering everything from serious accidents to the newsiest murders and robberies and the trials of those accused of committing them. I did that for about a month. Then Johnny Grosch, the sheriff of Orleans Parish, livened things up.

Sheriff Grosch, who had once been chief of detectives for the New Orleans police, had made news earlier in the decade when he testified before U.S. Senator Estes Kefauver's televised hearings on law enforcement and the Mafia. Kefauver called several sheriffs to explain why they were so rich. Grosch had testified that he'd made his money by accumulating rewards for catching bank robbers during the Depression, as well as from successful bets on "boat races."

"Boat races?" inquired Kefauver.

"Yeah, Senator," the sheriff said. "You know. Tips on fixed races that the jockeys told me about when I was pulling security duty at the fairgrounds racetrack."

Now Grosch was hoping to replace the reform-oriented deLesseps "Chep" Morrison as mayor. That's probably why he whispered to me and the *Picayune*'s veteran night police reporter, Joe Lucia, that the worst bad guys in town were in Grosch's old office, the New Orleans Police detective bureau.

Grosch told us that senior police detectives had been conspiring with burglars to steal safes from the lakefront homes of big-time gamblers. According to Grosch, the detectives, in their unmarked cars, served as lookouts while their safecracker partners broke in the homes. He said the gamblers weren't reporting the thefts because the safes were stuffed with winnings of which the Internal Revenue Service was unaware.

Lucia and I broke the news of Grosch's accusations. Grosch then held a press conference on a bridge over a city canal and invited all the papers in town.[8] As Grosch spoke, a deep-water diver dove under the bridge with a cable and hook, then surfaced holding an empty safe. The sheriff explained that one of his prisoners, an informant nicknamed "the Cricket," had told him the safe had been tossed over the bridge and into the canal by a detective who was complicit in the gambler-robbery caper. Another inmate at the Jefferson parish prison, this one named Roach, had confirmed the story.

Tips from Roach and the Cricket led to additional safes being fished up from bayous and beneath bridges. Of course, Grosch could have dumped those safes himself, as props for his case against City Hall. It wouldn't have been the first time he was suspected of planting evidence. But they had served their purpose for Grosch, acting as a sort of informal announcement of his intentions to run for mayor, and placing a police scandal squarely in the lap of the incumbent.

The safes had also served a purpose for me. Once that first one was pulled from the muck, my orientation to the police beat had ended. Most of my reporting thereafter was focused on allegations of police wrongdoing, a more dangerous pursuit than checking the daily logs to see who had been arrested, but an altogether more interesting one.

MAYOR MORRISON, his chief of staff, and the police superintendent mounted a counterattack against Grosch by denying everything. Then they announced a personnel shakeup and the firing of a detective named Pershing Gervais.

---

[8] Grosch even included the *Item*, which had been persona non grata with him ever since Thomas Sancton (one of the most aggressive and talented reporters in New Orleans history, who went on to work for *Life* and edit *The New Republic*) had led the front page of the *Item* with information from Grosch about police payoffs, whorehouses, and gamblers. Grosch had considered the information off the record. Grosch had promptly sued Sancton and the *Item* for $1 million; quit answering phone calls from Sancton and Frank Hay; and banned both men from the parish prison. Grosch had probably granted the truce that allowed Sanction and Hay to attend the press conference simply because that allowed him to tell the story in an additional paper.

Gervais was canned not for robbing safes but for selling jewelry, baubles he'd obtained from God knows where,[9] as an unauthorized sideline. (The Morrison administration also claimed Gervais was being fired because he took a trip with a woman who was not his wife, an offense for which New Orleans public servants historically had not been prosecuted.)

Morrison had picked the wrong scapegoat in Gervais, a tall, strapping Frenchman who talked like a Brooklyn cab driver. A former chauffeur for the mayor and police chief, Gervais did not go quietly into private life. While we were portraying him in the papers as an outcast rogue cop, Gervais began a new, twenty-year career as a valuable informant for federal agencies such as the Internal Revenue Service and the Justice Department. The Feds were highly interested in what Gervais had to say about "the element" in New Orleans—the folks in boxing, racing and handbooks; the merchants of gambling, prostitution, and drugs; and the details of the protection money those groups paid to politicians and police officials.

Yet Gervais was never too busy to tutor me in the underside of the criminal justice system. When I confronted him with the implication that he was one of the "bad guys," he shrugged that there were worse. His willingness to name names after he was fired transformed him from a disgraced policemen to an informed source for background, one of those "persons close to the investigation" who revealed the substance of the story, or at least what he wanted us to think it was.

Other than Gervais's dismissal, Grosch's charges never came to much—no cop was ever indicted for what he claimed they'd done—but they ignited a fire that the afternoon newspapers fanned in their search for more scandal.

If the morning *Times-Picayune* was depressingly dull, the afternoon papers were relentlessly hysterical. The *Item* fought a daily

---

[9] When a reporter friend of mine introduced his fiancée to Pershing, he complimented her engagement ring, but added, "I could have got it for you cheaper, honey."

war with the *Picayune*-owned *States* to find the best crime story with which to lead the front page of their afternoon editions. The *Item* had become much more competitive after it was sold in 1949 to young David Stern III, whose family had owned dailies in New York, Philadelphia, and Camden, New Jersey, but Stern still needed to sell papers. He looked for headlines about police misbehavior to attract readers.

Battling for street sales, the *Item* sold its final edition with market reports and boxcar headlines in a green wrapper. The *States* did the same but wrapped its final edition in peach. The wily Frank Hay of the *Item* and the supercharged Jack Dempsey, who worked for the *States*, scrambled to give their papers an exaggerated angle, evocative of the *Front Page* days of Chicago newspapers.

It was my job to shovel up after the elephants once the parade had passed. By the time I was writing at the end of the day for the next morning's paper, some of the headlines that had screamed in the afternoon were so small they made it into the back pages of the *Picayune* if at all.

IN THE COURSE OF COVERING A SIMPLE TRIAL that Hay and Dempsey ignored, I met a remarkable judge.

J. Bernard "Buddy" Cocke had been the district attorney of New Orleans for several terms before he was elected to the bench. On trial before Cocke was the manager of the public housing authority, a political hack from the "Old Regular" Democratic organization who was accused of drunk driving. Although two uniformed officers testified they arrested him after they noticed his car weaving in traffic, two bartenders swore the man had looked all right to them when he left their saloon just five minutes before he was arrested, having ordered only one drink. The elderly defendant, who had waived his right to a jury trial, testified to something vague about a defect in his steering mechanism.

"Not guilty!" the judge declared at the end of the testimony. "Court's adjourned."

When I went back to Judge Cocke's chambers to introduce myself as a new reporter on the beat, he was doffing his robe and lighting a cigarette. At fifty-seven, Buddy Cocke was short and paunchy, with a wrinkled face, tiny bloodshot eyes, and a bulbous nose. His distinctively rich voice reminded me of my grandmother's—instructive, compelling, and insistent.

Pulling out a bottle of Old Forester, Cocke poured two drinks into shot glasses and shoved one my way.

"Of course, that fellow out there was probably guilty," he said.

I must have looked shocked, because he added, "He was one of my folks, from the Old Regulars. I felt some obligation to balance the scales."

"*Balance* the scales?" I asked.

"Well, yes, so to speak. I acquitted a silk-stocking type from the Boston Club last week, accused on the same kind of arrest. I let him go because it seemed marginal, not worth the embarrassment." Cocke wiped his mouth with the back of his hand.

"If any of the bastards you work for should ask you, Mr. Smith, you may tell them what I just said. But add this: I dismissed the case against one of their pals for *them* because it was problematic and I took pity. Then I dismissed one for *me*, because the courts are just."

He stubbed out his cigarette meditatively. "That's called Tit for Tat!"

Becoming Buddy Cocke's friend was a profoundly educational experience. He was my mentor about the workings of the criminal justice system. A lonely man, he welcomed company, even at breaks during a trial. His chambers were like a second home in which he kept books and newspapers, a hot plate to cook his lunches, and an ever-open bottle of booze to get through the day.

The son of a court bailiff, Cocke had grown up poor but graduated first in his law school class. When Huey Long took away the power of the New Orleans district attorney to name his own assistants, Eugene Stanley, then the DA, resigned. Cocke, who was his first assistant, followed him out the door. The two formed a private practice, but they nearly starved until the scandals that followed Long's assassination in 1935 changed public opinion. Stanley eventually was elected Louisiana Attorney General and Cocke was elected district attorney of New Orleans.

Although Cocke had been a victim of Longism, he also had an ingrained resentment of the Garden District nabobs. That left him suspicious of the intentions of most of the politicians whom they liked, especially Mayor Morrison.

His father's dependence on the Old Regular political organization, which had also been oppressed by Long, left Cocke with a parochial respect for politicians of a type that was fading from the scene—ward leaders who delivered coal, ice, and groceries to the poor, found them jobs, and then delivered their votes on election day. Morrison had sapped the influence of the old-time pols by creating his own organization to serve the grassroots, but in doing so he had picked up their bad habits—selling jobs, buying votes, winking at the gamblers and prostitutes—while still posing as a reformer and retaining the editorial support of the newspapers. The hypocrisy of the do-gooders drove Cocke crazy.

As district attorney, Cocke had sent several defendants to the electric chair. In spite of this—or perhaps because of it—he was quick to listen to claims that defendants had been beaten in custody, and the police hated him for it.

He was especially suspicious of the narcotics squad, whose members doubled as vice cops to raid bookies and whores. He was a tiger when it came to requiring the cops to prove the chain of evidence, especially when the defendant was black. He took seriously the claims of black defendants who said they had been entrapped by police who used informants to lure them to buy drugs and then threatened them with lengthy sentences unless they became snitches themselves.

Perhaps nothing offended Judge Cocke more than the "war on drugs" of the 1950s. He considered the drug problem overblown. He blamed the scandal-hungry papers for portraying addicts as "fiends" in order to scare the public and sell papers, and the police for boasting about the "street value" of narcotics they seized in highly publicized raids in order to glorify themselves. He was infuriated when the legislature passed a harsh law requiring judges to sentence offenders to a minimum of ten years, without parole, for possession of as little as a grain of marijuana.

Cocke waged a year-long campaign against the mandatory minimum sentences, noting in testimony before the legislature that many more users were being convicted than major dealers. He succeeded in getting portions of the laws modified. As a result, the New Orleans chapter of the NAACP honored him in 1953 with a dinner for his "service in the cause of equal justice." But few whites, and no one from the district attorney's office or the police department, attended. Perhaps that was a harbinger of the city's disgusting resistance the next year to *Brown vs. Board of Education*, the U.S. Supreme Court ruling that integrated America's public schools.

THAT WINTER OF 1953, I covered the most publicized murder trial of my time in New Orleans.

Jimmy Cooper, the owner of the famous Court of Two Sisters restaurant on Royal Street, was accused of killing his estranged socialite wife, Didi. The prosecution charged that one night while the French Quarter was flooded with throngs from a Tulane-LSU football game, Cooper had driven unnoticed to the Garden District home where his wife lived, choked her to death, and returned to his apartment above the restaurant without being seen.

From the day Didi's body was discovered, interest in the case was driven by the newspapers' competition to boost their street sales by suggesting new leads. As the case grew cold for lack of genuine evidence, the *States* began running a box on the front page each afternoon under the headline "Who Killed Didi?" The box displayed a running tally of the days and months since Didi had died and insinuated in inflammatory prose that the police and district attorney were derelict in their duty.

Eventually, Cooper was indicted, with the help of a stripper the cops had hired as an undercover agent. She testified that Cooper admitted the killing to her after she slept with him. The stripper's tale and other flimsy testimony, however, failed to convince the jury, and Cooper was acquitted in less than an hour. I wrote a terrific story about the verdict, then headed for a celebration at Cooper's restaurant.

By the time I returned to the paper, our lawyers, worried about a lawsuit, had sent word to the night city editor to strip all the color from my article, the biggest crime story of the decade. They feared my account of the not-guilty verdict and the impromptu party that erupted in the French Quarter after it might imply that the newspapers' bias had led to Cooper being wrongfully accused.

The censorship by the *Picayune* unhinged whatever fragile control I'd been able to maintain on my drinking. My dependence on alcohol had been increasing since the day a few months before the trial that Noel had announced she wanted to end our marriage.

Over its three brief years, our union had consisted primarily of worry over debt, excessive drinking by both of us, and mutual disappointment that we couldn't turn our problems around. By the time my Cooper story was trashed, she had moved out of our apartment, and I was drinking ever more heavily on the job.

Three months later, I quit the newspaper.

I walked into Healy's office and told him I was exhausted and needed a break. He grimaced, shook his head, and said he was sorry.

Then he said, "I believe we owe you a week's vacation.

"I'll phone downstairs, and you can pick up a check on your way out."

-19-
New Man at the *Item*

AS MY MARRIAGE FELL APART, my parents resumed theirs.

When Dad found a job as an attorney with the Veterans Administration in Nashville, my mother returned to the farm at Hendersonville. She had been away for three years, but the neighbors along Center Point Road acted as if nothing had happened. She might have been caring for a sick sister up north, as far as they were concerned.

My sister Robin had married James Burrow from Kentucky, a graduate student in history at the University of Illinois, the school Robin was attending on scholarship. Noel and I attended Robin's wedding.

Three of my cousins with whom I grew up had also married. I skipped all of those weddings. I was too busy drinking my way through divorce with even greater intensity than I had drunk during our marriage. It was not a good time.

When I was in New Orleans, the city was often called "the Crescent City" or "the City That Care Forgot." In 1954, at age twenty-seven, I was trying to forget my cares with a new relationship and a new job.

I had taken up with an unhappily married woman—call her Miriam—who was bored staying home with an incurably ill husband. Miriam had married the man when he had the kind of money and professional prestige I never had, but now he was an invalid, and I offered the drama Miriam needed to alleviate her boredom.

Meanwhile, three months after I had left *The Times-Picayune*, Henri Wolbrette, the managing editor at the *Item*, called with a job offer.

"I like your work," he said. "You have a feel for what's going on with the courts and the cops. But I know you drink a lot.

"Be careful out there."

Then, apparently blind to the irony, Wolbrette ordered me over to the Sho-Bar on Bourbon Street on my first assignment. While drinking all night on the *Item*'s dollar and listening to the music of Louie Prima and Keely Smith, I was to watch for cops who might stop by to collect a payoff. I never saw a payoff, but I certainly got buzzed.

In my second month at the *Item*, the publisher, David Stern, asked me to go on a scouting trip to the infamous Louisiana State Penitentiary at Angola, where convict labor manned a prison farm. In 1952, thirty-one inmates at Angola had slashed their Achilles tendons in protest against the prison's inhumane conditions. Stern had served on a citizens' committee that recommended the usual reforms for the prison, and he wanted me to see whether things were improving.

I had never been to Angola, so I had no basis for determining whether conditions had changed. Besides, the warden never let me out of his sight, so there were no whispered private interviews with an inmate or disgruntled guard.

But the prison clearly housed some emotionally disturbed prisoners, many of them black, trying to survive the darkest of depressions in the prison hospital. Some of the inmates were jazz musicians reared in Chicago or other Northern cities who had been busted on Bourbon Street for smoking a joint. (As expected, I didn't see a single inmate the warden could identify as a major drug dealer.) These urban types, who weren't cut out to cut sugarcane for ten years, faced a bleak future unless Judge Cocke prevailed upon the legislature to rethink their cruel sentences.

While I didn't see much in which Stern would be interested, I did see an inmate whose story I'd written when he was on trial before Judge Cocke. On my way out, I stopped to say hello to Louis Eugene

Hoover. He didn't seem to remember me, or remember anything to speak of, but I certainly remembered him.

Hoover was the drifter and male prostitute convicted of choking a prominent businessman to death during a Carnival-week homosexual encounter. The search for him, his eventual arrest, and the murder trial had all been big stories I had covered at *The Times-Picayune*.

When the businessman's body had been found in the Monteleone, police had launched an all-points search of the city for a husky young man in a striped sweater who'd been spotted leaving the hotel. The search ended with a dramatic press conference at police headquarters where Assistant Chief Melvin Dumont, smiling and fingering a small silver crucifix, announced how the suspect had been found.

It seemed that Dumont had prayed fervently, made a novena and asked the Mother of Christ for guidance in the case. The Blessed Lady had responded, directing Dumont to a corner near the Veterans Administration (VA) hospital. When Melvin and his chauffeur proceeded there as directed, he reported, there was Hoover, a burly youth with tousled hair, dressed in a striped sweater and waiting for a bus.

"So that's how it was, Chief?" I asked. "You were just driving along, you and your chauffeur, praying and driving, and there he was?"

"That's right, Al," Dumont said, crossing himself.

"May I come home and find my sweet old mama, laid out stone-cold dead in Lamanna-Panna-Fallo [a funeral home] if that ain't how it was. Answered prayers."

I couldn't publish the real story, but I knew it. Dumont's prayers had been answered—by Dr. Dick Stone, the VA's chief psychiatrist, who happened to be a drinking buddy of mine.

When Hoover had shown up at the hospital—records later showed he had a history of fleeing to VA hospitals after attacking his patrons—Stone's intake conversation with him had implicated Hoover in the murder. After a few hours of pondering his responsibility, Stone called police headquarters and suggested that if an officer should happen to go by the front steps of the VA at exactly 3:00 p.m. the next day, that officer might find a discharged patient who could answer whatever questions the police might be interested in asking.

And that was how Eugene Hoover *actually* came to be sitting handcuffed in the back seat of a police cruiser with Dumont. Sworn to silence by Stone, however, I couldn't tell the real story.

Hoover was tried in Judge Cocke's court. The key defense witness, a forensic shrink from Tulane whom Cocke despised ("He's a quack!"), gave us the lowdown on Hoover's mental condition.

"Your honor, the defendant is incapable of knowing whether he committed this crime," the doctor testified. "If he did, it was in the midst of a seizure of *Jacksonian* epilepsy."

At that very moment, Hoover emitted a long, low moan, stood up, flung out his arms, and began spinning in place.

I was seated behind Hoover, and I was shoved to the floor as deputies piled on him. Cocke banged his gavel. "Get the jury out of here!" he yelled to the bailiffs.

"See, Judge, that's a *Jacksonian* petit mal seizure!" the forensic shrink helpfully interjected.

"… and take this witness with you!" Cocke shouted. "In the meantime, doctor, kindly shut up!"

Smart as he was, Cocke didn't know everything. He was convinced the episode was staged. But when I saw Hoover at the Angola hospital two years later, he was clearly catatonic. "He's been that way a long time," the warden told me.

WHEN JOHN MCCLURE DIED shortly after I joined the *Item*, I lost a revered elder and mentor. By then I was something of an old-timer myself, with a summer intern assigned to my care. Hodding Carter

III, a Princeton student from Greenville, Mississippi, had been sent to us by his parents for a journalism lesson in a larger market than that served by the paper they owned. Already sharp about news and destined to be even more advanced on integration than his liberal parents, Hodding became my friend. But he didn't learn much from me. The only lesson I taught him that summer was how to drink martinis for lunch.

Two of my *Picayune* friends, Al Maund and Reuben Killebrew, had also migrated to the *Item*. Maund was writing editorials, and Killebrew was working on the Copy Desk under none other than Joe Marshall, the Navy chief who had held my head as I vomited at a drunken party.

Perhaps foreshadowing my own future with alcoholism, the *Item* fired Marshall for missing work because of drinking. A month later, I visited him, and he was on the wagon. When I reported to Wolbrette that Marshall was penitent, Henri sent me to tell Marshall he could return to work.

The *Item* was generally a tolerant place, although it had stupidly fired Ewing Poteet, its music and theater critic, for signing a petition asking the New Orleans City Council to end the segregation of public transportation.

Herman Drezinski, the atheist religion editor, was luckier than Poteet. One morning, Wolbrette had teased the normally lovable Drezinski, who fell into a rage and hurled his typewriter at him. When Wolbrette ducked, the typewriter sailed through an open window and crashed to the street below. Herman's only punishment was being forced to continue using that typewriter, three keys of which were forever stuck as a result of their trip through the window. The managing editor sent Drezinski an apologetic note, but reported, "Unfortunately, there is nothing in our budget for a replacement."

Wolbrette didn't tease me, but he nearly got me killed.

One day I had written a story about friction at the highest levels of the Police Department. After I left the copy on Wolbrette's desk, he and I chatted awhile, and I happened to mention that the top two assistants to Joseph Scheuring, the police superintendent, had agreed that if Scheuring was forced to resign over the ongoing graft probe, whichever of them was named his successor would retain the other as first deputy. I'd been told this off the record by one of those deputies, Guy Bannister, at breakfast that morning.

Two hours later, as a newsboy dropped off late editions of the *Item* and the *States* in the Criminal Courts Building pressroom, the *Item*'s telephone operator called me with an alarming message.

"Chief Bannister was in the office asking for you, and he looked mad enough to shoot somebody," she said. "We told him you were at police headquarters."

Picking up the fresh paper, I saw why he was angry. Wolbrette had inserted Bannister's off-the-record comments into the story's lead and then bannered it on the front page under my byline.

Rushing out of the pressroom to find Bannister, I met him striding down the hall. Dressed in a gray suit and a straw hat with a huge pistol flopping at his side, he had the determined pace of a man on a mission. I managed to get out "I was just coming to explain" before he swung at me.

Once, twice, and then I was down—sliding along the marble floor toward the feet of two astonished detectives standing in an office doorway.

I decided not to get up until Bannister was gone. I was relieved to see him turn away.

"Freedom of the press is not a license to steal," he muttered over his shoulder. It was an appropriate comment, but he had slugged the wrong guy.

I was on the phone with the culprit Wolbrette, angrily recounting my "brush with the law," when the two detectives who'd seen the fight asked me to hang up. They had an urgent request from Superintendent Scheuring. He wanted me to swear out a warrant against Bannister for assault, and he would arrest Bannister himself.

I refused. Bannister, a former chief of the FBI's Washington D.C. office, had recently been recruited by the mayor to "get to the bottom" of all the graft charges. He was an outsider in the police department. He had been promised independence, but then was placed under Scheuring, which immediately suggested his hiring had been mere window dressing. By fouling up my story, Wolbrette had risked giving City Hall the chance to fire Bannister, who was the reformers' last best hope of exposing the graft system.

After a night of watching television broadcasts report "rumors" of an altercation between Bannister and me, the "good guys" patched up their differences. Bannister apologized to the *Item*'s publisher and to all of us who had caused him to make a fool of himself, and I went back to expanding my experience as a police reporter. (I don't think I knew the term "investigative reporter" back then. I thought it was the task of all reporters to investigate.)

-20-
On the Way Out

A MILE OR SO FROM THE CRIMINAL COURT BUILDING, another reporter, Tom Sancton, and I began sharing a vigil with Carlos Marcello and his lawyer as they waited for a last-minute reprieve of orders to kick him out of the country. Marcello was the foremost organized crime figure in New Orleans. He was not quite native to the city—that was what the deportation orders were about—but he was sufficiently indigenous to be the Mafia's go-to guy in the Gulf region.

My first contact with "the Little Man" came while he was awaiting deportation in 1956. He smiled nervously and talked baseball scores while we waited for phone calls concerning his future. Authorities in the Eisenhower Justice Department wanted to kick him out of the country as an alien. They claimed he was born to his immigrant parents in transit from Sicily to New Orleans; his attorneys said Marcello had always lived in New Orleans.

The reporters and the mob guys both called the diminutive millionaire "the Little Man," but Marcello stood tall in the gambling and prostitution rackets. Marcello was boss of a billion dollar criminal syndicate developed under the tutoring of New York Mafia chieftain Frank Costello.[10] I was never sure if Marcello dealt in drugs, but his numerous properties—he laundered his dirty profits into motels, restaurants, coin machines, and land development—were well-known to the police, who "bugged" his offices for years. He was finally convicted of bribery and sent to a Missouri federal prison.

---

[10] In the 1930s, Governor Huey Long had invited Costello to set up slot machines in Louisiana for which Long would provide protection in return for hidden payoffs. FBI records later made public showed that the arrangement continued when Earl Long was governor.

In Marcello's last years, still in federal prison, there were accusations, never proven, that he was complicit in the assassination of President John F. Kennedy.

In New Orleans, I lived near or associated with two other characters who would attain national notoriety over the killing of President Kennedy.

I once lived next door to Clay Shaw, a tall, prematurely white-haired, and quietly gay man who was a leader in international trade and a champion of architectural preservation. In the late 1960s, Jim Garrison, a New Orleans district attorney, ran an outrageously phony prosecution of Shaw, trying to link him and Marcello in a conspiracy to kill Kennedy. I knew Garrison, having occasionally joined him for a drink or dinner at "Clean" Gluck's on Royal.

Garrison also alleged, perhaps correctly, that Guy Bannister, who by then had been forced from the police department, had run anti-Castro agents into Cuba for the CIA. (Bannister, incidentally, also had had contacts with Lee Harvey Oswald in New Orleans before Oswald was arrested for assassinating Kennedy.)

All of these men are portrayed in the Oliver Stone movie *JFK*. Stone's version of the Kennedy assassination unfortunately is based largely on Garrison's questionable book, *On the Trail of the Assassins*. But the scene in which Bannister beats up an informant is quite authentic, I would say.

AFTER A YEAR OF CONTINUED HEAVY DRINKING, I blacked out one afternoon while driving from police headquarters to the *Item* office. When I came to, I was still driving aimlessly around the lakefront, with no memory of why I was there. That night, my friend Dick Stone, the VA psychiatrist, admitted me to a ward at Touro Hospital.

While I was hospitalized, Stone recommended a therapist, Dr. Ed Knight. I began to see him weekly. The routine was always the same: I'd ride a streetcar to the corner of Napoleon and St. Charles near Dr.

Knight's office, then pop into a bar to fortify myself with a stiff drink before showing up for our talk. Our sessions were also remarkably similar: I would talk nonstop for an hour, and Dr. Knight would mostly listen.

Occasionally, though, the quiet Dr. Knight said something perceptive. He told me I drank because I was "thirsty," and noted that I seemed "reluctant to close the curtain" or "leave the stage."

Two months into my counseling with Dr. Knight, I was promoted to assistant city editor of the *Item*. My job was to open the newsroom at 5:00 a.m., check the overnight local stories for something bold and eye-catching, and get the city stories shaped up for the first editorial conference at 8:30.

I told Dr. Knight that because of my promotion, I would be too busy with work to continue our sessions. He congratulated me and wished me luck. And as I walked out the door, he called after me, "You may want to come back someday."

ONCE I'D BEEN PROMOTED, the *Item* expected that with my background in crime, I'd be able to develop a shocking Page One yarn each day that would goose the sales of the Final edition. Between the early morning and the late afternoon, the *Item* ran a fairly respectable sheet. But for the Final, we liked pictures of ladies plunging from tall buildings, their skirts flying upward, or stories as risible as that of the frustrated, lovesick customer who chased a naked stripper down Bourbon Street as she screamed "rape!" (The waggish Killebrew noted that if the same story were to run in *The Times-Picayune*, the intended victim would have been quoted as yelling "Help, help, he's trying criminally to assault me!")

My job as editor was sufficiently flexible to allow me to check out the occasional story tip myself. So when we received an anonymous call that Earl Long, who was campaigning again for governor, had dropped dead at the Roosevelt Hotel, I assigned myself to follow up on it. Dashing down the *Item*'s steps, I sprinted several blocks to the Roosevelt, then raced to Long's suite and through an open door into his bedroom.

It might have been the story of the year, but Earl wasn't dead.

Less than a week before the election, on a cold January day, he was stuffing bundles of U.S. currency into the pockets of a black overcoat—Election Day money, I guess. Underneath the turned-up brim of a porkpie hat, he shifted his gaze between the stacks of money on the bed and the out-of-breath reporter who burst in on him. His teeth clinched on a cigarette, convinced that I was a reporter, something worse than a robber. Long's hard face nevertheless softened.

"Dead?" he said. "No, sir, *I'm* fine. It's little 'de la Soups' Morrison that's dead. Tell those bastards you work for not to cry, but I'm yore governor, again."

As Long and I rode down on the elevator together, he was still shifting bills around. The traffic cop on the street was under the command of Long's opponent, "de la Soups" Morrison. The light was against us as we tried to cross, but the officer blew a whistle, stopped the traffic, and waved us across.

"Good afternoon, Governor Long," the cop shouted. "It's in the bag Tuesday!"

IN LATE 1956, I TOOK A JUNKET TO NEW YORK for the world premiere of the Elizabeth Taylor-Rock Hudson movie *Giant*. I remember a sparkling chat with Michael Todd, then a Taylor husband, but I don't recall seeing the movie. I was in the theatre, sleeping off the drinks I'd had on the plane. I wrote the story from the publicity packet.

A few months later, I spent a morning in the bar at the St. Charles Hotel, drinking absinthes and listening to Robert Penn Warren explain that Willie Stark, the political kingfish in *All the King's Men*, was not to be confused with Huey Long. "Huey Long was a real person," he said patiently. And then, somewhat disingenuously, "How do I know what was in a real person's mind?"

In June 1957, my third year at the *Item*, the city editor bought my hunch that we were going to take a bad hit from Hurricane Audrey and gave me the go-ahead on a Sunday, a day we didn't publish, to post reporters on the coast and around the city. When the storm struck, claiming six hundred lives, we had the staff in place to produce a spectacular set of stories. But my twenty-four hours of preparation had been fueled by whiskey. The hurricane over, I was so exhausted that I checked into a hotel, a block away from the office, and slept until the next day.

I charged the room to the paper.

WHEN ALEC GUINNESS WALKED INTO the police station with me, he was already a famous actor in England. It would be only a year before *The Bridge on the River Kwai* established him as an international star. But that day not a single cop in New Orleans had ever heard of him. Several figured him for a British bobby in plain clothes. One officer inquired if he spent much time at Scotland Yard.

"As little as possible," was Guinness' enigmatic reply.

Only when I explained that my guest had just finished a film with Grace Kelly were the cops impressed. Living in a spotlight of their own, our police were always cordial to other folks in show business.

I had interviewed Guinness that morning at his hotel. He had just finished shooting scenes in North Carolina for *The Swan*, with Grace Kelly, his first Hollywood film. Unlike many actors, he had little interest in talking about himself, which made the interview difficult.

On the other hand, he was intrigued by my job as a police reporter and seemed touched that I had volunteered to leave my usual beat and interview him because I was a fan. I was astonished when he and his director, Peter Glenville, accepted my invitation to join me for the last few hours of that day's shift on the police beat.

This was at the peak of my compulsive drinking in New Orleans. I wonder now—how much of the darker truths about that police beat did I spill to Guinness and his friend that afternoon?

Did I tell Guinness about the brown envelopes that were slipped into the precinct lockers—envelopes stuffed with cash collected every week from madams and bookies and pinball owners? (If you don't like it, rookies were told, tell it to your priest.)

Did I mention my friend Eddie, the detective we had linked to a whorehouse? Did I tell him that Eddie came by the pressroom to wish me a merry Christmas, then went home and blew his brains out?

What about my interview with the new Crime Commission chief, another former FBI agent, this one from Chicago, who'd been hired by New Orleans reformers? Did I mention that when I'd asked him the difference between crime in Chicago and crime in New Orleans, he'd replied, "Well, in Chicago, the mob *controls* the Police Department. In New Orleans, the mob *is* the Police Department."

When we began our rounds, Guinness didn't say much. He observed everything, and he didn't want to stop looking. We went everywhere—homicide, narcotics, the coroner's office to see an autopsy of a murder victim—and, finally, to a lineup in the darkened basement, where the cops heckled the wretched suspects on a stage. He balked at only one opportunity—to sit for a test on the brand new lie detector. "*Never*!" was his emphatic reply. "You'll never get the truth from me!"

We might have analyzed the afternoon's adventure at dinner that night, but when he called with an invitation, I pleaded fatigue and declined. It was a polite way of saying I was too drunk to come out on the street.

The next day, I called in sick.

The day after that, the city editor phoned with an ominous request. I was to provide a medical excuse for my absence, in writing. So I put on some clothes, found the New Orleans coroner, and persuaded him to write a note affirming my poor condition.

When I came into the office, threw the note on a desk, and announced I was going back to bed, it was the last straw. The *Item* had had enough of me.

When I arrived at work on the third day, I was told it was time to leave. I was presented with a letter stating that I was being dismissed "for cause." The editor, George Chaplin, handed me a severance check for $1,700, asked me to sign it, and then took it back. It was for the exact amount I owed the paper's Credit Union.

My days and nights in New Orleans were over. Exactly ten years to the month after I left Vanderbilt, my parents drove down from Tennessee, took me home, and persuaded the superintendent at the Nashville Veterans Hospital to admit me for a thirty-day stay.

Unlike Guinness, I had no clue what my next act would be.

-21-
Russellville, Free State of Logan

"HOW LONG HAVE YOU BEEN AN ALCOHOLIC?"

The question, posed by the admitting doctor at Nashville's VA Hospital, startled me.

"*Me?*" The man must have been talking to someone else. "I'm no alcoholic.

"Sometimes I just drink too much."

So much for self-awareness.

My thirty days at the VA passed slowly. There was no treatment, no therapy, no mention of Alcoholics Anonymous. Since I didn't know how to play poker or bridge, I just sat and read in the hospital library as I waited to get back to my life.

RELEASED FROM THE VA, I had no place to go but my parents' farm. But I was restless to leave as soon as I could figure out where to go. So I welcomed a visit from Eliot Frankel, a friend from Vanderbilt days.

Eliot was now a producer for *The Huntley-Brinkley Hour*, NBC's national nightly news program. The correspondent John Chancellor was being transferred from Chicago to New York, and Eliot wanted to know if I'd come to Chicago and try out for the job.

I thanked Eliot for the opportunity, but told him I'd prefer to stay in the newspaper business.

The truth was I didn't believe I could face a camera without a drink.

MY FATHER DROVE ME TO *THE TENNESSEAN* OFFICE. To my amazement, the editor there seemed interested in me and promised to call at the next opening.

A call came, but it wasn't the one I expected. It was the columnist, Elmer Hinton, letting me know about a job editing a weekly paper in Russellville.

Why not? I thought. I could work there until I found a job in Nashville. But first I needed a clarification.

"*Which* Russellville?" I asked. "The one in Kentucky, the one in Alabama, or the one in Arkansas?"

THE RUSSELLVILLE THAT NEEDED AN EDITOR was the one in Kentucky, a town of some six thousand people sixty miles north of Nashville. I was hired as editor of the weekly *News-Democrat* after a single interview with Mrs. Byrne Allen Evans, the publisher.

Mrs. Evans had survived a string of eccentric editors. Perhaps she was so desperate she felt no need to ask why a former assistant city editor of one of the largest afternoon newspapers in the South was suddenly available.

As Ailene Chambers, a Vanderbilt graduate, Mrs. Evans had come to Russellville to teach at Bethel College. She married the local editor, and in the 1930s, they bought the paper from Albert Gallatin Rhea, brother of Thomas Rhea, a prominent political figure.

The Rhea family had controlled the paper—and dominated Logan County politics—for more than a hundred years before hard times in the Depression forced them to sell. Even after the change in ownership, the Evans family continued to align the paper with the Rhea political faction and its allies.

I knew nothing about Logan County or its politics on that first Monday of January 1958 when I got off the bus from Tennessee and checked in at *The News-Democrat*. But by mid-morning I had found a guide.

A handsome, cheery man named Jim Lyne stopped by and invited me to join him later for introductions at the Logan County Courthouse. He also arranged for me to rent a room at the home of his widowed mother, Myrt. The widow Lyne lived within walking distance of the paper and the public square, which was convenient for me since I didn't own a car. (It wasn't until the next day that I discovered I would need a taxicab to find a bootlegger.)

ON THAT FIRST VISIT TO THE COURTHOUSE, Lyne introduced me to Emerson "Doc" Beauchamp, a local political boss.[11]

A red-faced man with bloodshot eyes and a bourbon belly, Beauchamp greeted me with a beguiling smile.

"I suppose you're a Democrat," Doc said in a gravel voice I would soon learn that politicians and reporters loved to imitate. "Miz Evans wouldn't hire any other kind, would she?"

Doc, of course, knew the answer better than I. It didn't take me long to figure out that he knew the preferences of every adult in the county and most of the children.

Although he lived in Russellville and rented an apartment in Frankfort, the state capitol, Beauchamp owned a farm in Schochoh in southeastern Logan County and always listed his occupation as "farmer." Schochoh was where he voted—"early and often," according to his political enemies.

That day, Lyne and I watched as Doc tried to influence an election. He wasn't trying to steal it (although his foes certainly believed he knew how to do that). Instead, he was trying to persuade the Logan County Fiscal Court's six magistrates that they should accept Guy McMillen as the new county road foreman. McMillen had just finished a term as sheriff and could not succeed himself.

Unfortunately for Beauchamp and McMillen, County Judge Homer Dorris, the chief executive of the fiscal court, had another

---

[11] "Beauchamp" was pronounced "Beechum," except by toothless members of the electorate, who addressed Doc as "Mr.Meetchum."

idea. He favored John Q. Hite for foreman. Although Beauchamp and
Dorris were usually allied, their split over appointing a road foreman
had left the magistrates deadlocked three to three.

County road foreman was an important post. Whoever held it
looked to the county judge and the fiscal court's dominant faction for
guidance as to where to deliver gravel along the back roads of rural
Logan County. The foreman dumped the loads as directed, and also
where he deemed it to be politically helpful. Some farmers, for
example, might think they were due a load of free rock on their
private driveways. If the foreman agreed, he would oblige.

I quickly learned that Doc's political power extended past Logan
County's borders. Beauchamp chaired the county Democratic
organization, which controlled all but one of the elective offices in the
courthouse. In a statewide Democratic primary, he could dependably
deliver a two thousand-vote margin to the candidate of his choice. In
a tight race, those votes might elect the candidate he favored.

A canny operator in the corridors of the capitol, where he started
his career as a twelve-year-old page in the state legislature,
Beauchamp was one of the half-dozen Kentucky kingmakers who
could elect a governor.

But Beauchamp didn't always win.

After serving a term as lieutenant governor, I learned,
Beauchamp had shelved his own ambition to be governor in 1955 and
instead backed Court of Appeals Judge Bert T. Combs for the post.
Beauchamp reasoned that Combs, from the mountains, seemed, well,
more gubernatorial. Combs ended up losing that 1955 race to former
governor Albert Benjamin "Happy" Chandler, who reclaimed an
office he had given up in 1939 for a seat in the U.S. Senate.

Furious over Beauchamp's support of Combs, Chandler had
vowed after that 1955 election to exile Doc. "I'll send old Beauchamp
back to his farm in Logan County and build a fence around him,"
Chandler told the voters. And that's what he did.

When I came along, Doc was plotting a comeback. It began where he had started as a kid: at the grassroots.

BEAUCHAMP'S WORLD WAS FILLED with citizens who were chafed because he had out-maneuvered them in the precincts. But the short, rumpled man was so humorous and good-natured in victory that it was hard to stay mad at him between elections.

My new friend Lyne, who was married to Beauchamp's niece Lucy, was Beauchamp's lawyer and "pencil man," that is, he tabulated the official returns on election nights. (Lyne could score with either end of that pencil, I eventually would learn. "I don't know how many winners came from the eraser," he admitted one tipsy evening.)

Lyne ran the First Federal Savings and Loan Association and also was the attorney for the Evans family and *The News-Democrat*.

Lyne was a prince of the city, but he had been defeated for reelection as county attorney in 1957 by Joe Wheeler, a young lawyer with strong connections. Wheeler's two brothers-in-law were Granville Clark, the city attorney, and Carl Page, the local General Motors dealer. Clark and Page had manned the polls all day with volunteers, then stood over Lyne at the courthouse that night, never averting their gaze, until he counted himself out.

THAT FIRST DAY OF MY EDITORSHIP, before the magistrates broke for lunch at Higgins' Cafe, Beauchamp courteously introduced me to his friends and rivals alike, including county Republican Party Chairman Lawrence Forgy. The Republicans, who were in the minority, sought to maintain ballot security in "the Free State of Logan."

"Free State?" said Rayburn Smith, a Beauchamp crony I also met that first day. "That's just slang talk about politics from soreheads who think we make up the rules."

Rayburn was a lanky fellow, soft-spoken and slow to smile, with a bald head and the doleful countenance of a country undertaker. I assumed the bulge under the arm of his brown suit was a pistol, but it turned out to be an inner jacket pocket stuffed with notes he had jotted on the backs of envelopes.

A part-time farmer like Beauchamp and a deacon in the First Baptist Church, Rayburn was also the best poker player in Logan County. I'd soon learn that when he passed the collection plate on Sundays, folks jokingly wondered if it was the beginning or the end of his work week.

Rayburn's election skills were honed early in his youth. "I started driving the old folks to the precincts when I was thirteen," he would later tell me.

"I guess I didn't vote 'em until I was fifteen or sixteen."

When I met him in the hall that first day, Rayburn was chatting amiably with Joe Wheeler, the man who had defeated Beauchamp's man Lyne for county attorney, and Fount Shifflett, who had lost to Beauchamp's candidate for sheriff. Like Doc, his chieftain, Rayburn kept his enemies close.

When Beauchamp's friends ran state government in Frankfort, Rayburn was the governor's go-between to channel political messages to the engineers at the district highway garage in Bowling Green. Every six months he was also the bagman who collected money to cover election expenses from the highway workers and other state employees in the area.

Chandler had fired Rayburn for his support of Bert Combs in that 1955 governor's race. Rayburn was back on his farm at Oakville on twenty-four hour call as Beauchamp and the leader of their state Democratic faction, Earle Chester Clements, plotted to end the Chandler interregnum. When I met them, they were planning another Combs race, this time with Doc on the ticket as the Democratic candidate for agriculture commissioner.

APPROACHING *THE NEWS-DEMOCRAT* OFFICE on foot from Mrs. Lyne's house the next morning, I noted that it was as old-fashioned in appearance as it was in process.

A glass storefront bore the name of the paper in large letters. Visitors were greeted by "Tookey" Kemp, the secretary and society editor, who strategically sat near the front door. Dan Knotts, the ad manager, had a desk out front, as did the circulation manager and the bookkeeper. Between my little office and the visitors stood a tall cabinet stocked with stationery and poster board we sold as a sideline.

I felt as if I were back at Castle Heights writing stories for the *Cavalier* to be printed on the hot-type press at the *Lebanon Democrat*. *The News-Democrat* was still printed with hot lead and Linotypes. Photographs were sent to Bowling Green, thirty miles away, to be cast in zinc cuts, mounted on wood blocks, and returned to us the next day. Two sections and press runs of about 3,500 copies were the norm for our press.

The "back shop" work was done by Eugene Carnall, the press foreman; his assistant, Johnny "Popcorn" Carter; two Linotype operators; and a job printer. When not getting out the newspaper, the back shop men worked on commercial jobs—catalogs, handbills, business cards, church bulletins, even paper ballots.

The paper was printed on Wednesday. On Wednesday nights, cars would circle the town square like fireflies until Knotts came out with a stack of papers to sell. Most of the Wednesday night customers were subscribers who would receive the paper in the mail the next day, but driving downtown to read the front page "hot off the press" was a tradition that hundreds of Logan countians enjoyed.

TWO MONTHS AFTER I ARRIVED, Russellville stalled out in a winter snow storm that fell across the upper South. I collected a paycheck on Friday and promptly bought a bus ticket to New Orleans. Two days later, drunk and asleep in a French Quarter doorway, I was roused by a cop beating his nightstick against my feet. He didn't recognize me, but it would have made no difference. I had to sober up somewhere.

When they released me from the drunk tank six hours later, I walked over to the Napoleon House Bar and borrowed $20 from the owner, Peter Impastato. I once had lived in an apartment above that bar, but now I didn't live anywhere in New Orleans. I bought a bus ticket home with the borrowed money and concentrated on staying sufficiently sober to board the bus.

Back in Russellville, I mumbled an apology to Mrs. Evans for leaving town without letting her know I'd be gone. I told her I'd left town because I was lonely and wanted to see a sweetheart I'd left in New Orleans. I didn't mention that the woman, my girlfriend Miriam, was still married to her invalid husband, or that when I showed up she had kicked me out of her house, screaming and cursing.

Mrs. Evans could have told me she knew I was lying and fired me. Instead, she gave me a curious look.

"Well, let's get back to work," she said. No doubt she now knew what she must have at least suspected all along: that I was an alcoholic, so near the bottom I could no longer function after a few drinks. And I knew that she knew. And she knew that I knew that she knew.

Mrs. Lyne, my landlady, was not so tolerant. While I was gone, she had discovered a drawerful of empty whiskey bottles in my room.

"Mr. Smith, suppose you fall asleep with a lit cigarette and burn us up?" she said. At her age, she couldn't sleep for worrying, and she had called her son, the lawyer. I would have to move out, she said.

When Jim arrived, he helped me pack my things and drove me down to an old hotel on the town square, a three-story brick pile called the Kaintuck. When I entered the dark lobby, lit by a few dim fluorescent bulbs, I swallowed hard.

The walls were dark with nicotine stains. Faded prints hung over the sagging couches and broken-down chairs. Two old men were dozing in front of a black-and-white TV.

I rang a bell at the front desk, and one of the sleeping men got up and announced that he was the room clerk. For $10 a week, paid in advance, he gave me the key to a second-story room with a bath. I shakily signed the register and asked him to call a taxi.

When the taxi driver brought me back from the bootlegger's house, the night clerk had arrived, and the old man who was the day room clerk had returned to his lobby chair. Desperate for someone to talk with who would neither reproach nor fire me, I asked the day clerk if he would like to have a drink, and he accepted.

Edgar Reed, my drinking companion, turned out to be a retired bookkeeper who boarded at the Kaintuck. Rolling up his sleeves, he displayed three wrist watches on each arm. He told me he traded in watches, mostly with traveling drummers and farmers who came to town to sell or trade animals or other wares on Jockey Alley which ran behind the courthouse.

"Would you like to buy a watch?" Edgar asked me.

"No, thank you," I said. "I already have one."

"Well, then, we'll just have that drink."

He followed me up the steps to my new home.

-22-
"They Steal Votes in Logan County"

AFTER A MONTH OF OFFSTAGE HORSE-TRADING, the deadlock at the Logan County Courthouse over the road foreman's post suddenly ended. One of the fiscal court magistrates changed his vote to favor Guy McMillen, and Doc prevailed. The loser, John Hite, was a good sport; he bought McMillen a bottle of whiskey.

I soon discovered, however, that the fight over the road foreman post was nothing more than Doc Beauchamp's warm-up for the May 27 congressional primary.

I was covering the returns for *The Paducah Sun-Democrat* as well as *The News-Democrat* when I got a call around 9:00 election night from Bill Powell, the Paducah editor.

Powell said it looked to him like the incumbent, Noble Gregory of Mayfield—Governor Chandler's man—was the victor. The margin was slim, however, and there were a few precinct returns missing from Logan County.

Those totals were probably being held back because Doc supported the challenger, Frank Albert Stubblefield, a Murray salesman. Stubblefield was refusing to concede until Doc told him he had lost.

"So," Powell asked me, "is it over?"

It was over, but Powell was wrong about the outcome. At the courthouse, a jubilant Beauchamp, sweat circles beneath the arms of his khaki shirt, told me the last precincts had been counted.

"Al, I just got off the phone telling Frank Albert the news," Beauchamp said in that raspy voice. "He's the new congressman. I think we've beat Mr. Gregory by about three hundred votes overall."

The vote in Logan County turned out to be 443 for Gregory, 2,274 for Stubblefield.

And when all the votes district-wide were tallied the next day, Stubblefield's overall winning margin was 341 votes.

THE NEXT DAY, A HOWL WENT UP from the Gregory camp, and Governor Chandler called a press conference.

"Everybody knows they steal votes in Logan County," Chandler cried. "I'm ordering the state police to go over there and arrest somebody for fraud."

This was getting interesting. My first Kentucky election was looking a lot like my first one in Louisiana. But instead of Earl Long switching the outcome for his nephew Russell, Doc Beauchamp was playing tricks on Chandler and Noble Gregory.

But I knew we were on the anti-Chandler side, so I wrote the election headline for the Russellville paper this way:

STUBBLEFIELD WINS;
CHANDLER SENDS TROOPS TO LOGAN COUNTY

To call the state police detectives "troops" was a shameful evocation of Chandler's courageous dispatch of the National Guard to keep order in near riots at the beginning of integration in the Sturgis schools. But I was inhaling an anti-Chandler bias with every breath I took around the Logan County Courthouse.

Memories there were still raw over Chandler's defeat of Thomas Rhea in a gubernatorial primary twenty-three years earlier. Never mind that in the general election of 1935 more votes were cast for Chandler's Republican opponent in Democratic Logan County than there were registered voters. Forget that Rhea and Chandler quietly patched up their differences in at least one election after 1935, or that

Rhea's family in Logan County had gone over to the Chandler faction because of a row with Beauchamp.

To defeat a congressman who Chandler backed was a sweet triumph for the Beauchamp camp in western Kentucky. They were determined to deny Gregory victory, a recount or a court order or criminal charges be damned!

Chandler and Gregory lost their appeals, which were fought out in the Calloway County Courthouse at Murray, the challenger's home court. Stubblefield was seated.

THEN CHANDLER WON AN INNING AGAINST BEAUCHAMP.

The governor's ally, State Auditor Mary Louise Faust, reviewed the fees collected by Jim Lyne while he was county attorney and by County Clerk Bailey Gunn, one of Beauchamp's closest friends. Miss Faust concluded that the two men had improperly retained nearly $100,000 in surplus fees and demanded they repay the fees to the county.

I bannered Miss Faust's claim in the paper. Lyne and Gunn denied the charge, of course.

Interest in the story grew as the fiscal court magistrates hungrily considered what they could do with the missing money if the pair coughed it up. Eventually, Lyne and Gunn repaid the fees after they reached a negotiated settlement with the state.

My unrelenting focus on the story, combined with Mrs. Evans' willingness to stand with me against her political friends, gave us a chance to display our independence. Evenhanded coverage for friends and foes alike will win a newspaper respect for being unafraid to make enemies in pursuit of truth.

The story created a bond between me and my new boss. I decided she was smart, shrewd, and tough. And she was learning I could do more than drink whiskey.

WITH MY PUBLISHER'S ENCOURAGEMENT, I livened up the paper with a political satire column structured as a letter to the editor from a fictitious rural reader who signed himself "Cousin Charlie." Each column began, "Well, Miz Evans ..." and then carried on for several hundred words with observations about the news and the local folks who made it.

Some quotes were from real people; some were from characters I invented. Charlie's wife, "Minnie," often weighed in, and a "Wicked Cousin Odrow" offered comically dark quips at the expense of the community's big shots. An old sage named Uncle Edgar—based on Edgar Reed, the elderly clerk at the Kaintuck Hotel—also made frequent appearances.

AS ALL THESE POLITICAL STORIES PROGRESSED, I was learning more about my new county.

Named for a Revolutionary War hero and Indian fighter, Logan was so large in pioneer days that more than twenty other counties ultimately were carved from its original borders. In the early nineteenth century, when Kentucky was still "the West," Russellville was a frontier of "civilized society," with private academies, churches, gunpowder and rope factories, and lawyers who followed the settlers to resolve land grant disputes.

Good land meant everything in the life of Logan County. This was not the Kentucky where thoroughbred horses frolicked in white-fenced bluegrass fields beside pretentious columned mansions, as one might find in Lexington. This was not plantation country. But there was no richer soil than south Logan's, and the owners expected to dominate the decision-making at the courthouse and beyond.

LOGAN COUNTY'S HISTORY WAS IMPORTANT to its future. At least, that's what the Clarks said.

Granville Clark, the city attorney, and his mother, Margaret, who headed the Woman's Club, began preaching to the paper's new editor. If the community was to be vital, they said, it needed to look both ways: ahead, of course, to work for improvements, but also behind, to commemorate those aspects of a colorful heritage worth celebrating.

Granville Clark's law office was once the Odd Fellows Hall. A convention of Confederate sympathizers had met there in late 1861 to secede from the Union. Kentucky was accepted into the Confederacy, but the act was apparently in name only. The Commonwealth was occupied by federal troops for most of the war. Around the corner, the old Nimrod Long Bank on Main Street, robbed by the Jesse James gang in 1868, still stood. A mural depicting this robbery hangs in the lobby of a successor bank. It is perhaps the only financial institution in America whose artwork commemorates an assault on its cashier.

Preservationists in Logan County had saved the core buildings of a Shaker colony at Auburn in the eastern part of the county. And a replica of a log church near Adairville in the southern part of the county memorialized the Great Revival of 1800, part of the so-called Second Awakening of Protestantism in the United States. Those revival services took place on the banks of the Red River near the site of an 1806 duel in which Andrew Jackson killed a Nashville lawyer.

When I came to Russellville, Mrs. Clark was in the midst of an attempt to block the city council's efforts to extend a street through the middle of the town square's central park. She waved her umbrella threateningly at council meetings whenever she heard the mere suggestion that the statue of a Confederate soldier standing guard might be torn down.

The Clarks had no trouble persuading me that a street through the park was a bad idea. I was still Graeme's boy. Recognizing my grandmother's spirit in both Mrs. Clark and Mrs. Evans, my first editorial cause at this little newspaper was to exhort our readers to understand the importance of historic preservation.

I was on my best behavior for a while—meaning that I was sober—and I respected and supported the burst of civic energy that the Clarks' cultural efforts released. I also was catching on to the economic ambitions that banker Earl Davis and his mentor, Marvin Stuart, had for the town.

Stuart, who ran a small loan business in a little shopping center he owned, co-chaired with Davis the Chamber of Commerce's efforts to attract new industry. They were proud of recruiting Rockwell, a nationally recognized company.

But Stuart and Davis wouldn't take just anybody. They impressed me with a story about rejecting a Yankee "high-binder" (or con man) who wanted to build a glove factory in town.

Davis laughed as he remembered that the man talked about the county's black population but then mumbled over the details. It wasn't clear whether this venture was a plant that would employ blacks, which Davis favored, or one that would make gloves to sell to blacks. Either way, Stuart said, he and Davis believed the "Negro glove factory," as they called it, would turn out to be a sweatshop. So they pointed the stranger westward, toward Hopkinsville.

Russellville had Red Kap, a "cut and sew" garment operation. But what Davis sought was another Fortune 500 company that would employ large numbers of both black and white Logan countians.

Davis was an old-fashioned conservative Republican from a family that sided with the Union in the Civil War. He noted archly that the Democrats never hired blacks for those coveted political jobs at the state highway garage. "Beauchamp and his buddies talk to the colored folks about Roosevelt and Truman and Social Security and food stamps," Davis said. "But they keep those state jobs for white folks."

AT NIGHT, I GOT TO KNOW OTHER REAL CHARACTERS who lived at the Kaintuck. Some of them, only slightly disguised, popped up in Cousin Charlie's letters.

John Henry Marion, a retired livestock trader, entertained me with tales of returning to Russellville with railroad cars of mules he bought in Kansas City to sell on Court Days.[12] I loved his story of a desperate country fellow who showed up at Jockey Alley, the trading area behind the courthouse, with a truck full of cats to swap for guns, knives, dogs, and clocks.

Jim Gordon was a gentle little man of exquisite Southern manners. An alcoholic surveyor, by the time I knew him, he recalled better days when he was a member of Todd County's landed gentry. He remembered when families of his social class camped together in tents for several weeks in the summer in the beautiful woods near the Cumberland River, and recalled that the best moonshine whiskey was sold out in the dark beyond the torch lights at country revivals at Sharon Grove.

I remember "Long Barrel" Page, a carnival operator who left word never to admit his estranged wife past the lobby.

And Chester, who would rather talk to himself than to us.

And Mrs. Traughber, a husky lady with a scowling face who spent some anxious evenings at the hotel while her civil case was on the courthouse docket. She carried a crutch around to substantiate her claim that she'd been injured in an accident, but I never saw her lean on it.

The Kaintuck's proprietor during my tenancy was J.M. Richard, an "import" like myself who had moved to Kentucky from South Carolina. His accent was so strong that he always made hotel reservations by Western Union or U.S. Mail. When he tried to make them over the phone in those Jim Crow days, he said, the hotel clerks refused him rooms because they thought he was a black man from the Carolina coast speaking Gullah.

Although Richard was considered something of a slicker, he'd been outsmarted by the county jailer, Joe Gunn Gregory. Richard had bought Gregory's lease on the Kaintuck during the American Legion's annual Logan County Fair, when the rooms were filled with

---

[12] Once a month, people from Logan and surrounding counties brought all kinds of wares to sell in an alley behind the courthouse. The days of those sales were called Court Days.

carnival folks. Later, as the vacancies increased, no one believed Richard's claim that he hadn't known about the fair.

Richard recovered the cost of his initial investment by strictly controlling his heating system. The Kaintuck's big coal-fired furnace was not turned on until November 15, and it was cut off April 15, no matter how chilly the weather.

BEFORE MY TIME, JOE GUNN GREGORY, THE EX-JAILER, had been the subject of an unsavory story in *The News-Democrat*. It was reported that he taken some lady prisoners to the picture show, then moved them over to his hotel to work out their fines by "entertaining" his other guests, so to speak.

Several years after he was defeated, Gregory was trying to be reelected jailer and asked me to help him write an advertisement. As I recall, Gregory made two campaign promises.

The first was that he would "live in the jail"; in other words, he wouldn't leave the inmates unprotected at night from his brutal guards.

The second was that "my wife Lucy will be the cook."

Lucy Gregory may have been one of the better cooks in the county, but I don't recall that Gregory ever regained the office.

ONE BITTERLY COLD NIGHT THAT FIRST WINTER, I met a young lady—let's call her Lois—in the Kaintuck lobby. A smiling country girl with a salty wit, Lois had a bruise on her cheek. When I asked her about it, she told me that if I thought she looked bad, I should have seen her boyfriend. She'd split his face with a heavy ashtray.

It turned out that Lois, an ex-Marine, was fleeing the consequences of a spat at a honky-tonk near Fort Campbell and had decided to hide out at the Kaintuck. The next night, Lois moved in with me, apparently operating upon the theory that two against one improved her odds of survival. But it wasn't long before she disappeared from my life.

A year later, Lois stopped by the hotel to say hello. She said the ex-boyfriend had never reappeared.

"What do you think happened to him?" I asked.

"I don't know," she said.

"Maybe I killed him." She was one tough Marine.

-23-
The Good Times Guy

MANNING TAYLOR FIRST SHOWED UP on the front page of *The News-Democrat* in 1958 when he succeeded in coaxing one Oakley Cisney out of the cave where he'd been hiding and into the hands of the police, who were waiting to arrest Cisney on a murder charge.

A tenant on Cisney's north Logan farm had been shot dead in a dispute over a still, and Manning was part of a posse searching for him. Hunting down murder suspects was probably not on the list of Manning's job responsibilities as a runner/clerk for Jim Lyne. (Manning was working with Lyne to complement the law courses he was taking at Cumberland, my dad's old law school in Lebanon, Tennessee.) But wherever Manning Taylor went, excitement seemed to follow.

Manning was a rugged, self-assured man with steel-gray hair and pearly white teeth. He put on more airs than the average ambulance chaser while he was working for Lyne, but he must have felt entitled. After all, Manning had always been a child of privilege.

Manning grew up in Russellville, the son of Coleman Taylor, an attorney who had mentored Lyne in his early law practice before leaving Russellville to become general counsel of a carpet company in New York.

As a child, Manning was what today might be referred to as "over-indulged," but used to be called "spoiled." When he crashed the red roadster his parents gave him for his sixteenth birthday, they bought him another. Manning was the best-dressed of all the local kids, always attired in suits from Loveman's, one of Nashville's finest stores.

Following a stint in Culver Military Academy and service in the Army, Manning ran into a bit of difficulty with a stock scheme and a company called "Smoke Eaters." But his parents came through again. They financed his return to Russellville. They set him up with his beautiful second wife, Nancy, and his handsome little boys in a stately old home downtown. And they enrolled him in Cumberland to study law.

After Manning's daring escapade ended in Cisney's capture outside the cave, there was talk that Cisney had just been defending himself against the tenant, who had been beating on Cisney pretty hard before he pulled out a pistol and shot him.

Nevertheless, the newly forged legal team of Lyne and Taylor defending Cisney was no match for "Skye" Howell, a special prosecutor hired by the victim's family to prosecute Cisney. An experienced criminal lawyer, with an addiction to pain medication that stimulated some intense speeches when he wasn't on the nod, Howell pulled out the stops during the trial. He nearly fried Cisney, but the jury settled for a life sentence.

When Cisney escaped from the penitentiary at LaGrange, Kentucky, a year later, it seemed to me the law had little interest in chasing him down; the consensus was that he had been over-sentenced in the first place. Eventually he died in another state.

EVEN IF HE COULDN'T SAVE CISNEY, fortune continued to smile on Manning, and he shared his luck with friends.

An oil boom in Green County, Kentucky, inspired Manning to turn his talents to hustling leases. Horace Durwood, an elderly local man who had made money speculating in oil out West, offered his assistance. Durwood had returned to Russellville intending to practice pickup law with a dusty license from his youth, but on the side he tutored Manning in the basics of the petroleum game.

Soon Manning was a high-stakes player, and his Black and Gold Enterprises was the talk of several counties. He seemed born for the shill, promising a quick way to make big bucks. Just the turn of a switch on one of his rigs sparked bidding for leases on land all around it, even if he drilled a dry hole.

Leaving the front yard of a farmer who might have declined to sign a lease, Manning would bend down, seize a pebble, pop it in his mouth, and suck on it. Then he would stick the pebble in a side pocket and head for the gate. By the time Manning opened his station wagon door, the farmer would be chasing after him, screaming "Gimme back my rock!"

IN THE FIRST FLUSH OF FINANCIAL SUCCESS, Manning bought a carpet for one church, a pipe organ for another, and gave his old car to Jimmy Lee, his yardman.

He and Nancy hosted some glittering parties. Once while I was taking Antabuse[13] and on the wagon, I attended one of them. My host hurt my feelings by saying, "The paper's a helluva lot more interesting when you're drunk."

A few days later, when a highway contractor named Norwood Kemp told me the same thing, I fell into a depression and off the wagon. So I must have been in a fog when Frank Goad Clement, then the governor of Tennessee, arrived for a visit with the Taylors.

By that time, I ordinarily didn't miss much in town. I had developed rapport with the police, and what they didn't know, I usually picked up on the street or at the Kaintuck. But Clement had come and gone before I heard that he and Manning had been as drunk over at the Taylor manse as I was at the Kaintuck.

Had I not been too shaky to leave my room at the hotel that weekend, I surely would have sought an interview with Governor Clement, introducing myself with a nostalgic account of working with his aunt, the elocution teacher my Granny Graeme had hired before

---

[13] Antabuse is a medication sometimes prescribed for people who are trying not to drink. Drinking while taking Antabuse results in severe nausea, cramps, and sweating. The drug must be stopped for two weeks before one can drink without the serious side effects.

the American Legion speech contest back when I was a teenager. Or I could have dropped the name of my high school friend, Walter Durham, who was by then a Sumner County, Tennessee, business leader who supported Clement as a progressive.

Instead, I heard about the governor's partying with Manning from Dick Hite, who lived down the street from the Taylors. A tall, droll fellow who ran a concrete paving business, Dick swore that when he had dropped by for a neighborly beer, he found Clement and Manning talking on the telephone to Fidel Castro.

This was 1959, the year after Fidel's insurgent forces swept the corrupt Batista government from power in Havana and astonished Americans saw a photograph in *Life* of a rebel firing squad executing a portly police chief.

"... And to secure this heroic revolution," Hite said he heard Clement tell Castro, "I offer you the services of my trusted friend, Colonel Manning Taylor, late of Culver Military Academy and of the armored warfare forces of the United States Army. Colonel Taylor is just the right commander to retrain the Batista army, redirecting its loyalties to Your Excellency. Currently he is practicing law and managing his oil properties, but Colonel Taylor preserves his contacts with high Pentagon officials and is *au courant* with the latest theories of commanders at nearby Fort Campbell."

Although Manning had the star-quality looks of a John Wayne or Ronald Reagan and similar acting talents, he was never a silver bird in the Army. Rather, he was a "Kentucky Colonel," a commission to be obtained for the price of a postage stamp on a letter to Frankfort from an accommodating precinct captain. If there had been such a conversation between Frank Clement and Fidel Castro—witty Dick Hite narrated the adventures of Manning Taylor with such entertaining gusto I never demanded footnotes—then the governor was enhancing the resume.

Country Editor

MY FIRST REAL FRIEND AT *THE NEWS-DEMOCRAT* was Tookey Kemp, the receptionist, society editor, and obituary writer.

When people in Logan County died, Tookey often generated two obituaries: one for the paper, with details from the funeral homes, and another she shared only with me.

In a low voice, she told me the unprintable elements of the deceased's life that she thought I needed to know. Those spicy stories kept her from falling asleep at her Royal typewriter over the humdrum birth dates, marriages, occupations, club and church memberships, and immediate survivors that made up the publishable obituaries. Like my new friend Dick Hite, Tookey and her merry gossip, which was seldom malicious and only slightly racy, distracted me—somewhat—from thoughts of New Orleans.

Tookey's stories mixed the dead and the living. There was the departed farmer who served on the fiscal court who was said to be so lazy he only took a Saturday-night bath if his wife gave him one. The farmer's cousin, an attractive widow, was the mistress of a prominent fellow who sang in the church choir. The singer was unhappily married to the niece of the patron who set him up in his career.

These convoluted stories helped me understand the many connections between people in the county. They also taught me to be careful what I said.

The wife of a former sheriff named Reuben Kemp, Tookey was born Ella Louise Milliken, the daughter of another sheriff who had left Tookey and her spinster sister, Rena, a farm on the north side of Russellville. Rena was away most of the year teaching business courses at Union College, the little Methodist school in Barbourville, Kentucky.

Reuben had fallen out with Doc Beauchamp and, as a result, was out of the courthouse. By the time I came along, he worked for a local real estate salesman named John Moore in an office down the street from the newspaper.

A gruff, dangerous-looking man of few words, Reuben's limited charm was focused on promoting Moore's farm sales "At Absolute Auction" as *The News-Democrat* ads described them. Always dressed in a dark suit, white shirt, and tie, Reuben carried a concealed pistol to work in the early mornings and a half-pint of whiskey home in the late afternoons.

I wouldn't have bought a garden tomato from Reuben. It was clear by his scowls that he disliked me, even before Tookey whispered that he had warned her not to get too friendly with the new editor.

Tookey told me that, after Thomas Rhea died in 1946, she and Reuben, as well as the four Rhea children, were among the losers in a power struggle between Beauchamp and an alliance of Rhea loyalists led by John Albert Whitaker, a U.S. Representative from Russellville. Whitaker had been county attorney for two decades before succeeding Earle Clements in the House of Representatives in 1947. When Whitaker died suddenly in 1950, Doc was left to rule Logan County politics largely unchallenged for the next two decades.

Despite her husband's admonition, Tookey was my confidante, an invaluable guide to understanding Logan County's history and people, especially its leaders. When folks she thought I should know came by the newspaper, she made sure I met them. And Tookey seemed to know everyone. We were lucky to have her and her cheerful, inviting personality, welcoming scores of people who came to our office on Main Street.

MRS. EVANS, IN ILL HEALTH THE DECADE I KNEW HER, seldom left home, but her two daughters were in and out of the office.

Dorothy, the wife of ad manager Dan Knotts, and Virginia Belle ("Beedie"), who was married to a Presbyterian minister named Harold Knox, shared ownership of the paper with their mother and their brother, Byrne Evans, a lieutenant colonel who had elected to stay in the military after World War II.

Dorothy was a thin, sickly young woman with a teenage daughter. She was a skilled Linotype operator but wasn't given to working unless someone quit or was fired. Beedie kept the books, but she had two young sons to care for as well as her duties as a pastor's wife. The Knoxes lived in a parsonage, but the Knotts family lived with Mrs. Evans. Byrne was living abroad on an Army post.

Every one of them received money from the paper.

IT WAS UP TO TOOKEY AND ME to produce enough copy to fill the paper, which usually ran fourteen to sixteen pages. We had help from our correspondents in the incorporated towns—Auburn, Adairville, and Lewisburg—and writers from a dozen smaller communities with names like Spa, Lickskillet, and Chandlers Chapel.

Most of the correspondents' reports were traditional rural newspaper fare about the comings and goings of neighbors. These writers had their own lingo. Those visitors who stayed for a while might be described as "bedtime guests." If a bunch showed up for a meal, the copy might read "covers were laid for twelve at lunch." If a social gathering was successful, "a good time was had by all."

A legendary country correspondent from the Mud River community, a Mrs. Pillow, made it into Kentucky historian Thomas Clark's book, *The Country Editor*, with her account of a neighbor who, reaching for a country ham in the smokehouse, fell "up to her armpits" into a barrel of molasses. Mrs. Pillow's closing advice: "Friends, be careful where you buy your molasses."

Editing Mrs. Silvey's "Doings from Dunmor" and other reports from across the county took me back to *The Times-Picayune*'s State Desk, where my boss Fred Corwin taught me to respect the cabbage crop in Copiah County, Mississippi, and the blessing of the shrimp boats at New Iberia, Louisiana.

BUT RUSSELLVILLE WAS NO NEW ORLEANS. I was physically closer to my Kentucky writers and our three thousand readers than I ever had been in my earlier career.

In rural journalism, unlike at the big dailies, there is no guard in the front lobby, no elevator separating the newsroom from the folks on the street. Visitors who are mad over something don't sign in; they barge in.

Running a small town paper is very personal. The country editor who criticizes the mayor or the county attorney in print may be sitting next to him or her at the Rotary Club lunch the next day. Their kids play ball or go on Scout trips together; their spouses may work in the same office.

If you can't stand confrontations, editing a rural newspaper will take the starch out of you. If you stick to telling the news in full, the unpleasant facts you publish will keep you on a hot skillet with somebody.

The flip side? Some of your readers may agree with you.

Early in my first year as her editor, Mrs. Evans, to her credit, asked me to liven up the paper with editorials on the local issues I was covering. I gladly obliged. She was a fervent Democrat but let me know she would be pleased if I needled the incumbent Democrat office holders to show our independence and to keep them straight.

I knew that *The News-Democrat* should be something more than dependably partisan. I wrote features about public figures, in business as well as politics, starting with Page One stories on three different women—a gasoline distributor, the secretary to the county judge, and a woman police court judge from southern Logan County. If my fledgling comments on the editorial page offended some readers, surely these ladies and their many friends would defend me. "He's not *all* bad," I hoped they would say.

OUR COVERAGE of the Frank Stubblefield-Noble Gregory congressional primary and court challenge attracted many readers. One day after the affair was settled, I ran into Rayburn Smith coming out of Perry's Cafe.

Playing the innocent, I asked, "Rayburn, how does a vote counter spoil a paper ballot?"

Obligingly, he explained. When a race was close, he said, he taped a piece of lead under an extra-long fingernail so he could scratch the name of a candidate his side opposed.

"For God sake's, Rayburn, shut up!" snarled Bailey Gunn, the county clerk, his lunch companion. Shooting me a glance, Bailey said, "Rayburn, you're making me nervous."

Mrs. Evans told me that Rayburn was so adept at manipulating elections that Bert Combs had dispatched him to Louisville during Combs's 1955 race against Happy Chandler for governor. Rayburn's job was to instruct Combs's Jefferson County precinct workers on how to keep the other side from playing dirty tricks. "Combs figured Rayburn was really up on that subject," Mrs. Evans said.

Like Tookey, Rayburn became another of my tutors and a source for important local history, especially about Logan County politics. He was especially helpful in teaching me about the Rhea family, Beauchamp's predecessors.

The Rheas had dominated elections, banking, and the newspaper business in Logan County for more than a hundred years. They had served in Congress, in the judiciary, and in state offices at Frankfort. Thomas Rhea, Beauchamp's mentor, lost a historic race for governor against Chandler in 1935 in Kentucky's only primary runoff for that office. He went on to serve as one of Franklin Roosevelt's floor managers at the 1936 Democratic National Convention.

One early summer day in 1958, as I left the courthouse, I saw Rayburn squatted on his haunches in the yard, sucking on a weed. I stopped to ask him a question about Tom Rhea that had always puzzled me.

"Tell me, Rayburn," I said. "How did Mr. Rhea get by? I know he was sheriff twice, a highway commissioner, and state treasurer. But the Rheas sold *The News-Democrat* to the Evans family in the Depression, and they lost a bank. He wasn't a lawyer, so how did he live between elections?"

Rayburn took a chew on that straw, then spit it out.

"Awwwww," he said mournfully, in a voice so soft I leaned over better to hear. "Mr. Roosevelt sent him money, I reckon."

"What on earth for?" I asked.

Rayburn wiped his forehead with his arm. "Mr. Roosevelt just liked him, I guess."

ON PRESS NIGHTS, as Dan Knotts delivered bundles of papers around town, I took a bundle to Perry's Cafe where I usually went for a late supper.

Elvis Perry, a portly gent with a fetching smile, sold hamburgers, puny salads, bakery pies, and two kinds of stew. This basic fare was also available behind a side door for "colored." The place was so segregated that I never saw a black face inside it. Nor was there a restroom for black customers, although I don't remember one for whites, either. When "Popcorn" Carter, our assistant press foreman, got his dinner at Perry's, he and I ate the same food. We just couldn't eat it together.

At Perry's front counter, where I deposited my stack of freshly printed *News-Democrats*, rows of gleaming pistols were for sale in the glass display case. I never bought one, but I witnessed those who did. When Elvis made a firearms sale, no paperwork was exchanged—just dollar bills.

Southern Deposit and Russellville's other bank, Citizens, offered checking accounts as a service. They made loans, sold certificates of deposit, and accepted savings deposits on which they paid no interest. The other incorporated Logan County towns each had small banks, all of them zealously committed to remaining independent.

Entrepreneurs found credit hard to come by; the financial sector and its regulators were still in shock from the Depression-era crash of Banco Kentucky in Louisville and its Nashville partner, Caldwell and Company. But the Russellville banks were generous with small "character" loans. I learned this the day I threw myself on the mercy of young Bob Kirkpatrick.

An IRS agent had come to my office to personally inform me that the federal government did not consider those bar bills I'd run up in New Orleans while "researching" my 1949 *Newsweek* article on jazz to be legitimate tax deductions. Bob cheerfully loaned me $100—about a week's salary—to pay the tax bill. I breathed a sigh of relief as the agent left with my payment in hand. My new employer would never know the identity of the stranger who sat in my office while I stepped down the street to get a quick loan from the heir apparent to the Southern Deposit Bank.

RUSSELLVILLE LOOKED LIKE MANY SMALL TOWNS in the South. A public square (which was round) sat in the heart of town with streets radiating outward. *The News-Democrat* office was on Main Street, not far from the square, in a narrow building between a drugstore and the gas company. We faced Page Brothers Auto Company, once the old Russellville opera house. Up the street were the Logan County Hardware and Furniture Store, a plumbing company, a dress shop, drugstores, Leedom's, Klein's, and two other clothing stores. On both sides of Main Street near the square were small appliance stores, another hardware store, and a small gas station aptly named Parkview.

Margaret Clark had triumphed in her battle with the city council over the fate of the square; there would be no street running through it. Instead, the park acquired new iron benches and beautiful landscaping, and the fountain began flowing again and became the center of attention in downtown Russellville.

By the late 1950s, preservationists had succeeded in erecting markers noting that Russellville had been the home of four pre-Civil War governors of Kentucky, and six of its sons had gone on to become governors of other states.

Yet there were fights left to come against the boomers and their bulldozers.

The biggest dust-up was over plans to build a new courthouse. The old one wasn't beautiful but it was an authentic example of nineteenth century architecture. The proposed substitute, a brick and concrete block structure, failed under fire from the Clarks and their allies.

"Al, you're just not fighting hard enough. Your editorials are tepid!" Mrs. Clark scolded.

"I don't know why Mother talks that way sometimes," her son Granville said. "It's that old Harrison blood in her."

He referred to an ancestor, Benjamin Harrison, who had been President of the United States (1889-93). Or perhaps it was Benjamin's grandfather, William Henry, who died after one month in office in 1841. I never knew which.

-25-
Boomers

IN THE 1950s, MARVIN STUART AND THREE OTHER local businessmen sent five hundred letters to major corporations boasting about Russellville as an attractive site for industrial expansion.

Logan County's cheerleaders couldn't claim it would be easy to excavate the ground to build a plant. Russellville and North Logan were rocky with thin soil and the fertile farmland of south Logan was too valuable to use for industrial development. But the town elders insisted the potential work force would be loyal to their Yankee supervisors if they were treated well, a euphemistic way of saying there would be no unions or disagreeable confrontations over work conditions and wages. Hundreds of Southern towns offered similar promises about their workers.

Before I got to Russellville, Stuart's team already had landed Rockwell, a Pittsburgh-based aluminum die-casting plant, which was constructed in 1956. Rockwell employed two hundred fifty people.

At least as important as those jobs to the community's future was the plant manager, Harry Whipple. A brusque bear of a man, Harry brought with him his two brothers from Pennsylvania to help hire and train the work force and two patents of his own design for die-casting machines.

Harry was a profile in paternalism. He treated his workers to bus trips to baseball games in St. Louis and Cincinnati. He leased a ramshackle motel on Kentucky Lake and fixed it up as a weekend resort for Rockwell employees. Harry never missed a wedding or a funeral, and he walked around the plant with a wad of cash in his pocket, always ready to peel off a few bills for any employee in trouble.

When he drove visiting company executives out of town for steak dinners, Harry invited me along. I think he wanted to impress his bosses that the local editor was in his pocket. If so, he was right. And I loved the steaks!

The Rockwell plant's Christmas parties were command performances for Marvin Stuart, banker Earl Davis, and me. After the carols and Santa's gift to each child, Harry would announce a bonus or salary hike. Then it was Harry's turn. Grateful workers would present him with a gift, something on the order of a long rifle or a painting of the plant. Harry would pull out a handkerchief as big as a diaper and dab at his eyes, all three hundred pounds of him shaking with emotion.

When Rockwell needed more water, Mayor Taylor Fuqua and the six Russellville City Council members voted for the city to run new water and sewer lines to the plant. N.C. "Pete" Hancock, the council member designated as utilities commissioner, supervised the work.

Hancock, a chunky, blustery fellow who operated hardware and furniture stores occupying almost an entire block downtown, thrived on the challenge. The first time we met, he was sweating in the hot sun in khakis and an undershirt, helping his crews dig another pipeline north of town to a new water reservoir to be named, appropriately, Hancock Lake.

With no river or deep wells—only a town creek—Russellville had to expand its treatment plant and network of pipelines to avoid losing out in the Southern competition to lure Northern industries. The small towns of the South offered reasonably priced land well-suited to industrial development, government-sponsored incentive deals, and docile workers who would not join unions. But without a good water supply, a plant wouldn't come.

Before Russellville and Rockwell found each other, the local industries were a garment plant, a cheese plant, and the Bilt-Rite Company. Bob Guion had started Bilt-Rite while he was still in high school as a place to make dog kennels, but that small business had evolved into a factory, first for making venetian blinds and then to make wire for huge poultry houses.

Those little companies, together with grain mills, a pallet plant, and a hosiery mill in the county's smaller towns, did not have enough business to hire the increasing number of job seekers. As Logan County's farms rapidly mechanized, there wasn't enough agricultural work to employ all of the younger generation. Without more industrialization, it appeared the county would lose its children.

That's where Whipple became Russellville's important advocate. Once Rockwell had hired all the workers it needed, Harry could have tried to keep out the competition to protect the labor pool for himself. Instead, he told prospects that Logan County had enough workers to support their businesses as well. He let them know that with their farm backgrounds, the workers they could hire in Logan County would be quick to master new machinery, eager to please, and appreciative of work that paid decent wages.

"Follow my lead and treat these folks well," Harry said, "and you will thrive."

When Harry turned the spotlight on the Northern scouts, with questions about their companies' labor records, their financial stability, their intentions for growth, and the sort of incentives they expected, they realized that Harry held the key to the door. Without this rough, tough man's approval, they didn't stand a chance of locating here.

Whipple was not greedy; the folks who needed jobs were not his chattel in a holding pen. He wanted to see the community prosper, but he valued his version of labor peace—that is, no unions—and wanted newcomers who were willing to preserve it by "doing the right thing."

From the viewpoint of the town leaders, it wasn't long before this big-hearted Pennsylvania Dutchman had become one of us. He was the human prize when we recruited Rockwell.

ALTHOUGH I CONTINUED TO MISS NEW ORLEANS, my curiosity about this rural life was whetted by the little dramas I encountered at the courthouse, school board meetings, and city council sessions.

The slow-talking mayor, Taylor Fuqua, was an interesting contrast to the charismatic Chep Morrison, who had dominated New Orleans politics during my life on the papers there.

Fuqua was stolid but focused. He owned a small bus line that grew from his early Russellville days as a farm youth turned taxicab driver. Back then, when he went to meet the passenger trains, the thugs who were there first with their jitneys beat him up and tried to drive him away. But he kept coming back.

Nothing daunted Fuqua. His first bus service was a limousine he ran between Russellville and Hopkinsville, thirty-five miles west. During World War II, he bought real buses to carry passengers to Tennessee and across southern Kentucky. He invested in cheap real estate, but sent his son Billy to expensive Washington and Lee University and on to law school.

In an audacious race for mayor, Fuqua triumphed in an upset against proud Jesse Riley, a well-to-do farmer, insurance, and real estate salesman from the Beauchamp camp. Riley extended his hand to Fuqua at the courthouse on election night.

"Well, Taylor," Riley said, "you won."

Fuqua removed his ever present unlit cigar and replied, "That's what I meant to do."

TUESDAY NIGHT CITY COUNCIL MEETINGS were my primers in municipal management. I learned from discussions of garbage collections, zoning disputes, fire trucks, police radios, potholes, broken sidewalks, and plans for low-cost public housing.

At the courthouse, the fiscal court magistrates, sometimes called squires, debated county road maintenance—that is, which roads would get the gravel, a principal matter of rural patronage. They discussed fixing rickety bridges, and firing animal wardens who couldn't keep the peace between the dogs and the sheep.[14]

With county and city schools to cover, as well as the county sheriff's office, the state police, the courthouse, and the police and city governments of four towns, I had my hands full. Don Neagle was a young reporter for radio station WRUS, the popular daytime-only AM station. Facing the same heavy load, Don agreed to my suggestion that we quietly split the work. We'd each cover different events and then share our notes. And if either of us picked up anything off the beaten path—a tip that deserved research, or "investigative reporting" as it is called today—we agreed that would be that person's story to pursue independently and perhaps report as a personal "scoop" with no hard feelings.

We never bothered to divulge this understanding to our respective bosses. Don's boss was W.P. "Winkie" Sosh, a tall, authoritative church elder who owned the station with an out-of-state partner. I admired Sosh. But I was aware that his Baptist sensibilities were troubled by my frequent appearances at public occasions with liquor on my breath.

Mrs. Evans, on the other hand, resented Sosh for siphoning revenue from what had once been the paper's monopoly on local advertising.

So it was best that Neagle and I keep our plan secret from both the public and our owners. Over the years, Logan County citizens got news reports that were twice as good as they might have been because Don and I were collaborators rather than competitors.

---

[14] There is a story about sheep-killing dogs in *Kentuckians are Different*, a book by Marmaduke Beckwith Morton, a former *Nashville Banner* editor born on a Logan County farm during the Civil War era.

A candidate for the fiscal court giving a stump speech was heckled by a farmer who demanded to know how he might vote on a proposed county dog law.

"What about the dogs?" the farmer insisted. "What about the dogs?"

To end the confrontation, the candidate assured his audience that he would favor a law "that protects the sheep.

"Of course," he added thoughtfully, "I also want a law that will be fair to the dogs."

THE LOGAN COUNTY TOBACCO FESTIVAL[15] was an annual event each October in Russellville, and *The News-Democrat* was a big supporter.

When I first came to Russellville, Gene Riley was festival chairman. Gene, an electrician who owned an appliance store, was always quick to leave his store down the street to come rewire a Linotype if it broke down the day we put out the paper.

In return for his generosity, Gene received in-kind payment from me. I labored without compensation to write features for the Tobacco Festival tabloid that we inserted in the paper. While the festival committee paid us for printing and insert charges, the tabloid ad revenue went to pay festival expenses, not us. The features I wrote, with the help of the community's history lovers, always highlighted the county's past—schools, statesmen, doctors, soldiers, and the like.

On the final day of each year's festival, people lined Main Street for a parade of school bands, kids on horseback, farm tractors, Joe Gunn Gregory's steam-powered antique thresher, Gene Riley riding an elephant, and a flatbed truck on which hounds barked at a terrified raccoon crouched atop a ten-foot pole.

Even then, a few eyebrows were raised about celebrating a crop already being questioned for its possible harmful impact on our health. But I believed Logan County's farmers, who grew three different kinds of tobacco and spent the money they made from that crop in Russellville and the county's other towns, deserved a day of appreciation, and that's what I opined in the paper. Besides, any function that pulled 7,000 folks into Russellville was a sign that we were a wide-awake town, invigorated *and* invigorating.

No doubt I fudged those attendance figures by several thousand when I wrote about the festival in the paper. That might suggest that a liquor habit wasn't the only thing I had inherited from my father. Like my dad in the 1920s, I, too, had become a boomer.

---

[15] After the repeal of the tobacco subsidy program and a great consolidation of growers, the event is now called the "Logan County Tobacco and Heritage Festival."

ONCE FRANK STUBBLEFIELD WAS DECLARED the official winner of the Democratic congressional primary in 1958, he and his wife Odessa made a low-key appearance at the Tobacco Festival. His primary win meant he was as good as elected, as he had no significant Republican opposition.

The Stubblefields had a quiet dinner with Doc Beauchamp to discuss Doc's expectations of what patronage rewards might be in the offing from Washington, such as the naming of postmasters. When dinner was over, Jim and Lucy Lyne invited the Stubblefields to spend the night at their home, but Frank and his wife declined. Frank explained that they were already checked in at a comfortable corner room on the second floor at the Kaintuck Hotel, which was where he had always stayed when he was on the road selling pharmaceuticals and other goods to drugstores. I guess he wanted to show the folks in Logan County that he was the same old Frank.

I was impressed when he asserted that the Kaintuck was still good enough for him. The next day, after the Stubblefields bid me goodbye in the downstairs lobby, I informed J.M. Richard, the proprietor, that I wanted to upgrade my own accommodations.

"How about the room the Stubblefields just left?" I asked.

"Five dollars more a week, and it's yours," Richard said.

That night after work, I changed rooms.

Logan County's ambitions to rise in the modern world were being realized: in the great Southern buffalo hunt for new jobs; in the preservationists' fight to save the park and other historical sites; in Doc Beauchamp's determination to come back as a political power.

And that night, I was doing pretty well myself.

I was comfortable, in a better bed where my new congressman had just slept. The room had a nicer view of the town square, where the fountain flowed again and the yellow chrysanthemums still bloomed in October. I was living in what I would call, from then on, the Stubblefield Suite.

-26-
Wyatt and Combs

WHEN WILSON WYATT CAME TO TOWN IN 1959 to talk about his race for governor, he told me he hoped to visit each of the state's one hundred twenty counties. Over iced coffee at Howard's Drugstore, he handed me a campaign card. Wyatt told me he began each day with the same number of cards. That way, come nightfall he could count the remaining cards and determine how many folks he had shaken hands with since breakfast.

In his early fifties, Wyatt had been the mayor of Louisville during World War II and a leading lawyer since he was in his thirties. He was so stylishly dressed that Governor Chandler claimed he wore spats and mockingly called him "old ankle blankets."

Until I met Barry Bingham, for whose Louisville papers Wyatt served as counsel, Wyatt had the most patrician air of anyone I had encountered in Kentucky. "Wait until we get him on plowed ground," scoffed Chandler, who contended Wyatt's aristocratic demeanor would be no match against the "plain folks" personality of Lieutenant Governor Harry Lee Waterfield, a weekly newspaper publisher and farmer from Hickman County in far western Kentucky.

Waterfield was Chandler's choice to succeed him in the May 1959 Democratic primary. Hoping to be the designated champion of the anti-Chandler forces, Wyatt announced his candidacy early, in April 1958.

But Bert Combs soon announced that he would run again. As in his race against Chandler in 1955, Combs was backed by former Governor and Senator Earle Clements, leader of the anti-Chandler faction of Democrats that had fought Chandler since the 1930s.

Both Waterfield and Combs, "the mountain judge" from Prestonsburg in Floyd County, would appeal to rural voters, and Wyatt could count on overwhelming urban support. The problem for the anti-Chandler forces was this: In a three-way race, the split among Chandler's foes would make Waterfield the front-runner.

Drinking a second iced coffee to calm a bad hangover, I was in poor shape to entertain my visitor, Wyatt, a commanding presence at that drugstore counter. Though Wyatt came from a modest family background, he *did* resemble the stereotypical "city dude." Nevertheless, with his intelligence, legal skill, and leadership ability, it was no wonder that President Truman had appointed him a cabinet-level housing administrator, an important position as the country began building houses again after World War II to meet pent-up demand.

And Wyatt had managed Adlai Stevenson's bid for the presidency against Dwight Eisenhower in 1952. Stevenson was a gifted politician and orator, but Wyatt was an impressive personality in his own right. He belonged on the same stage with Stevenson, where he often was.

I was awed when this star of the Louisville elite explained how he planned to campaign until he had shaken hands with 250,000 rural Kentuckians.

But I was not too hung over to know who counted for most.

"Have you talked to Doc yet?" I asked Wyatt.

It was gravel-throated Doc who had given up his own gubernatorial ambitions in 1955 to support Combs. At the kickoff of that campaign, Combs had announced in a nasal twang his plan to raise taxes. Hearing that, Beauchamp had cast a scornful glare at Clements and their sidekick, former Governor Lawrence Wetherby.

"And y'all said *I* couldn't make a speech!"

As it turned out, Wyatt didn't visit Doc on this trip through town. Thus Wyatt, a good fellow, avoided the duplicitous response Doc had given Noble Gregory, who had come to visit Doc during his campaign to defend his congressional seat against Frank Stubblefield.

"Awww, Noble, don't you worry about Logan County," Doc had assured the gentleman from Mayfield.

"You go on to them other counties and line up the support you deserve, and I'll take care of Logan County."

We know how *that* election turned out.

A FEW MONTHS LATER, I MET BERT COMBS for the first time as I climbed into the back seat of Rayburn Smith's car to join the two of them and Doc for a visit to the VFW Club. As he had been in the 1955 campaign, Rayburn was Combs' driver in west Kentucky.

Combs was usually reticent, more given to listening than making small talk. But he made us laugh by telling us about the time Rayburn had taken him to visit a tannery at Auburn during the campaign four years earlier. Rayburn had pushed Combs into a curing room where, he assured the candidate, there were five potential Combs voters working.

"It stank so bad in there Rayburn wouldn't go in with me," Combs said.

"He stood outside, but that was a short wait. I came out of that smelly place in just a few minutes, coughing and cussing."

But in a statement none of us would challenge, Doc said, "I'm satisfied you got the votes."

Doc always knew what was going on in an election. Ed Prichard, the Kentucky attorney who had spent years redeeming himself from a ballot scandal in his youth, told a story about the time Rayburn went into a panic when he discovered some Election Day monkey business by Beauchamp's foes at the Bucksville precinct in Logan County.

Calling from a grocery store payphone, Rayburn whispered, "Doc, they're stealing the Bucksville precinct!"

Seeming not to hear, Beauchamp gave his loyal lieutenant new marching orders.

"Rayburn, get out of there and go over to Auburn and see how the turnout is."

"But Doc!" Smith argued. "You're not listening. I said they're stealing the Bucksville precinct!"

"Oh, that's all right, Rayburn," Doc chuckled. "Tonight, we're not counting the Bucksville precinct."

Inside the VFW club, after the patrons met the candidate, my three companions sat down to enjoy a beer. No one said anything when I ordered a Coke. Judge Combs may have thought it curious to see a newspaper man sipping a soft drink in a veterans' joint on Saturday night. If the two locals knew that I was on Antabuse, they didn't mention it.

THE FOLLOWING JANUARY, after our little chats in Russellville, Wyatt and Combs finally concluded they both would lose if they did not form a team against Chandler's man, Waterfield.

Shown a poll that placed him last of the three major candidates, Wyatt agreed to take the lieutenant governor spot on a Combs-Wyatt ticket. This big political development was a front-page story in the cities and led the broadcast news all over the state.

The following morning, looking to localize the story, I phoned Combs at his Louisville hotel. When the telephone operator announced a call from Russellville, Combs, thinking Beauchamp was on the line, answered.

"What about Doc Beauchamp?" I asked. "He wants to come back to Frankfort as Commissioner of Agriculture. Will he be on your slate?"

"Sure," Combs said. "Doc knows everybody. He'll really strengthen our ticket."

The story was written and ready for the next edition of *The News-Democrat* when Beauchamp dropped by the office on press day to persuade me to kill it. He was affable about it, but he insisted that publicly linking him to Combs would alienate Waterfield voters who might otherwise vote for Doc as well. (After all, he *was* popular.)

I furiously objected. But when Dan Knotts, Mrs. Evans's son-in-law and our ad manager, agreed with Beauchamp, I knew I had to swallow the little doctor's bitter dose of practical politics. He was sixty years old and had been in politics all his life. I was thirty-two. What did I know?

Swallowing my wrath, I said, "Okay, Doc. If I leave the slating out, you've at least got to give me a new lead for my story. Tell me what you'll campaign for in the race for ag commissioner."

Lighting a cigarette, Doc smiled. "Not *for*, Al, … *against*. I'm running *against* brucellosis—that cattle disease."

"And what will you do about it if you win?

"I'll hire the best veterinarians money can buy—providing they voted for me."

COMBS AND WYATT BEAT WATERFIELD in the primary, despite harsh criticism from Chandler, who suggested it would be better for the state if the Republicans had won. Beauchamp swamped his three primary rivals. That fall, the Combs-Wyatt slate won handily over the Republicans.

And when Governor Combs announced an ethics code under which no member of his new administration was to accept any gifts more valuable than a country ham, Beauchamp supposedly replied:

"Governor, there is *no* gift more valuable than a Kentucky country ham."

Sick in the Sixties

BERT COMBS AND WILSON WYATT LED perhaps the most progressive administration in Kentucky history from 1959 to 1963. Exploiting a three-cent sales tax—it provided three times the revenue needed to pay for a veterans' bonus that had been authorized by constitutional amendment—the Combs-Wyatt team funded sweeping improvements throughout the state.

Plenty of money was allocated for education. An enormous new highway program supplemented the expanding federal interstate system. New parks were built and old ones improved. The forestry budget was doubled, and conservation laws were enacted. This being Kentucky, however, arguments over regulation of the coal industry would continue into the next century.

Wyatt headed an admirable economic development effort as Combs got nearly everything he asked for from the legislature: home rule, a meaningful civil service system, voting machines, the beginning of an educational television network (KET), modernization of the state library program, and construction of new airports and improvements at existing ones.

In Russellville, inspired by new tax breaks from the state and other inducements from Marvin Stuart and the city fathers, the Emerson Electric Company of St. Louis was building a large plant for the construction of hermetic (sealed) motors. Things were looking up in Logan County.

That's when I decided to throw away my Antabuse. I immediately fell into a serious relapse, drinking nonstop, alone or with friends from the ragged crew at the Kaintuck. After I missed work for several days, the city attorney, Granville Clark, who was becoming a friend, walked across the street from his office to the hotel with an offer.

If I would go to Western State Hospital in Hopkinsville for a month of treatment, Granville said, he would take over responsibility for getting the paper out while I was gone.

Granville's was an incredibly generous proposition, but I rejected it. I feared the stigma of a stay in a mental hospital. And I was not too drunk to forget that Mrs. Evans still held a grudge against Granville. He had invested in a failed attempt to start a daily paper in Russellville several years earlier.

More than anything, though, I just didn't want to stop drinking.

IN THOSE DRY DAYS, ALCOHOL WAS READILY OBTAINED from "the black bottom," a muddy neighborhood of crowded shacks, backyard privies, and stinking ditches where blacks sold half-pints of strong spirits for $2.

The "aristocrat" of the bootleggers was the elderly Blake Lamb, who was a cook and servant for a prominent Russellville family, the Gorrells, until he retired. Blake was not too ancient to come to the door when I knocked. But in hot weather, he might just holler, "Come in."

I would find him rolling out of bed. Occasionally a teenage girl, young enough to be his granddaughter, would be there with him.

One afternoon when I had interrupted his nap, he surprised me as he reached beneath the bed for the bottle with a compliment on a "progress" edition of The News-Democrat I had produced to mark the arrival of the Emerson Company.

"This here a pretty good town," Blake mumbled.

"Yes, it is," I agreed, with reservation. But that was a lie on my part. I hated it.

"I wouldn't live no place else," he said, reaching for my $2. "I wouldn't live in no town with no polices and no churches."

Late at night, when I didn't want to rouse a sterling citizen like Blake, I directed my taxi to Willie Jeff Fenton's cabin.

The father of many young children who slept crossways on a crowded bed in view of the door, he was one of four brothers his Pa had named "Willie": Willie Washington, Willie Madison, Willie Lincoln, and Willie Jefferson.

If I ever had a conversation with Willie Jeff as extended as the one where Blake praised Russellville, I don't remember it. Our dialogue was generally just a few words.

"Gimme a vodka," I'd say. Or maybe, "Gimme a whiskey," or "Gimme two half-pints."

Jeff would grunt "He-uh." Then I would whisper a sad "Thanks" and be on my way.

I HAD SPORADIC OVERNIGHT VISITS AT THE KAINTUCK from Lawrence Forgy, a chain-smoking gent from Lewisburg who came to town dressed in suit and tie. Lawrence, still the leader of the county's Republicans, came to Russellville to escape the monotony of running a country store with his widowed mother and the boredom of too many sober nights at home with his wife Mary and little daughter, Alice.

Lawrence had been a high school basketball star, which counts for a lot in Kentucky. He was fondly respected as such by the county's Democrats, who tolerated his boozing and forgave his Republicanism.

Friendly and courteous when sober, Lawrence was fun to fuss with over politics. On his Russellville overnights, he would tank up at the American Legion and VFW, then take a taxi to the Kaintuck, rent a room for the night, and find me to heckle.

"You know, they hate you up my way," he would say, referring to my pro-Democratic editorials, or the stories I wrote in support of a consolidated high school at Russellville to replace the aging high schools at Lewisburg and four other small communities. "You couldn't buy a meal north of Epley Station," a crossroads on the outskirts of Russellville.

"And at Lewisburg, wouldn't nobody feed you except at our house, and you'd have to come after dark, to the back door, where nobody sees Mary let you in."

Lawrence would occasionally pause in his needling long enough to wave me over to a corner of the Kaintuck lobby. There, he'd pour us each a drink from the flask in his pocket, offer one to the night clerk, then march me to a couch by the black-and-white television.

Then Lawrence would start talking again. "You remember my son Larry?"

Larry Forgy was a promising young valedictorian from Lewisburg High. Everyone in Logan County, regardless of their politics, believed Larry had a bright future, maybe even as governor. After struggling through college on scholarships, he was working as a Capitol Hill cop in Washington, a patronage appointment from Kentucky's Republican senators that was helping him pay for law school.

That question was a signal that Lawrence was about to start bragging on an engaging lad who was studious, good-natured, didn't drink much, and was even better looking than his father. I took it and ran with it.

"I never saw that kid," I said. "I don't believe you have a son named Larry."

Choking on his cigarette smoke, Lawrence would laugh incredulously. "Never *saw* him?"

That line meant it was time for us to climb the stairs to the Stubblefield Suite, where it was my turn to provide the nightcap.

Some mornings when I awoke, Lawrence was still there, still dressed in suit and tie, asleep across the foot of the bed like Willie Jeff's children.

In my loneliness, I was an equal opportunity host. One weekend during a Tobacco Festival, the circuit judge passed out in my armchair. He was Tom Noe, the son-in-law of Thomas Rhea. Friends joked that Mr. Rhea's only daughter, Lillian, a princess of the county, had chased Tom until he married her. After wartime service as a Navy officer, his connections quickly eased his way into the state legislature and then onto the bench.

When Tom stumbled into my room, looking for a drink after the festival parade, we hardly knew each other. Neither of us was aware of how desperately sick we were, or that we would soon share a battle against the disease of alcoholism, or that one of us would win and one would lose.

While Judge Noe and I became close friends and he guided me to new horizons in journalism, Lawrence Forgy contracted tuberculosis and gave up whiskey on his own. After Larry Forgy came back to Kentucky, Lawrence never took another drink, and Larry almost became governor.

IN THE 1960s I ACQUIRED THREE HEROES NAMED JOHN.

I was thrilled when John Kennedy campaigned in Bowling Green. From a seat I proudly claimed in a section for the national press, I had a clear view as Kennedy thanked Mayor Bob Graham for a moldy green Kentucky ham. Looking at the ham, Kennedy wittily commented, "We say the bravest man in the history of New England was the first who ate an oyster."

Standing in the Russellville square on a hot fall day, Kentucky's popular U.S. Senator, John Sherman Cooper, tried to make the case for Kennedy's opponent, Vice President Richard Nixon, but the audience was skeptical. Cooper finished an awkward speech and sat down.

Almost immediately he jumped back up. Ignoring the microphone, he shouted, half apologetically, "Oh yes … one other thing folks, that I forgot to mention. I'm on that ballot too. Heh, heh. Now don't forget to vote for me!"

I admired Cooper and even persuaded Mrs. Evans we should endorse him. He was all wrong about Nixon, but he was loyal to the party, and on many things, he was so right. He was one of the Senate's most liberal Republicans.

"Kentucky politics are the damnedest," or so goes the poem "In Old Kentucky." Cooper bore that out. I was astonished when I read in *Time* that the Kennedys' first social engagement after the election was a dinner at the home of Cooper and his wife Lorraine.

My third hero in the early 1960s was John Clark, the administrator of the Logan County Hospital. Again and again, he intervened to stop my drinking sprees. Undiscouraged by my resistance to his cousin Granville's suggestion that I commit myself to Western State, John offered—nay, *demanded*—that I submit to the care of his local hospital.

More than once, Clark sent a rescue team, Winston McReynolds and Hiram Wilson, to kidnap me from my cave at the Kaintuck. They would push me into their van as I clutched a book I was too cockeyed to read and an overnight bag they packed for me. Upon arrival, I was hustled up to the hospital, undressed, and put to bed with the help of a nurse wielding a hypodermic full of knock-out drugs John had ordered in the name of an agreeable doctor. Next day, the doctor, accompanied by John, would set about devising a plan to return me to work sober.

Before John took personal charge as my caregiver in the early 1960s, I suffered through one terrible mishap at the hospital. In 1958, I was admitted with a genuine case of flu by a doctor who didn't know about my alcoholism. Cut off from the booze, I went into the DTs. A nurse found me barefoot in my pajamas in the elevator; I explained that I was going to walk down to the hotel a mile away to get some more books to read. She was alarmed, of course, but had she seen the snakes and bats in my room, she would have called a cab.

When I regained consciousness several days later, I was still strapped to the bed. But the scary creatures had vanished, and the doctor said I wouldn't have to go to Western State after all.

WHY DIDN'T MRS. EVANS FIRE ME? I'm not sure.

Beasley Thompson, a former editor of *The News-Democrat*, was by then editing a larger paper in Athens, Alabama. But he always seemed happy to drive up to Russellville when Mrs. Evans summoned him after I went on a bender. He'd spend two days at his old job, collect my entire week's salary, and then spend a night drinking at the American Legion before returning to Alabama. I never knew how he managed that, but he performed ably in more emergencies than I can remember.

Perhaps the reason I was retained as editor was because most readers liked my writing. Or maybe it was because after each drinking bout, I'd accumulate weeks of sobriety like a bank account of good behavior I could draw on to reclaim my reputation. Inevitably, though, I'd eventually give in to depression, take a drink, and keep at it until word got out that "the poor boy is sick again."

Then, once more, John Clark would send Hiram and Winston to the rescue at the Kaintuck.

–28–
The Hospital That Was Ours

SAVING ME FROM A DRUNKARD'S DEATH was not John Clark's only special talent as CEO of the county hospital. He knew how to meet his patients' needs, whatever they were.

Once, during one of my "guest" stays in 1962, I heard John enter the room next to mine, where a woman had been moaning through the dinner hour.

"Hi, Mrs. Stratton," I heard John say. "I've brought you a little something you'll like better than what's on your plate." There was a silence, and then I heard him say, "Nurse, bring me some ice, please."

Leaving Mrs. Stratton's room, John paused in my doorway.

"What the hell were you doing in there?" I asked. The woman's moans had stopped.

"Just fixing her a little dose of what you've had too much of," he said. "It can't cure what she's got, but it may help her for a little while."

To ease the agony of a woman dying from cancer, John Clark created a cocktail hour.

When the police made a rare raid on the bootleggers in the Bottom, they called for the paper to take a picture of the loot. After the photographer left, they set aside a few bottles as evidence, then divided the rest among themselves and the other authorities. They always remembered to take some whiskey to John.

JOHN CAME BACK HOME TO RUSSELLVILLE after serving four years in the Pacific during World War II. He returned to a job with Dr. John Pepper Glenn, a surgeon who had set up a small hospital before he left for the Navy.

Now, twenty years later, Glenn's little hospital had become a home for nurses, and Mrs. Stratton and I were patients in a crowded fifty-bed hospital that the county built with assistance from federal Hill-Burton funds.

John didn't possess the typical credentials of today's hospital administrators. His qualifications were his association with Dr. Glenn, for whom he had been a chauffeur, and the training as a laboratory and x-ray technician he had gotten with his GI Bill benefits. After a few college types faltered at the hospital's helm, the fiscal court settled on John for the job. He gave the hospital nine years of the best leadership it would ever have.

His Army experience helped. He scavenged a stream of surplus property from Fort Campbell—jeeps, tractors, mowers. He bought kitchen utensils, including a giant colander, which was often out on loan for church spaghetti suppers. He once bought enough surplus paint to meet the hospital's needs *and* completely redo the county courthouse.

John was tall and red-faced, a rough-talking, fortyish fellow usually dressed in khakis. He was not your typical executive. But he was a Samaritan for all seasons.

Daughter with a baby out of wedlock? Send the young mother to John; he'll give her a job while Granny keeps the baby. Another girl broke, with a semester needed to finish nursing school? No worries; Earl Davis will approve a loan from the bank because John guarantees he'll hire her. Dad hurt his back? Tell John Clark; he'll make him a night watchman.

THE ENTIRE COUNTY WAS PROUD OF THE HOSPITAL. Its modestly paid staff was assisted by volunteer "Pink Ladies," only one of whom ever hissed at me, "You should be ashamed." The dawn of integration in the 1960s was signaled by a smiling young dark face among the teenage Candy Stripers.

On every patient room's door, a brass plate proclaimed that the furniture was a gift—from a homemakers' club, or the VFW auxiliary, or the Ladies of the Order of the Eastern Star. The general surgery equipment in the operating rooms, if not scrounged from Fort Campbell surplus, might have been paid for by the American Legion Fair Board. Harry Whipple's Rockwell was prominently represented by the bigger pieces, soon to be joined by more modern machines given by Emerson Electric.

All of the county's doctors—there were no more than ten—sent their patients to the Logan County Hospital. They took turns covering for each other and the emergency room when needed.

One Sunday night, the police called me to the scene of a terrible car wreck where five people had been critically injured. The rival funeral home directors, their hearses serving as ambulances, had raced to the scene for a rescue or darker business. They brought the injured to the emergency room, where a full staff was waiting.

Those rural docs had left their farms and families, donned scrubs, and were standing at the ready to help our two surgeons, Dr. Glenn and Dr. Harris. Those two men positively *hated* each other. Yet they and the other docs teamed that night as angels of God to save the lives of five strangers.

NO ONE DIED THAT NIGHT, as I had not died when my compulsion to destroy myself was interrupted by Clark and those country doctors. Weeks after that spectacular wreck, when John came to the newspaper office with a plea for me to help *him,* I was glad to oblige.

What John wanted was a fiscal cure for the increased overcrowding at the hospital, where often as many as thirty patients had to be treated on beds in the halls. The solution to the problem was a bond issue financed by a tax on county residents. And that tax would have to be approved in a general election.

"Do you think you can write enough stories and editorials to persuade your readers to vote 'Yes'"? John asked.

I told him I would try.

The proposition called for a 20 cent tax to retire enough bonds over twenty years to finance a $1 million, fifty-bed annex to the existing hospital. That expansion would double the size of the current facility. The fiscal court was willing to put the tax question on the same ballot with Kennedy, Nixon, Senator Cooper, and his opponent.

But everyone involved knew that Logan countians were notoriously tax-averse. And two-thirds of the voters would have to vote "Yes" for this particular type of tax to pass.

For me, it was payback time.

Over the next three months—stone-cold sober—I wrote reams of words on behalf of my first great crusade in Logan County. Outside the office, I helped organize teams of volunteers to work every precinct on Election Day.

On election night, after the presidential and senatorial votes had been counted (Kennedy and Cooper carried the county), Rayburn Smith, Lawrence Forgy, and County Clerk Bailey Gunn announced on behalf of both political parties that it was getting late. The election officials were exhausted, they said, so the vote counting for the hospital issue would be suspended until Wednesday morning.

I was outraged, but the courthouse officials were adamant. I was still fussing at Gunn, who was locking up the clerk's office when Doc walked in.

I protested to Doc as some sort of higher power. I had a Wednesday noon deadline for the paper's election issue, and I needed those totals. But when Gunn assured me they would resume counting early Wednesday morning, Doc, politely but firmly, all but suggested I run along.

I joined the same gang of election officials the following morning for breakfast at the Parkview Restaurant. Rayburn and Lawrence said they knew I had a busy day ahead of me, so I needn't go to the courthouse with them—they would bring me the hospital results as soon as the counting was over.

True to their word, the old foes showed up at the paper two hours later, and both were smiling.

The hospital tax, which Rayburn and Lawrence had both supported in a rare moment of unity, had passed. The requisite two-thirds of the total 9,000 votes cast, plus a few more, were recorded "Yes" on the hospital bond issue.

"Good for Logan County!" I exclaimed. "It's a great day!"

"Your old paper just about put it across," said Forgy.

"Them editorials were a right smart of help," Rayburn agreed.

"I never worked any harder," I said, congratulating myself. "I wrote an editorial and a front-page story on the need every week."

"You've got a lot of readers," said Smith, as the old boys walked out.

BY SUNSET, I HAD FIGURED IT OUT.

As Virginia Edwards, the elderly county treasurer who was a tabulator, stood watching through the haze of her usual post-election hangover, Rayburn and Lawrence had tossed the "No" ballots in a "Yes" pile and the scant number of "Yes" ballots in a "No" pile. It was the old shell game.

Miss Edwards, who was dead honest, thought she knew which pile of ballots was which, so she just watched as sly Lawrence and slick Rayburn took it from there.

I didn't see it happen. But when I quizzed courthouse insiders about my suspicions that the vote totals just couldn't be right, every one of them just laughed, responding to my questions with a "No comment" or a smarmy "What makes you think that?"

That was easy: History is what made me think that. There had been elections in the past where Logan County was said to have reported more votes than it had registered voters, and where precinct records reportedly showed dozens of votes had been cast by the residents of neighboring counties.

At the post office a few days later, I confessed my suspicions to an old-timer, Clay Franklin, the manager of the local garment company.

"You're right, Al," Clay said. "Our farmers will never vote for a tax, no matter how much they love that hospital."

But Clay told me that since all the local doctors wanted to expand the hospital, and since those doctors gave campaign money to both sides in elections every six months, the county politicians felt they had a bipartisan duty to improve the county's health care.

"Don't worry about it, Albert," he said. "I was here when they had the election to build the hospital.

"They stole that one too!"

THE NEXT YEAR, VOTING MACHINES replaced paper ballots, thanks to legislation sponsored by Governor Combs, in whose cabinet Doc served.

The change gave Doc occasion to observe famously, "Instead of precinct workers, what we need these days is good mechanics."

PART TWO
Recovery

-29-
Surrender

I WAS TOO HUNG OVER to sit in the business sessions at a summer convention of the Kentucky Press Association in 1962, so I slipped out to a secluded spot on the bank of Kentucky Lake. Hoping either the air or the sunshine would ease my pain, I flung myself on the grass.

The day before, I'd ended a week of heavy drinking. An annoyed Dan Knotts only agreed to drive me to the meeting at Kentucky Dam Village State Park on condition that I not drink while we were there. The unspoken reason I insisted on the trip was hope of recognition at the awards dinner that night.

I was suffering the consequences of going "cold turkey"— cutting off the alcohol without a few spaced drinks to slow the shakes, calm the stomach, and, I hoped, ward off the DTs. Face down in the grass, I knew that a drink would fix my nausea, but it might also get me fired.

As the dry heaves began, I propped myself on my elbows. Nearby, an old lady was standing at the water's edge with a fishing pole. She threw out her line, then cast a curious glance at me.

"You all right, son?" she asked.

"Yes, ma'am," I said. "Just got a little sick after breakfast."

"I'm Mrs. Nolan," she said. Next, a signal that I wouldn't have to lie, that she had seen enough inebriated writers and editors in her day that she recognized a disabled reporter when she saw one, "I own the Hazard paper."

Then she recast her line and turned away.

THE NEWS-DEMOCRAT'S ENTRY in the Kentucky Press Association contest was a series of stories I wrote for a special edition about the opening of the Emerson Electric plant. Eighteen families had moved from St. Louis to Russellville to get the assembly lines up and running and to train two hundred new local employees.

I didn't drink as I prepared those stories. I had narrowly dodged a disaster, however. A primitive antidepressant had gotten me through all the stories, but almost ruined my career.

I woke up in horror at 3:00 a.m. on the day we were to go to press with the special edition. Throwing on my clothes, I walked across the square to the paper, switched on the lights, and snatched the last of my Emerson stories from a hook on the Linotype where I had hung it at midnight.

Sure enough, I was crazy when I wrote it. I *had* interviewed the new plant manager, Ed Johnson, but he'd never said at least half of what I'd written about our conversation. The quotes were imaginary, fantasies generated not by whiskey but by the mood drug.

By the time I cut off the lights and left the paper, I had penciled out the inventions in the Johnson story—flattering lines about "lovely Logan County" and "looking forward to entering an Emerson float in the Tobacco Festival," as well as assurances about hiring blacks. Back in my room, I dropped the little pill bottle into the trash.

THERE ON THE LAKE BANK, neither Mrs. Nolan nor I was getting anywhere. We were there an hour, but she hadn't caught a fish, and I was feeling no better.

"You ever been to Hazard?" she asked.

I hadn't been anywhere east of Louisville, and Hazard was in the mountains. "No ma'am," I said.

"Well, if you ever do, come see me," she said. Then she walked away.

That night at the banquet, I still could not eat anything, but I sipped iced tea until my name was called. "And the award for Best

News Story of the Year goes to 'Emerson Electric Comes to Logan County,' by Al Smith."

LATER THAT FALL, still employed at *The News-Democrat*—the award had won me a reprieve—I took up with Wendell Dole, a new "guest" at the Kaintuck. He and I sometimes chatted in the lobby until Jack Parr came on the TV and Wendell went upstairs—or out on other business.

Wendell was a criminal—a burglar with safe-cracking skills. His work sometimes took him out at night.

Thin, with sallow skin and a greasy cowlick over his forehead, Wendell usually dressed in a black shirt, dark trousers, a black jacket in cold weather, but never a tie. It was more a uniform for work than a wardrobe.

Wendell had an angry-looking blind eye, the result of a heroic effort to save some Navy shipmates in an explosion. He was decorated for bravery, but that did not shield him from penitentiary time for various felonies. Prison had been profitable, however. His Navy pension continued, funding lucrative sessions at craps and cards.

On work nights, Wendell sometimes exited the Kaintuck via the fire escape, conveniently located next to his third-floor room. Lest this unnerve other Kaintuck boarders, Wendell quietly got the word out that he was just trying to avoid surveillance by parties unknown. No need to worry: A professional thief does not spoil his own nest. Observing that our landlord, J.M. Richard, accepted Wendell on these terms, so did the rest of us.

Nevertheless, when I heard the police radio crackling one Sunday with an all-points alarm to apprehend Wendell Dole, it seemed almost foreordained. He was wanted for a break-in and safe robbery at the Zeinmeister Wholesale Grocery of Greenville, Kentucky. Five thousand dollars had been stolen by two men believed to have been Wendell and Dred Gray, a wallpaper hanger who was also from Russellville.

An informant's tip had led the state police to set up a watch on a car hidden at a quarry north of town. When Wendell and Dred Gray returned late Saturday night to swap that car for the one they'd been driving, the state police officers ambushed them.

Wendell, believed to be the driver, got away through the woods, but Dred Gray, passed out on the back seat after drinking a bottle of scotch taken at the burglary, was nabbed along with the stolen cash.

Late that Sunday afternoon as I left the Kaintuck, I saw Wendell's lawyer, Skye Howell, stopped at a traffic light. Howell, who was so fat he looked stuffed, was in that peculiar sweat that other attorneys said was drug-induced.

"Where have you hidden Wendell?" I asked Howell in the brassy, sassy tone of my New Orleans crime beat days.

Howell opened the passenger door and grunted, "Get in."

Five minutes later, Howell and I were in the backyard of a cabin in the Bottom. A ragged Wendell emerged from a chicken house and slid into the back seat.

"Whatcha say, Big Al?" he greeted me.

"How much did we lose, Skye?"

"$5,000," muttered Skye.

"Oh, my God!" Wendell groaned.

Skye Howell's next move was to drive Wendell to a better hiding place: behind the little Muddy River Baptist Church out on the Bowling Green Road, east of Russellville. The game plan, Skye explained, was to elude the police roadblocks and drive Wendell ninety minutes north to Calhoun, Kentucky, where he could give himself up to the McLean County jailer.

Surrender in Logan County was not an option, Howell said. Wendell was due in Calhoun for a trial the next week on charges of stealing shotguns from a local hardware store. Out on bond from that caper, and now in deeper trouble, Wendell and Skye feared that

Logan County would not agree to transfer Wendell in time for the Greenville trial. That would mean that Wendell's uncle, who posted the bond at Calhoun, would lose his money.

While I was digesting this shadowy conversation behind the church, I realized I was trapped with these two dangerous rogues. They would never take me back to the hotel until Wendell was in jail in a far-off county.

Wendell refused to go on this frightful trip around the roadblocks without a half-pint of liquor and the comfort of his sweetie, a Mrs. Banfield.

"Don't tell Mrs. Banfield about the liquor—she don't like drinking," Wendell said. He figured on doing his tippling during rest stops along the way. I was to carry the hidden booze and provide it whenever we peed in the bushes.

Dole insisted that the half-pint be vodka. "That way she won't smell it," he said—a myth among alcoholics, of course.

An hour later, all the requirements met, Skye and I collected Wendell from the rear of the church. We put him in the backseat with Mrs. Banfield, a gray-haired lady who was several years older than Wendell. I was on the wagon, but I had possession of the vodka, and I slipped it under the front seat between me and the maniacal lawyer at the wheel.

Ten miles north of town on a deserted back road, Skye suddenly pulled over and stopped the car.

"I have an announcement," he declared.

"For the record, I am making a citizen's arrest of Wendell. I am taking him to jail in McLean County to face trial next week. You, Al Smith, and you, Mrs. Banfield, are my witnesses. If the police should try to halt us, I have no intention of risking gunfire. I will stop immediately and give this story.

"Any questions?"

"I have an announcement," said Wendell.

"What?" Skye asked.

"I have to pee."

About 5:00 a.m. Monday, back in Russellville, Mrs. Banfield wearily got out of the car, noting she had to open her grocery store in two hours. Skye assured her that the boy we left at Calhoun would be safe; the *boy*, who was forty-five, had been in worse places. Skye said Wendell might beat the case at Calhoun, but if he was to get a proper defense on the Zeinmeister case, Mrs. Banfield would need to work on securing Skye's fee.

In front of the Kaintuck, Skye pulled out the vodka bottle and drained what was left. Maybe it would carry him until Perry's Drugstore opened and he could refill his prescription for the stronger stuff.

A FEW MONTHS LATER, Skye managed to get Dred Gray, the paperhanger charged in the burglary, acquitted of the crime. He convinced the Greenville jury that Wendell had pulled off the safecracking by himself while Dred was passed out drunk in the backseat.

Dred went on to marry Jane, the girl who testified at trial as to his changed character. (She feigned pregnancy while on the stand by wearing a pillow beneath her dress.) Dred and Jane joined Brother Joe Carrico's Post Oak Baptist Church after Carrico also testified on behalf of the "reformed" Brother Gray. Dred stayed straight and became a business success.

Wendell copped some kind of plea, served some more prison time, and doubtless emerged with a hoard of cash from gambling. He married Mrs. Banfield and never came back to the Kaintuck. I gratefully lost touch with him.

THAT MONDAY AFTERNOON I was still on the wagon, despite the hair-raising trip to Calhoun. I was walking back to the Kaintuck from the newspaper office when I saw Judge Tom Noe, my occasional Kaintuck drinking buddy, buying gas at the station on the square. I was about to speak when Noe said, "Let's go to an AA meeting."

"All right," I said. And I slid into the front seat of his Impala.

I had never been to an Alcoholics Anonymous meeting. I had forgotten there was a group in Russellville, and I wasn't aware that Tom attended. But I had nothing else to do.

The meeting was in a basement of the First Christian Church. There, in a smoked-filled room, were twelve men and women, some of whom I knew, laughing about stupid mistakes they had made. They said they were "sick and tired of being sick and tired." That resonated with me.

I had never seen drunks who seemed happy not to be drinking. These people talked of God as a "Higher Power," not the God I'd heard Brother Anderson preach about back in Sarasota, but a God of "one's own understanding" that could help each of us stay sober.

That was all. There were no promises like "I'll never take another drink." The pledge was simply to stay sober, "one day at a time."

An hour later, back in Judge Noe's car, I was startled at what I had done.

I had told eight friends and four strangers, "My name is Al, and I am an alcoholic."

Like Wendell, I had surrendered.

–30–
Sober Summer

"ONE DAY AT A TIME."

From October through Thanksgiving and on to Christmas, 1962, that's how I stayed sober: one day at a time.

Then, so pleased with my first sober holidays in nineteen years that I felt I deserved a reward, I accepted a few cups of spiked milk punch at a New Year's Eve party and was soon drunk.

That sent me home again to Here We Are farm, but only for a few days. My mother drove me back to Russellville on my thirty-sixth birthday.

"Good luck, Albert," she said, handing me 50 cents for breakfast as I got out of the car. Once inside *The News-Democrat* office, I opened the cash register and took out a five-dollar bill, replacing it with an I.O.U. It was enough to last me until payday.

That night I went back to an AA meeting. The old-timers who greeted me were amused, not angry, as I told about my slip.

THE NEXT DAY I FLEW TO LEXINGTON with Oscar McCutchen, a Russellville florist, for a consultation with the president and vice president of the University of Kentucky (UK) about an educational windfall Russellville had received.

Thomas P. deGraffenried had grown up in Russellville but had gone on to live in New York, where he was legal counsel for a shipping line. When he died a bachelor, he left $1 million to his hometown, to be spent "on education of the citizens at large."

McCutchen, who aspired to be mayor, was well connected at UK, his alma mater. We met with Frank Dickey, then UK's president, and A.D. Albright, a vice president, about how best to invest and use our legacy.

Sam Milam, the "dean" of the Russellville bar, had sought and received a ruling from a New York probate court that under the will, the city council and mayor—not the city school board—were the "citizens at large" that deGraffenried had intended to spend the money.

I had a special emotional stake in the outcome of these discussions: Before his death, deGraffenried wrote a Russellville cousin praising a special section of stories *The News-Democrat* had published about early Logan County schools. The cousin had pleaded with deGraffenried for a gift to renovate the local country club, but deGraffenried declined, promising instead to leave a "gift" to Russellville in his will. He didn't say how much.

THE NEW YORK COURT HAD RULED that the circuit court in Russellville would oversee the spending of the gift. That meant that my new brother in AA, Circuit Judge Tom Noe, would be very much in the public eye as the people of Russellville and Logan County wondered how the politicians would slice the deGraffenried cake.

That spring, Noe was up for reelection, and the challenger and his friends were spreading the word about his alcoholism. Tom's fate in the judge's race depended in large part on his ability to convince the voters he was repentant and reformed.

I did my best to help him.

Every weekend, Tom, his wife Lillian, and I crossed the county together. We stopped at country stores, ate at school suppers, and attended ballgames and funerals. Whatever the occasion, Tom and I— both sober—made ourselves noticed in the crowds when candidates for statewide office showed up.

Most people in those days viewed alcoholism as a moral issue and knew very little about AA. But I was not above whispering to the right people that the Judge Noe and I attended "those meetings."

The News-Democrat reported that Judge Noe had sensibly approved the city council's plans for spending the deGraffenried money. Whether that helped his chances in the election, I don't know, but I tried.

I admit it: In that election, I was shamefully partisan. I was very grateful to the man who took me to the basement of the First Christian Church for an AA meeting that changed my life.

TOM NOE WON THE PRIMARY. That night, as the courthouse crowd was clearing out, I went upstairs to congratulate him.

I found him sitting in the dark, alone in his little office next to the courtroom. On the desk was an open bottle of vodka.

Had he deceived the voters? Had he stayed sober just long enough to win, planning to go back to the bottle at the end of election night?

I never thought so. I think Tom was chronically depressed. Today's antidepressant medications, together with AA, might have relieved his dark moods. As it was, I will never know how many days of sobriety AA alone gave him. But I believe they were many. In those days, he was an exemplary judge.

Six years later, after several more "stumbles" or lapses, Tom finally lost his reelection bid. The voters had lost patience, I guess. But I never did.

I owed him too much.

BY MIDSUMMER 1963, SIX MONTHS "DRY," I felt I was pitching a no-hitter against the demon from the distilleries.

But don't misunderstand me. Although I had become a teetotaler, I was not a prohibitionist.

In AA, I accepted the idea I was suffering from what a doctor friend in the program called "the disease of alcoholism." I came to believe I suffered from an ailment that, like diabetes or a severe allergy, could kill me if I continued to drink. But I also believed there were those who could manage moderation, and I bore them no resentment and certainly no feeling that their enjoyment should be banned by law.

Looking to improve my future as a sober journalist, I flew to Jackson, Ohio, to see my cousin McGregor Smith, Jr. He had taken a leave from his job at *The Miami News* and was in Ohio to outfit an Airstream trailer and a Ford truck for an Airstream-sponsored trip around the world. He, his wife Jackie, and three small children would be gone for a year.

"When you get back," I said after we had chatted awhile, "would you like to invest with me in a weekly newspaper?"

McGregor was quick to answer.

"Goodness, no," said the son of one of Florida's top business leaders. "That sounds too much like business. I grew up with that, and it's not for me."

I was disappointed in my cousin's reply. That evening, I joined McGregor's young family for an ice cream supper at a Methodist church. As I watched his kids play afterward in a little park next door, I wondered if I would ever love a woman again or have children of my own.

In my bed in a motel room that night, so close to the lounge that the music was keeping me awake, I began to wonder what my next step was. I thought about the bar in the lounge, but that was no longer for me.

Pretty quickly, I turned out the light and said the Serenity Prayer I had learned in those basement meetings.

"God, grant me the serenity to accept the things I cannot change, courage to change the things I can, and the wisdom to know the difference."

I decided I would not try to push for a solution. I would turn my life over to my Higher Power, God "as I understood him." Then I fell asleep.

-31-
"Clean Ned"

IN THE SUMMER OF 1963, the Logan Courthouse was still buzzing over an upset in the Democratic primary for governor. Young Edward T. Breathitt, Jr., only thirty-nine, had defeated the old warrior Happy Chandler, sixty-four, by a landslide. Breathitt's 60,000-vote margin dashed Chandler's hopes to be governor a third time and ended his colorful political career.[16]

Breathitt was a Hopkinsville attorney who was little known until Governor Combs chose him to defend his administration's progressive programs and maintain the three cent sales tax that funded them.

Ned had a strong reputation for integrity. He had also served as Combs's personnel commissioner, overseeing the new civil service, or "merit," system. Those factors led some to call him "clean Ned." His stunning victory was a sign of the state's confidence in him, as well as an endorsement of Combs and a rebuke of Earle Clements who had split from his protégé, Combs, and Combs' choice of Breathitt.

The factional break among Kentucky's Democrats into pro- and anti-Chandler camps, which was a factor in state politics for a generation, began after the 1935 governor's race, when

---

[16] Breathitt also won in the general election that fall, but barely. He defeated the Republican, Louie Nunn, by a mere 13,000 votes. Breathitt's patron, Combs, was nearly his undoing. In late June 1963, Combs issued an executive order prohibiting state-regulated establishments, such as restaurants, hospitals, parks, and hotels, from discriminating against blacks. With much of Kentucky still hostile to the idea of civil rights for blacks, the measure was deeply unpopular, and the backlash against Combs hurt Breathitt.

Chandler defeated Russellville's Thomas Rhea for the Democratic nomination and went on to win the first of his governorships. Clements, who was from west Kentucky, had managed Rhea's campaign in that race and become the head of the group opposing Chandler.

The anti-Chandler faction was a factor in Kentucky politics for a generation, and Clements—a west Kentucky politician who himself was elected governor in 1947—had headed it. When Clements was elected to the U.S. Senate in 1950, Lawrence Wetherby of Louisville succeeded him as governor, but Clements retained leadership of anti-Chandler forces.

In the 1963 primary, Clements incredibly backed Chandler. Clements and Combs had fallen out over bad publicity about a highway contract in 1960. Earle was still so mad he could not bring himself to get on the same side with Combs again, virtuous as Ned Breathitt appeared to be against the battle-scarred Chandler.

ALTHOUGH A CLEMENTS DISCIPLE, Ed Prichard, a brilliant attorney, was a strong supporter of Breathitt. He was working his way back to the inner circle of state politics after briefly going to federal prison in 1950 for stuffing a ballot box in Paris, Kentucky, his hometown.[17]

"Happy Chandler is the leader of the Republican wing of the Democratic party," Prichard liked to say, referring to Chandler's frequent support of Republican candidates against his Democratic foes. (In the general election that year, Chandler backed Breathitt's Republican opponent, Louie Nunn.)

---

[17] Prichard's amazing career of rise, fall, and redemption, is well told by UK historian Tracy Campbell in *Short of the Glory*, University Press of Kentucky, 1998.

THAT 1963 SPRING PRIMARY drew me closer to Doc Beauchamp and to Rayburn Smith, his "bag man."

During the five years I'd been in Russellville, Rayburn had guided me through the mysteries and machinations of the Logan County Courthouse. He and I had become friends, as had Beauchamp and I.

Doc, a kingmaker in that anti-Chandler faction, was now joined at the hip with Combs's protégé Breathitt. He was on the Breathitt ticket as the nominee for state treasurer and was a cinch to be elected.

In 1963, I was no longer the naïve newcomer I had been when I first met Doc and Rayburn. I better understood that Doc had a special relationship with my publisher.

Yes, she had encouraged me to print the full story about the pro-Chandler auditor's efforts to collect unpaid fees from Doc's courthouse cronies when I had first arrived in town. But Mrs. Evans never forgot that she owed Beauchamp for a favor. When she had fallen ill with cancer a few years before I became editor, Doc had voluntarily served as interim editor of *The News-Democrat.*

In the elections that followed (Kentucky then had some kind of election every six months), the county Democratic Party, which Doc controlled, regularly charged a sizable amount of advertising at the paper.

After the polls closed, Dan Knotts would deliver the bill to Doc. The next day, Beauchamp would visit Mrs. Evans at her house.

In his courtly fashion, he would ask, "Miss Ailene, how much do you want to contribute to the party?"

Mrs. Evans would reply, and that number was quickly subtracted from the amount the party owed.

Beauchamp would then pull out a clutch of bills, no doubt harvested from the faithful by the dependable Rayburn, and peel off the balance the party owed Mrs. Evans.

Gradually, I had become an accepted Sunday morning visitor at Doc's Russellville home, where his closest buddies crowded the living room or front porch to gossip about politics from the courthouse to the White House. Earlier in the morning, before the visitors arrived, Doc would have called special friends who were political leaders in Louisville and each of the grand regions of the state.[18]

Harry Caudill, the lawyer and Appalachian advocate who lived in Whitesburg, Kentucky, once recalled Doc's conversations with his father, a county clerk.

"They were always plotting the political death, damnation, and destruction of Happy Chandler," Harry told me.

WESTERN KENTUCKY WAS STILL "the Gibraltar of Democracy" in 1963—that is, the First Congressional District was staunchly Democratic. Citizens of the district who loved politics had plenty to watch and enjoy during that primary campaign.

Chandler would sing "My Old Kentucky Home" at campaign appearances. Ed Prichard, standing in the back of Breathitt rallies, would hoot "He's clean! He's clean!" about his man Breathitt, suggesting that Happy was not.

Rayburn and other Breathitt supporters carried around a caged goose with a sign that mocked Chandler and charged that he had illegally shot a bird in a wildlife preserve.

---

[18] These included Smith Broadbent, Cadiz; Willie Foster, Mayfield; J.R. Miller, Owensboro; the Paxtons, Paducah; "Miss Lennie" McLaughin and John Crimmins, Louisville; the Turners, Breathitt County; Dr. Benjamin Wright, Whitesburg; and congressmen Carl Perkins, Hindman, and Bill Natcher, Bowling Green.

Rayburn told of seeing two small boys trying to read the sign.

"What it say, Br'er?" the younger brother reportedly asked.

The older boy struggled to read it. "Hap...Hap...Happy...Kuh...Kuh...Killed...My...My...Pap..."

Suddenly the boy figured it out. "Happy Killed My Pappy!" he shrieked.

The smaller boy's mouth flew open.

"Why the son of a bitch!"

A BREAK FROM POLITICS AND HISTORY that busy year of 1963 came when Harry Whipple invited me to fly with him and his boss, Lloyd Dixon, to Lexington, Kentucky. Dixon, Rockwell's executive vice president, wanted to buy some horses at the July Keeneland sales.

During a late lunch in a motel bar, Whipple ordered a beer. Dixon asked the waiter, "Will it bust this place up to bring me a coffee?"

"Bring Al a coffee too," Whipple grumped.

Turning to Dixon, Harry said, "Al's a drunk."

My face surely flushed.

"Hell, that's nothing," Dixon replied.

"So am I."

I soon figured it out. Whipple, Rockwell's bull of the woods, had tricked me into a sober weekend so I could watch another recovering alcoholic—this one a multimillionaire—spend $300,000 on colts for his stable in California. Moral: Success in recovery comes in different packages.

The incident made me think of quiet Buck, who brought AA to Russellville. In the group's early weeks, Buck would sit alone on Monday nights in the basement of the First Christian Church,

AA's "Big Book" on the table in front of him, waiting for someone who needed help.

Buck had once owned several grocery stores but lost them because of his drinking. He had started over as a produce clerk, working for someone else, but sober, thanks to AA. Compared to gregarious, hard-charging Dixon, quiet Buck was just there to help others talk.

The same month as my encounter with Dixon, I met Mac, an AA old-timer who was sponsoring my friend Judge Noe. Mac was from a prominent Bowling Green, Kentucky, family, but he managed to drink his way from a vice presidency at an oil company to a night clerk's job in a motel.

Once securely sober, Mac had opted for a new career at a less stressful pace than pumping gas on a national scale. He got a job carrying the U.S. mail on a rural route. What did he tell the government about his past?

"I told them the truth," he said. "But I also said I wasn't that man anymore, and that I had friends who would testify to a new life in our fellowship."

Mac's humble workdays were followed by inspiring nights of taking the recovery message to other alcoholics. I was moved by the choices he made to change his life by helping others change theirs.

When we met, Mac had remarried a wealthy woman and moved into her home. She had accepted him for who he was, not who he had been. Driving by their house, I marveled at the symbolism in their two-car garage: her Cadillac sitting beside Mac's beat-up, dusty Chevrolet.

There was a lot of love, service, gratitude, and acceptance in their story.

I was hoping to find the same in mine.

–32–
Epiphany

IT ISN'T BOASTING to suggest that because our paper emphasized heritage and preservation, many Logan County citizens were proud of their history. So, increasingly, was I.

The county had been home to ten governors (four of Kentucky and six of other states), six U.S. senators (three representing Kentucky), four chief justices of the Kentucky Supreme Court, five U.S. congressmen, and two presidential cabinet members.[19]

But in a town with an increasing number of historical markers, there was none proclaiming a president among Logan County's sons. So it was exciting when Alice Dunnigan—an early black journalist who was herself a Russellville native—reported in the early 1960s that the new Vice President of the United States, Lyndon Baines Johnson, was descended from a couple who had left Logan County by wagon in the 1800s to seek their fortune in Texas.

Alice Dunnigan's LBJ story was catnip to the folks in the Logan County Historical Society, not just because the man who was just a step away from the presidency had a Logan connection, but also because a daughter of the county knew Johnson and was herself a national success in journalism.[20]

---

[19] Many of these prominent leaders first came to Russellville to "read law" under older, pioneer attorneys. Disputes over land grants to Revolutionary War veterans fueled business at the courthouse which originally served a vast section of what was called "the Green River Country."

[20] Ms. Dunnigan was the first black reporter to be given White House press credentials and the first black female to be a member of the U.S. House and Senate press galleries. Her contributions to journalism are now noted by a historical marker in Russellville. I first heard of her when she spoke out about civil rights at President Kennedy's first nationally televised press conference. A former school teacher, she borrowed a typewriter at the Russellville Post Office to write an application for the wartime job that took her to Washington.

I wrote about Johnson's Kentucky roots, just as I had with other stories when the members of the historical society brought them to my attention.

Besides the historical markers—which the state erected, imprinted with text our local amateur historians wrote—buildings from other times still in use reminded us of our past, thanks to the work of preservation-minded citizens.

The core buildings of the South Union Shaker colony at Auburn, which had stood for more than a century, had been saved and restored.

A replica of a log church near Adairville, in the southern part of the county, memorialized the Great Revival of 1800, part of the so-called Second Awakening of Protestantism in the United States. (Those revival services took place on the banks of the Red River, near the site of a duel in which Andrew Jackson killed a Nashville lawyer in 1806.)

Also saved were a few early nineteenth-century "row houses" on Russellville's Main Street, not far from what was left of two colleges that went out of business during the Depression. And north Logan countians had protected a burial site, long known as the "Lost City," which bore evidence of three separate Native American cultures.

Eventually, with help from friends, I was able to chart the stories of fifty-six Russellville homes with connections that justified their placement on the National Register of Historic Places. Several of these history enthusiasts wrote for the paper and were especially valued contributors to the annual Tobacco Festival edition.[21]

BY 1963, I WAS EVER MORE INTRIGUED by Logan County's history and involved in its economic development efforts. But as my

---

[21] They included Mrs. Wells Vick, Mrs. Curry Hall, Ms. Maybelle Morton, the Reverend Edward Coffman, Evelyn Richardson, Maurice Linton, Henry Duncan, Jim Lyne, Marie Turner, Jim Turner, and Algie Smith—names that may mean little to my readers, but deserve a space here. Those people inspired my readers and my recovery.

"no hitter" year rolled on, I decided to approach the Louisville and Nashville papers to see if I had a new future in the big city.

Norman Isaacs, *The Courier-Journal's* executive editor, had shown he was interested when he commissioned me to write an article on rural journalism for the *Bulletin of the Society of American Newspaper Editors*.

Still carless (for that matter, I had no driver's license either), I took the bus to Louisville for an interview. Isaacs said he'd like to hire me if I were interested. First, though, I would have to be cleared by two of his rising managerial stars.

George Gill and Michael Davies, both talented men, were Isaacs's young tigers. But I, too, had been a young tiger—at *two* big-city dailies—and had managed reporters when I was younger than they.

Reflecting about the Isaacs interview on the bus for Russellville, I rebelled at the thought of further scrutiny by Bingham company managers.

It was like being back at Vanderbilt again. I was different from many students on that campus, and I made little attempt to conform. No fraternity if that meant some sort of social test. No classes unless I taught them (admittedly, a bad joke which concealed the real truth—I was an alcoholic). I did it my way, or I didn't do it at all.

I admired *The Courier-Journal* immensely and was flattered when Isaacs sought my opinion about small papers. But I was startled to conclude that I wouldn't be happy working for Gill, Davies, or even Isaacs himself.

That night I called Nat Caldwell, the top reporter at *The Tennessean*.

I had first met Nat when I was boy; my father had called him the best reporter in Tennessee ("even if he is a Socialist"). He had come back into my life when he visited *The News-Democrat* the first year I was in Russellville. *The Tennessean* had assigned him to write stories promoting TVA development and the creation of jobs in his paper's circulation area. He was impressed with Russellville's new industrial plants and was writing about them for a special edition on progress in the Tennessee Valley.

Nat and I had become warm friends. He was my role model. He was the kind of "engaged" journalist I wanted to be for the rest of my life: a reporter with a purpose who made things happen, even if he sometimes became a part of the story.

I asked Nat to set up a meeting for me with his editor to talk about a job at *The Tennessean*, the same paper that had encouraged me to wait for an opening when I got out of the VA hospital in 1957.

"I will if you really want me to," Nat said that night. "But I don't see why you should start working again for someone else who picks your stories and tells you how much to write.

"Think about it, and call me back next week."

After he hung up, I began to wonder if any of those city guys really wanted me, or if I wanted them.

Hanging on the wall by my roll-top desk was a framed copy of an ad I had written about Russellville for that "Progress Edition" of *The Tennessean* on which Nat was working when we had first reconnected.

Over a green-tinted map of Logan County, the ad's headline read "LAND OF LOGAN." The ad's text extolled the community's diversified attractions, beginning with its history.

"Where Jesse James robbed a bank, and Andrew Jackson fought a duel ... Where the Great Revival of 1800 was preached on the banks of the Red River ..."

Musing over those words I had written five years earlier, I realized I had used Logan County's history to stake a claim for its future. I was predicting new growth for new times in a region where we were building industry to balance agriculture and create jobs to keep our children at home.

Snapping off the lights, I locked the office door and headed across the square toward the Kaintuck, wondering if I knew what the hell I'd been writing when I had put together that ad.

Up in my room, reflecting on the day, the epiphany came as I turned off my room lights.

Why would I leave a community where they had taken me in—a drunk, itinerant editor no one knew?

The people of Logan County had saved me from myself: first in the local hospital, and then again when I asked for help in a church basement when it wasn't even Sunday.

They read my paper when I told them their schools weren't good enough. A lot of folks disliked my politics, but our circulation was growing.

What was this place I was trying to leave?

Somewhere that night, between consciousness and dreaming, I told myself that Logan County was a microcosm of Kentucky, maybe even of the world.

There was no bigger job than the one I had.

THE NEXT MORNING, OVER BREAKFAST at the Parkview, I asked Tom Noe to help me think about becoming an owner of *The News-Democrat*.

"What would it take to buy 5 percent of the paper?" I asked him.

"Wait a minute," Tom said, "Not 5 percent.

"You want ten."

Mrs. Evans and I really liked each other in those days. Still, when I called her with my proposal, she screamed in alarm. She said I would leave her nothing to live on. I didn't say anything different, so she calmed down.

A week later, she phoned back. She and her three children had talked it over, she said, and had agreed to sell me a 10 percent share.

We valued the paper's worth at $150,000. I would pay her $15,000: $7,500 down on January 1, 1964, and $7,500 more in equal payments plus interest over the next four years.

She didn't ask me where I was going to get the $7,500. The answer would have been that I had saved $1,500 in those first sober months and would borrow $6,000 more from my father on an open unsecured note at 7 percent interest.

By then, Dad had sold the farm to the developer of a subdivision. The new Old Hickory Lake had made the property valuable. The best money my father earned in twenty-four hard years after we left Florida was when he sold the land of his dreams.

BY EARLY NOVEMBER, MRS. EVANS AND I had worked out our deal. On November 22, I was leaving a Kiwanis Club luncheon when I heard that the president had been shot and killed in Dallas.

That night, Judge Noe and I drove to Clarksville, Tennessee, for an AA meeting. On the way there and returning home, all the radio news and commentary was about John Kennedy's brilliant career and tragic ending.

When we pulled up in front of the Kaintuck, the judge had a suggestion.

"Let's go get a bottle," he said. That's the tempting voice of alcoholism—cunning, baffling.

"Of course not!" I protested, angrily.

As Tom drove away, I watched until I saw him circle the town square and head up Main Street toward his house on the hill, not toward the Bottom where the bootleggers lived.

In New Orleans, The
Times-Picayune editor,
George W. Healy, Jr., an
intimidating man, but he
gave me my first break.

With the super Sanctons
in 2009: Thomas, Sr.,
ninety, star of New Orleans
journalism, former New
York editor, and son,
Tommy, Jr. Rhodes scholar,
jazz musician and Time
Magazine correspondent.

In Russellville, the Kaintuck Hotel where I lived for five years until sobriety, sanity, and ambition for change took me to a better place.

Governor Lawrence Weatherby and Lieutenant Governor Emerson "Doc" Beauchamp. Doc's "seminars" on courthouse elections taught me Kentucky politics.

Vote counting in Logan County: jailer Fount Shifflett, on left, and attorney A.G. "Ab" Rhea, on right, make sure Rayburn Smith gets the numbers right.

Republicans keeping watch on election count in Logan County are Lawrence Forgy, left and son, Larry. In center background is farmer Les "Jr." Page, who told me that his wife Virginia, would make me rich if I would just stay out of her way.

Bob Kirkpatrick, my go-to banker who put deals together.

The Logan County courthouse—my "graduate school" in political science.

The newspaper plant at Russellville, a renovated hardware store that won architectural awards.

With Aunt Dollie at dedication of renovated newspaper plant, 1973; the bishop prayed but it was Granny Graeme's spirit we remembered.

Maude VanCleve, with our daughter Ginny at Courts Hall. President Ford sent Maude a message of hope about her sister, Addie.

Courts Hall, the first
house we bought, up the
hill from the Kaintuck.

With Martha Helen,
Mother's Day, 1975,
at Courts Hall.

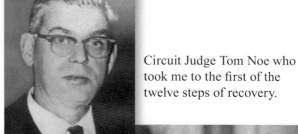

Circuit Judge Tom Noe who took me to the first of the twelve steps of recovery.

Granville Clark, who helped me in the worst of times and lived to see my best of times.

George Street Boone, the Todd County attorney who introduced me to his circle of interesting and successful Kentucky friends.

Swearing in as ARC chairman by U.S. District Judge Edward Johnstone on a Bible held by Martha Helen, at Granville Clark's law office in January, 1980.

The news gang in reunion in Russellville: Al Cross, Don Neagle, Jim Turner and I at a community-wide Don Neagle Appreciation Day.

From the "talent pool" of the old days in Russellville, we lunched and gossiped together. From left, Judy Murphy, Virginia "Gin" Lloyd, and Jeannie Leedom Bowles.

-33-
Felts Finer Folks:
The Lunch Bunch

WHEN I BECAME A PART-OWNER of *The News-Democrat* in 1964, the front-page announcement of my investment created a little buzz about "change" around the lunch table at Felts Finer Foods.

Felts had the tastiest food in town: good country cooking that appealed to the male business and professional class who worked around the downtown square. As an owner of the paper, I could claim increased status with the other self-employed men who gathered there around a large Formica-topped table for daily lunch.

My companions often included Buddy Duncan, a druggist who was on the city school board; Joe Wheeler, the county attorney; Joe's brother-in-law, Granville Clark, the lawyer who had an investment in Dick Hite's concrete business; and Hite himself.

Dick called Granville "the brain," for the obvious reason that he probably had the highest IQ of any man in the county. Granville was also the landlord for Viola Felts, the lady who owned the restaurant.

Felts wasn't much to look at. The sign outside was usually missing several bulbs. Inside, the floor was linoleum, and the windows were grimy and stained from cigarette smoke.

But Felts always smelled way better than it looked. The air was heavy with the aroma of fried chicken—*good* and savory fried chicken—except at breakfast, when the scent of bacon, eggs, grits, and Viola's sausage and biscuits wafted through the often-opened doors. Felts' breakfasts were better even than anything you could buy at a McDonald's—if Russellville had had one.

CALVIN COLBURN, one of my lunchtime favorites, and his buddy Hite were active in the management of the American Legion's annual Logan County Fair.

The fair provided a cover of respectability for year-round gambling at the Legion's clubhouse. As in thousands of service clubs in "dry" American communities, illegal beer was sold openly across the counter. Poker games went on in the rear. And Calvin's slots clinked and clattered in concert with the thump of his pinball machines.

I liked Calvin. He was smart, straight, and funny. When a federal judge ruled that pinball machines were gambling devices, I pretended to be incredulous.

"Surely not," I said one day at lunch.

"Get in this truck," Calvin said.

He whisked me away to his shop on the Nashville Road. There, in a side room, he shoved aside his mechanic and twisted a few knobs and springs on one of the partly assembled pinball machines that filled the room. Lights began to flash all over the screen as it rang up numbers.

"Of *course* it's a gambling device," he said.

"That's all there are to it!"

Calvin then pronounced the verdict on the machine's future and his.

"I'm selling these suckers to the first fool who wants 'em."

And he did. Once additional industrial plants came to town, he sold his punchboards, pinball machines, and slot machines to an associate and expanded his candy and cigarette routes into an upscale food vending machine business with several thousand customers at area factories.

PRINTING THE FAIR CATALOG EACH YEAR, I should note, was a profitable little venture for my paper. So I never got in an editorial twist over the technicalities of what went on behind closed doors at

Russellville's private clubs. I knew what the reaction would be if I did.

Knock off the Legion and the VFW? Then what's next—a raid on the country club? That would be the concern of the lunch bunch. Sure, let the cops bust the black bootleggers, but not too often, lest it look like discrimination.

It wasn't enough, but I eased my conscience by urging the new Emerson Electric manager to hire blacks for his assembly line. He demurred on grounds that Emerson's St. Louis headquarters respected the mores of a little town where there were no African-Americans working in banks, retail stores, the highway department, or the Rockwell plant.

But as the times changed, so did Emerson Electric. By the late1960s, Emerson had become an "equal opportunity" employer, as had the other plants in the county. As Ed Johnson, Emerson's manager, admitted, "LBJ twisted our CEO's arm in the Rose Garden. He reminded us that our military contracts had to be renewed."

I ATE AT LEAST ONE MEAL EVERY WEEKDAY at Felts with Chick Ray and Joe Copple. There were other restaurant regulars from whom I picked up tips, but Chick and Joe were the oldest businessmen and among the more interesting. They brought the juiciest gossip from Main Street, and weren't always discrete about other folks' finances.

Chick and Joe were important figures whose approval the town's leaders[22] sought for any undertaking that touched on finding more jobs, electing candidates for office, or adding taxes.

---

[22] When I came to Russellville, the local businessmen on the city council included a garage owner, a dry cleaner, the owner of a furniture and hardware store, a miller, a gasoline distributor, and the mayor, Taylor Fuqua. The only professional man, a general practitioner named Dr. L.E. Johnson, usually sided with the majority but never got any heat for their errors. He often dozed through the council meetings but always received the most votes on Election Day. I guess the citizenry interpreted his sleeping spells as a commitment in civic life to that fundamental rule of medicine, "First, do no harm."

Although neither of them ever ran for anything, they had an opinion about everything and were the loudest voices—cranky, often amusing, sometimes sharply insightful—in the small-town Greek chorus that dined at Felts.

Chick and Joe had little formal education, but from the two of them, as well as Marvin Stuart, Earl Davis, and the guys who went to college—Granville, Bob Kirkpatrick, Bill Fuqua, and dear Tom Noe—I soaked up a common sense approach to business.

MR. RAY WENT HOME FOR LUNCH, but he ate breakfast at Felts. More accurately, he smoked a lot of Chesterfields during breakfast hours and drank many cups of Viola's free-refill coffee. He doused each cigarette in a separate cup and left a very small coin under the saucer of the last drink.

Ray's nickname arose from the wholesale poultry business and block of low-rent real estate behind the courthouse that he inherited from his father. He introduced himself as Stanford Ray, but everybody called him Chick, except a few renters and other respectful types who addressed him as "Mr. Chicken Ray."

Chick's friend, Copple (pronounced "couple"), dined twice a day at Felts, sharing gossip with Chick at breakfast and with anyone who joined the table at lunch. An elderly bachelor, he headed the family-owned Coca-Cola Bottling Company. He had a lady friend, but spent a lot of time with "the boys" at Felts.

Copple's niece, Wilba Ruth Freeman, and her husband S.J., referred to Copple as "Uncle Joe," and most of his Felts buddies did as well.

During football season, Uncle Joe and Chick went to Vanderbilt games in one of Chick's Buick Rivieras. I use the plural because Chick boasted that he traded cars every time the tires wore out.

And why shouldn't he? To hear him tell it, he just brought his old car into Carl Page, the Chevrolet-Buick dealer, and swapped it for a new one. The charge? Carl's cost, "plus $100 or so," Chick claimed. I never had the nerve to check that out with Carl.

I rode with Chick enough to know that Uncle Joe was accurate when he described him as a "nervous driver with a timetable." Chick allotted only so many minutes to get to Springfield, Tennessee, then on to Greenbrier, to Ridgetop, and to the stadium in Nashville, clocking himself all the way.

Uncle Joe's innocent descriptions of people and places were funny. The country club was "the golf course." The veterinary clinic was "the dog kennel." Social workers were "the give-away ladies," and the phone book sales force was "the yellow people."

Uncle Joe was on the board of the local savings and loan association, and, along with Chick, was a director of the Citizens National Bank.

"Chick doesn't really run the bank," Uncle Joe would say, "even though he acts like he does. I don't run it either. Earl Davis runs it.

"We get paid to listen to him tell us what he's doing."

Referring to those directors' meetings, Uncle Joe joked that they'd spoiled him. He didn't like to sit down at a table "unless there is a check under the plate."

UNCLE JOE, A SELF-MADE MAN, was slightly envious of Chick. After all, Chick had inherited a family business.

"Chick is a business success all right," Joe would say when he was in a spiteful mood.

"He's hung on to everything his daddy left him."

Not to be out-scorned, Chick would whisper to me that the real spark in the Coca-Cola Company was Joe's brother and partner, Sam Copple, who died before my time.

"Sam had all the personality," Chick would recall. "Joe was just the bookkeeper."

Joe Copple thought of Chick as a tightfisted slumlord with little interest in civic causes, but Chick fooled him with a crusade for a new library.

It began when Chick lost a leg to diabetes. During his recovery, Chick read all the paperbacks and mysteries he could find in the library, which was then located in the old bank building the James Gang had robbed. Bill Fuqua's wife Marcia and lawyer Sam Milam's wife Justine were organizing support for a tax initiative for a new library, and an appreciative Chick Ray agreed to *lead* the drive—to the absolute amazement of Uncle Joe.

"Chick never finished a book in his life," Copple grumbled.

But Chick went on to head the new library. In declining health, he gave his last years to creating an institution of genuine value to Logan County. The library remains, in my mind, a memorial to Chick and the friends who persuaded him to lead them in building it.

When he died, Chick left plans for his family to clear the Jockey Alley property, thus silencing Uncle Joe's witty line that Chick charged rent for those awful, overcrowded shacks "by the door."

I ENJOYED JOE COPPLE'S STORIES about coming to Russellville from Clarksville with his brother Sam.

The first time they applied for a local loan in the 1920s, they were denied. The banker had lost money on a Nehi drink plant and didn't think there was a future in Coca-Cola.

When the Ku Klux Klan thrived in Logan County in the very early 1920s, the Copples, who were Jewish, and the Hite family, who were Catholic, spied on the anti-Semitic, anti-Catholic, anti-black meetings of the Klan. They listened through a hole in the wall as Klansmen ranted in a rented hall.

At one of the biggest Klan outdoor sessions—a gathering complete with hoods and fiery crosses—they scattered nails along the campground trail, punctuating all that windy hate with the hissing sound of tires going flat.

The Klan and its newspaper were finally defeated in a county election in 1922 by the Tom Rhea Democratic organization. By then, Joe Copple was a "strong Rhea man."

The friendship went both ways. Uncle Joe told me how Mr. Rhea took him to the construction site of Fort Campbell at the beginning of World War II to meet the general in charge.

"When I visited the White House last week," Mr. Rhea told the general, "Mr. Roosevelt was very pleased to hear from my own lips just how good a job you soldier boys are doing with this project."

Rhea paused for a bit, then continued.

"General, I also told the president I have an Israelite friend—little Joey Copple here—who is a veteran himself and would like to do something to help the war effort."

Pause.

"Joey can bring his soft drinks right over here to the base."

And that's how the Russellville Coca-Cola Bottling Company won the franchise for the Kentucky side of Fort Campbell in the 1940s. That's what made the Copple brothers rich.

TOWARD THE END OF HIS LIFE, UNCLE JOE YEARNED for a simpler time when there was a Rhea barber shop and an anti-Rhea barber shop and you could still hear the familiar sound of pistols thumping against the wall as customers hung up their jackets.

During one of our last meals at Felts, he complained that there were so many new folks in Russellville he could no longer call everyone by their first name as he strolled downtown.

"Take that girl waiting on our table," he said. "I don't think I know her.

But as the waitress walked away, he mused under his breath, "I guess I do know her. I think she's a Young."

"How do you know, Uncle Joe?" I asked.

"Well," he said, "she has a Young back."

Crusades

I WAS FAST BECOMING THE PUBLIC FACE AND VOICE of the paper. Believing now that I had a future in the community, I began to take even more interest in the needs of the county.

At lunch I was often at Felts, but occasionally I slipped away for a sandwich elsewhere with L.J. Northern, the federal soil conservation officer who educated me about Russellville's water problems.

He explained to me that the town didn't have an adequate supply of water to support its expanding industrial base. But Northern thought he had a solution.

The federal agency Northern worked for was building a network of earthen dams in the Mud River Watershed Conservancy District. These dams originally were intended to create small lakes for farm use. But several large multipurpose dams on the drawing board had the potential to rescue the city-sponsored factories, where many farm people worked, from shutdowns during droughts.

Northern—joined by the chairman of his district directors, Jewell Graham, and my friend Oscar McCutchen—had proposed that one of the large dams be built to create a lake just north of Russellville that would provide more water for the town, as well as recreation for Boy Scouts at a proposed new camp to serve twenty-six counties in western Kentucky.

In Owensboro, headquarters for the Scout region, McCutchen had already won a favorable response from the Scout leaders who were looking to build the larger camp. Those leaders included an insurance company executive with political ambitions named Wendell

Ford and J. R. Miller, a utility manager and influential player in Democratic Party politics.

I soon was writing news stories and editorials in support of regional cooperation on the common goals of improving the water supply and building the Boy Scout camp.

Over the next five years, with leadership from a new mayor—businessman Wallace Herndon—and City Attorney Bill Fuqua, the lake was built and 1,000 acres were purchased and developed for the Scout camp. Soon Camp Wildcat Hollow served some 2,000 Boy Scouts a year.

And a $300,000 federal grant paid for pipelines to pump water from the lake to the city of Russellville for purification. The land costs for the camp and the lake were raised through donations from private citizens and area industries. All of this was celebrated and recognized in the paper when seven key local leaders were named Men of the Year at the dedication of the Scout camp in 1969.

IN 1964, A LIBERAL—OR AT LEAST A NAÏVE LIBERAL—was someone who actually believed that Barry Goldwater, the U.S. Senator from Arizona who was the Republican nominee for the presidency, was a threat to the election of Lyndon Baines Johnson, who had been president since Kennedy's assassination.

Reader, I was that kind of liberal.

I wanted to do all I could to help Johnson get elected. I was an ardent supporter of civil rights and the War on Poverty and an enthusiastic believer in Johnson's vision of a "Great Society." I was sure that Goldwater, if elected, would roll back the clock on Johnson and Kennedy's programs. He might even sell the TVA to private power companies.

So when shrewd old Doc Beauchamp invited me to chair President Johnson's election campaign in Logan County, what did I do? I tossed ethical concerns to the wind and said, "Sure."

Doc quickly mustered several super dependable co-chairs, including Becky Bouldin, a deputy county court clerk, and Nell Gorrell, the wife of a popular farmer with strong Democratic ties.

Taking up the challenge, I offered the Beauchamp Democrats an idea for a big fundraiser: a celebration of Doc's sixty-fifth birthday in June.

We would sell tickets to a barbecue at the football stadium. The entertainment would feature Grand Ole Opry stars from Nashville, with speeches honoring Doc and appeals for the election of LBJ and his vice presidential candidate, Hubert Humphrey.

After years serving in elected or appointed offices in Logan County and the state capitol, Beauchamp had compiled an extraordinary Rolodex. It became the source of addresses for hundreds of invitations. Soon we had thousands of dollars in ticket sales and dozens of pages of advertising (which benefited the paper).

Lester Flatt and Earl Scruggs from the Grand Ole Opry were booked. I managed to wrangle a presidential discount from their manager, Mrs. Scruggs.

"Is President Johnson going to pay us," she inquired tartly, "or will you?"

"Doc's Day" gave me the chance to meet the famous Ed Prichard.

Tall and heavyset, Prichard rolled out of one side of a state police car, catapulting the short and light Governor Ned Breathitt out the other.

After a lavish lunch for visiting dignitaries, "Prich," as he was called, appeared to fall asleep on the platform in the hot sun. I learned it was a trick he pulled in courtrooms and classrooms, always waking up with a wry grin to quote all the speakers who had orated while he seemed to doze.

Over the years after our meeting in Russellville at "Doc's Day," Prichard and I became close. I helped found what is now called the Prichard Committee for Academic Excellence, which has followed his lead in a decades' long campaign to improve education in Kentucky.

But the Sunday after Doc's Day, I was furious with Prichard. Doc's buddy, the political genius, had paid us with a cold check.

"Doc," I said, "I'm going to harass Prichard until we get every penny back."

"Naw, Al," Doc said. "Don't do that. Just forget it. Prich is okay. He'll make it up to you some way."

Doc was in a good humor, as well he might be. We had delivered him the $10,000 we had cleared from the birthday party. As we spoke, he was packing the bills into a cigar box which he kept hidden under a telephone table in his parlor—for election expenses, no doubt.

"You weren't around, Al," Doc told me, "but I used to drive a Cadillac that the boys gave me when I retired as lieutenant governor. When the Cadillac got old, Prich bought it.

"That check bounced too."

Doc smiled and rose to signal my visit was over. "Wait a minute, Doc," I said. "I'm not quite settled up.

"Nell Gorrell needs a new dress for the Democratic National Convention. It's been a hard year on the farm, and she's a delegate, remember?"

"Why, certainly," Doc wheezed, pulling the cigar box back out.

"Give her this with my sincerest thanks."

I took the $100 bill he handed me, nodded, and left.

So ended my first experience as an impresario.

WHEN JOHNSON CAME TO KENTUCKY later that year on a campaign swing across the South, I shook hands with him at a breakfast at the Seelbach Hotel. I was thrilled when he mentioned those Logan County ancestors in his speech. Earle Clements introduced Doc to the President as "the mayor of Logan County."

By the time Johnson had ended that day of speeches across Dixie, he had hinted that a new day was dawning in civil rights. More respect for black citizens was coming from a government headed by the tall Texan.

ANOTHER ISSUE SOON DEVELOPED IN RUSSELLVILLE. Employees at Emerson had asked the National Labor Relations Board to call a union election. That was on my mind as Bob Guion and I landed in his little company plane at the airport in Paragould, Arkansas.

I was convinced that Russellville's industrial expansion would be over when and if the first union contract was signed. Bob, a self-made man whose Bilt-Rite Company employed two hundred people in Russellville, believed that once a union breached the walls at Rockwell or Emerson, his company would be next.

Our trip to Paragould was a "union-busting" mission of a sort.

Bob had quietly volunteered to fly me to Paragould, as well as another town in Tennessee. In both places, Emerson plants had been struck over union contracts. I would see how the strikes had affected community life, then write stories on what I found.

Bob and I expected that the stories might discourage Russellville's Emerson employees from voting to unionize in an election the National Labor Relations Board (NLRB) had called.

Interviews with townspeople at Paragould and later in the day at Paris, Tennessee, provided the quotes I expected for the negative stories I wrote the following week. The consensus in both towns was that the strikes had hurt the communities and damaged labor relations, even splitting families.

No one had asked me to do what I did. I made the trip and wrote the stories because I agreed with Bob and others in town who had worked to recruit or build new plants: Being non-union was one of our community's biggest attractions to industry outsiders. I was passionately opposed to unionization in Russellville.

We weren't trying to keep wages down. We figured that competition for skilled labor between the "good" industries would push wages up without the hassle of collective-bargaining elections.

Of course, this wasn't how I felt when I was secretary of the Newspaper Guild in New Orleans. I had been convinced then that unions were needed there. But I didn't believe they were right for Russellville.

I was forthright about why I wrote the stories, and even mentioned that I had been a union member and officer in New Orleans.

Later that year, Emerson employees rejected union affiliation.

Not long after, the NLRB sustained a protest by the union and ruled that my articles had poisoned the election. The outcome was thrown out and another election ordered.

This time, I didn't need a lecture.

I wrote only a few straight stories and kept my editorial opinions to myself. The company won again.

This was a crusade the government said I had no business waging. Was it correct?

Perhaps yes, perhaps no. I think my First Amendment rights were violated. But the NLRB said I violated the workers' rights to a fair election, and that might have been true.

Fifty years later, the Emerson Electric plant continues to manufacture hermetic (sealed) motors for compressors at Russellville and has never unionized. While the company ultimately outsourced much of its production to low-wage foreign companies, which led to job cuts or plant closing in other small towns, its employment in Logan County remains stable.

INDUSTRIAL DEVELOPMENT was not my only cause in those days. In the early 1960s, I began a real push for school consolidation in Logan County, a crusade that would occupy me for years.

Bill Coke was a son of Logan County who had graduated from Yale with a degree in political science and from UK with one in agriculture. He had settled back near Auburn to partner with his father, Gaston Coke, to run a farm that had been in their family since land grant days.

Coke ran for and easily won a seat on the county school board. Soon thereafter, he recruited me as an ally for a renewed attempt to consolidate Logan County's tiny high schools.

Each of Logan County's small towns outside Russellville had its own high school, and Coke believed a single county school would better serve the county's educational needs. I agreed.

The state board of education was promoting school consolidation all over Kentucky, but in Logan County, the normal resistance from the rural communities was compounded by the fact that no new school could be built unless the voters approved a tax to pay for it.

When Lawrence Forgy and his Lewisburg friends noisily disrupted a pro-consolidation speech by a deputy state superintendent of education, the battle was joined. Coke and I succeeded in getting a special tax election on the fall ballot in 1964.

Bill Fuqua, city attorney of Russellville, was strongly in favor of consolidation. He courageously volunteered as a precinct worker on Election Day at Lewisburg, the hot-bed of opposition. This was over the protest of Lawrence Forgy.

"Bill, this will ruin your political career," Lawrence warned.

It didn't: Bill went on to become circuit judge and then a Kentucky Supreme Court Justice.

When the election returns came in, the school consolidation tax was beaten badly. My consolation was that the loss was not nearly as lopsided as the first election on the issue ten years earlier.

THE SCHOOL ISSUE DIED FOR QUITE AWHILE. But fifteen years after that vote, a new State School Building Authority coughed up the dough that the locals wouldn't vote to spend.

Logan County High School was built just outside the city limits of Russellville. The old high schools were rehabilitated as junior highs and earned respectable scores for student achievements.

When the brand new Logan County High School boys' basketball team won the state tournament, I had left Logan County, but it was all I could do to refrain from sending a taunting letter to my old paper.

I wanted to say, "I told you so."

-35-
The Skewer
and the Cause Lawyer

ON DECEMBER 5, 1965, *The Courier-Journal* reported the suspension of three Western Kentucky State College students over a free press issue. Two of the three students were from Russellville.

The next day, Granville Clark accosted me at lunch.

"What are you going to do about it?" he asked me.

The offense was a brief satirical article published by the three students, plus a fourth who dropped out of school before he could be suspended, in the second monthly issue of their mimeographed, off-campus magazine, *The Skewer.*

Titled "In Defense of Morality," the piece dealt with what it described as "the social practice of allowing men complete sexual freedom while requiring women to remain chaste." The article contained no obscene words but did use some blunt slang phrases.

"The piece is generally objectionable," the Dean of Students declared. "The school can't live with this."

Kelly Thompson, president of the college (which became Western Kentucky University the next year) denied the students' request to be reinstated.

Thompson said he had witnessed "unbelievable chaos and virtual anarchy" during a recent visit to the University of California at Berkeley. "I'm determined to prevent a Berkeley in Bowling Green," he said.

At Granville's urging, I instigated a complaint by Sigma Delta Chi, the professional journalism society, as a member of the Louisville chapter. Other complaints came from the American Civil

Liberties Union and Kentucky members of the American Association of University Professors.

None shook Thompson's conviction to stand his ground. He refused to meet with the *Skewer* students, who had all but apologized for the ruckus and admitted that their "hastily written" article was a clumsy piece of work.

It wasn't long before Thompson was confronted with the threat of a lawsuit from Granville Clark.

Granville was no longhaired, wild-eyed radical. He was the district governor of Rotary International and superintendent of the local Methodist Sunday School. But he agreed to take the students' case because he believed they had been denied due process of law and their First Amendment rights of free press and free speech.

Hearings involving the school's regents and President Thompson were scheduled during the Christmas holidays. Testimony focused on the college's dull, dispirited student paper, censored to the point that it was merely a mouthpiece for the administration. No campus magazine or paper offered students the opportunity for creative writing or the expression of opinions.

Granville summoned my friend Tom Duncan, a former reporter for *The Courier-Journal's* Bowling Green bureau. Duncan had nothing positive to say about the editorial practices taught by Western's journalism program. The Reverend Tom McGloshen, another Russellville friend, opined that *The Skewer*, while wretchedly written, was hardly obscene. Several faculty members also testified in behalf of the students.

President Thompson finally relented, and Western readmitted the students.

This action was too late to avoid several critical reports on the incident, one by Sigma Delta Chi (I was one of the signers), as well as an embarrassing editorial in which *The Courier-Journal* declared, "Western deserves the harvest it is reaping."

Granville, the outspoken professors, the critical journalists, and the rebellious students all deserve to be remembered for this exercise in First Amendment rights. This was much more than just another of the protests on American campuses in the 1960s.

Western's students were the big winner. Over the next few years, primarily under President Dero Dowing, the school reorganized its journalism program. It hired professionals from *The Courier-Journal* and *The Tennessean* to teach best practices and advise, with a very light touch, the school's student-produced publications and broadcasts. Academics with respected backgrounds in theory were recruited, and Western, opening its windows for the fresh air of freedom to inquire and debate, created a School of Journalism and Broadcasting that has become a state-designated Center of Excellence.

GRANVILLE, CHAMPION OF FIRST AMENDMENT CAUSES, was born in 1919. When I met him he was a pudgy, slightly-stooped guy with ruddy, freckled skin, and auburn hair.

He had captained the golf team as a student at UK, where future Lexington business wizard and philanthropist W.T. Young and the soon-to-be star of *The Courier-Journal*, John Ed Pearce, were his classmates.

They called Granville "Grumpy," not without reason. Granville was easily riled, drawling out his grievances in an exasperated inflection that could be funny if one was not the butt of it.

In some ways, all three of these worthies could have answered to "Grumpy," for that was the persona they shared. In each of them, a gruff exterior concealed a generous heart and a readiness to battle for convictions that were not always popular.

In later years, when I knew each of them rather well, I marveled at their similarities. Their voices and vocabulary were alike. They often began discussions the same way: *"I don't see how ..."* or *"I don't know why ...*" Their topics may have been different, but their discourse sounded the same.

Pearce complained about his salary at *The Courier-Journal,* whose publisher, Barry Bingham Sr., called Pearce the best writer he ever hired.

Young, whose horse Grindstone, won the Kentucky Derby in later years, was irritated with stuffy bluebloods in racing who were offended when he said the sport was "all about gambling" (he was advocating the addition of slots at the tracks).

Granville raged at state Attorney General Robert Stephens when he balked at filing a lawsuit to save a Russellville museum.

"I see you're just another goddamned bureaucrat," Granville told Stephens. (At least that's the way Stephens recalled it to me when he, Stephens, was chief justice of the Kentucky Supreme Court.)

Granville was good at business too. From his office, which had once been his father's funeral home, he counseled farmers and small merchants, advised a large dairy company, and drafted contracts for the Kemps, three Russellville brothers who were road contractors. At the same time, he managed his own interests: a concrete plant, a subdivision, and two farms his mother owned.

Granville represented the city school board and the telephone cooperative. Somehow he also found time to teach Sunday School and broadcast Friday night football games over WRUS, our local radio station.

But Granville's wife Mary Rebecca was right.

"Granville's true calling," she said, "is to be a cause lawyer."

In the 1960s, for example, Granville represented most of the homeowners and small farmers who lived in a long, narrow stretch of forested land between the Cumberland and Tennessee rivers in western Kentucky, which was known as "the Land Between the Lakes[23]." The Tennessee Valley Authority (TVA) was attempting to

---

[23] The lakes are Kentucky Lake and Lake Barkley.

buy out all the property owners through land negotiations or court rulings in condemnation suits.

Although he lost every case—to a government opponent that was the largest utility in the country, remember—Granville's clients benefited from hiring him because they got more from the court judgments than the TVA initially had offered them.

As word about his prowess at fighting the government reached south to Nashville, his new opponents became Vanderbilt University and the city's urban renewal agency.

Clark claimed the university and agency were bullying his new clients—"elderly widows of professors" and "little old ladies renting rooms to students to stay off welfare"—into selling their properties for low prices so Nashville could redevelop the land. I don't recall that he blocked the project, but I never heard any of the widows claim he disappointed them, so he must have gotten them reasonable settlements.

With the passage of the Medicare and Medicaid laws, Granville became my most reliable consultant on health care issues. His background as a former chairman of the county hospital board made him a valuable resource to me in the 1970s when I challenged developing plans to sell the hospital in Russellville to a new management company from Nashville, Hospital Corporation of America (HCA).

My deep admiration for Granville, however, temporarily faded into the background when I first read an article in the Sunday *New York Times* magazine about Muhammad Ali's Logan County ancestors, some of whom were white.

The story was by John Egerton, a gifted writer, who had owned a farm in the Land Between the Lakes and had been one of Granville's clients.

Suspecting the source of the Egerton story, I made an indignant phone call to Granville.

"Did you tell Egerton about Ali's ancestors?' I asked.

"Yes, I did," Granville said.

"I guess you know how embarrassed I am to learn about this in the *Times*," I said. "I like John, but I expected better from you, my friend who's been eating lunch with me all these years. Why didn't you tell *me*?"

"Well," Granville said, "I guess you never asked."

-36-
J.R. Miller and the Rise of Wendell Ford

WHEN LOGAN COUNTY'S LEADERS developed Lake Herndon and Camp Wildcat Hollow, the Boy Scout camp, in the early 1960s, they forged friendships with business and political people in Owensboro. Scout leaders there gave up their outdated regional camp for more land and a larger lake near Russellville.

My first friend in Owensboro was the dynamic and shrewd J.R. Miller. He headed the Green River Rural Electric Cooperative and was a major force in the Scout project. ("Major force" is actually a bit tame; Miller was more like a commanding general of any project in which he enlisted.)

I actually had met Miller several years before we started the Scout camp project, when I went to Owensboro with Rayburn Smith in 1958 for a barbecue honoring Doc Beauchamp.

At first I wasn't clear why J.R. wanted to honor an old-timer who'd been chased out of Frankfort by Happy Chandler. But after thirty minutes on the scene, I figured it out.

The picnic was a gathering of an enormous number of Chandler foes and Clements friends, and all the guests seemed to be supporting another race for governor by Bert Combs, Clements's protégé of the1950s. Beauchamp was everywhere. He made no speeches, but as he huddled and whispered with group after group across the picnic grounds, he was certainly heard.

Rayburn introduced me that afternoon to Wendell Hampton Ford, the son of an Owensboro state senator and a partner in an insurance agency with his father and brother. Noting that Wendell was the national president of the Junior Chamber of Commerce (the Jaycees), Rayburn said J.R. had big plans to make a political future for Ford. The party we were enjoying was probably as much a debut for Ford as a tribute to Beauchamp.

Who was J.R. Miller?

By the end of that picnic, I had learned that he was a native of Mississippi who'd been recruited to Kentucky to straighten out problems with the Green River Electric Co-op. When the co-op made him a good offer to be president, J.R. signed up to stay on.

The ambitious "man from Mississippi," as he was called, persuaded the farmer directors of the co-ops along the Ohio River in western Kentucky of the need for a huge power-generating plant at Henderson, Kentucky. Friends in Washington advised J.R. that if he wanted to secure the millions in low-interest loans the steam plant would require, he needed to get involved in politics.

J.R. jumped in, painting a vision of industrialization along the Ohio River, fueled by cheap electricity from the plant, to be called Big Rivers. That image was irresistible to the county courthouse cronies he began acquiring in western Kentucky's Green River country, known in political circles as "The Gibraltar of Democracy."

THOSE POLITICAL CONNECTIONS J.R. developed were valuable to Wendell Ford when he decided, after a spell as a top aide to Governor Combs and a narrow victory in a 1965 run for the state senate, to run for lieutenant governor.

In 1966, Ford's network of Jaycee members and Miller's allies among Kentucky's co-op directors set up an organization to hold off a potent rival, Attorney General Bob Matthews of Shelbyville, Kentucky. Matthews was pressuring county and commonwealth attorneys, as well as the many judges and other lawyers he knew, to back him in his bid for lieutenant governor, a job that frequently led to the governorship.

Meanwhile, in Frankfort, Governor Ned Breathitt was remaining neutral in the lieutenant governor's race. Breathitt's political friends, such as Doc Beauchamp, were free to support whomever they wished.

Folks in Logan County suspected that Doc wanted to help Matthews, but he was still holding his cards close when Ford came to my office that summer of 1966, nearly a year before the primary.

Doc, who was state treasurer at the time, was in Frankfort when Wendell visited. So I took the candidate to see Beauchamp's sister, Mrs. J.T. Linton, also known as Miss Allie Mae. Mrs. Linton had herself had a political career, succeeding her husband, a former county judge, when he died while a state legislator.

Ford and I found Miss Allie Mae extraordinarily gracious. Over tea and cookies, she recalled that Wendell's father, then a state senator, had given her his room in a Frankfort hotel when accommodations were scarce the first night of her first term in the legislature in 1948.

As we left Miss Allie Mae's home, Wendell said, "Well, that's one solid vote for me."

"Not so fast," I replied. "All she said was that your father was generous and helped her.

"She didn't tell you who Doc would help."

A YEAR LATER, I WROTE SEVERAL EDITORIALS in *The News-Democrat* endorsing Ford. I reminded readers that Ford was Owensboro's favorite son, and that Lake Herndon—which had proved crucial for supplying Russellville's industrial water needs—couldn't have been built without Owensboro's support.

I had nothing against Matthews, but I thought Wendell's experience was equivalent to Bob's. And if the next lieutenant governor should become governor, Russellville would benefit if that person was a neighbor from Daviess County, just sixty miles north.

By mid-morning Election Day, however, it became clear that Doc was running a stealth campaign for Matthews. His precinct officers kept finding excuses to join compliant voters behind the curtains.

At noon, J.R. Miller called Doc.

"J.R. was cussing so bad on that phone you could hear him from Doc's living room all the way to the kitchen," a Beauchamp henchman named Burvin Stanley told me.

Burvin was a heavy drinker in those days who had a job on the Alcoholic Beverage Control Board, thanks to Doc.[24]

The Ford-Matthews race "was the weirdest election ever," according to Burvin.

"Al, all morning I went in the booth with the old folks and pulled the lever for Matthews," Burvin told me. "Then Miller called Doc and changed Doc's mind.

"That afternoon, I yanked that lever for Ford until the polls closed."

Matthews carried Logan County, although J.R.'s call to Doc apparently kept the Matthews margin to eight hundred votes. Across the state, Ford was the winner by six-hundred fifty votes.

Over the years, leaders of a number of Kentucky counties told Ford they hustled up his slender victory margin.

"I always just said, 'You sure did,'" Ford cheerfully told me years later over breakfast in Washington. After his stint as lieutenant governor, Ford had become governor and then a U.S. senator.

But I knew better.

It was J.R. Miller who'd made the difference.

IN 1967, LEST I FORGET, THERE WAS ALSO a governor's race.

The winner, as Doc and J.R. had probably figured all along, was a scrappy county judge from Glasgow named Louie Nunn, the first

---

[24] Doc and I visited Burvin's one-hundred-year-old father one afternoon during the 1960 presidential campaign. The elderly Mr. Stanley roused from a nap long enough to tell me that he had voted for the other Al Smith in 1928 and lived to tell the story.

"Voting Catholic won't kill you," he said.

Republican to capture Kentucky's governorship since World War II. Nunn had given Breathitt a close race in 1963.

The loser in that race was Democrat Henry Ward, an honest, hardworking hero who had modernized and expanded the state parks system and supervised construction of parkways and interstate highways for several Democratic governors. Ward never went to college, but he was a respected Paducah, Kentucky, newspaper reporter by the time he was elected to the state senate in his twenties.

Ward had first been drafted by Governor Earle Clements, and had gone on to serve governors Combs and Breathitt as transportation and parks commissioner. After many years of service in the cabinet, Ward claimed he was due a crack at the governorship.

The kingmakers had agreed. They knew he was a colorless speaker with zero charisma, but there was no other option. Miller, Beauchamp, Breathitt, and their cronies across the state swallowed hard and backed an honest loser.

Happy Chandler, however, having no such qualms, jumped party lines and supported Nunn.

The grateful winner quietly gave Chandler an unmarked office in the capitol, complete with secretary. Nunn also made sure Chandler always had a state police trooper to drive him wherever he wanted to go.

-37-
Martha Helen

WHEN JOE STRONG AND HIS CANTANKEROUS WIFE Ona, began coming back to AA meetings, they seemed to have benefited from their thirty-day treatment at Western State Hospital, a psychiatric treatment facility in Hopkinsville, Kentucky.

Joe and Ona were less tense with each other, especially after Doc Beauchamp got Joe reinstated at the Agriculture Department. Joe had been fired after Ona called his boss there to report that Joe had threatened to kill her with a hatchet.

No one in our AA group believed there was a jury in Logan County that would have convicted Joe had he made good on his alleged threat. We all liked him, but we could barely tolerate Ona.

The Strongs were what Logan countians referred to as "decent people." Joe's father had been the sheriff at one point. He left Joe a nice farm, but Joe lost it because of his drinking. The Strongs needed help, and I tried to offer it.

Joe told me that his and Ona's teenage son Donny also had been in treatment at Western State. Donny was no longer catatonic, so long as he took his Thorazine.

I agreed to let Donny try out for a job at *The News-Democrat*. I had known Donny when he was in high school. I liked the boy, and I admired his pretty sister, who had married early and helped put her husband through college. Donny performed fairly well as an apprentice in our print shop, and he liked collecting the paper's Little League ball scores on the side.

One day, Joe stopped by the office to report that the "nice young lady at the hospital" had a proposition I would like. The state vocational rehabilitation agency for which she worked had funds for on-the-job training. Joe said the woman could reimburse me for some of the expense of teaching Donny the printing trade.

"Oh, I don't need that," I said. "Donny's coming along, and I'm not paying him all that much."

But Joe insisted. "Listen, Al, you need to meet this lady. She's a grass widow[25] with a lot of class.

"She might be able to help *you* as well as Donny."

I STILL DON'T KNOW whether Joe was suggesting that I could use a date or just that I needed a social worker myself. Whatever his intent, when a letter arrived from the "nice young lady" at Western State, I invited her to a morning meeting in Russellville the next week.

I heard Martha Helen Hancock come through *The News-Democrat's* front door and tell Tookey Kemp, our receptionist, who she was. I peeked from my back office to see if my visitor was presentable for a lunchtime appearance at Felts. More than reassured, I came out for an introduction.

At Felts, we ended our lunch with chess pie and ice cream for me and Viola's great pecan pie for Martha Helen. As I remember we talked ten minutes about Donny's case and two hours about our own lives.

Martha Helen heard about my alcoholic years, without flinching. I heard, with just a slight skip of my heart, that she was recovering— she hoped—from thyroid cancer. She told me she was preparing to leave her counselor's job at Western State Hospital for Nashville, where she would study for a master's degree in social work at a branch of the University of Tennessee.

I learned that Martha Helen, who had grown up in Hopkinsville, Kentucky, had spent a scholarship year at Lindenwood College, a women's college near St. Louis, before transferring to Austin Peay

---

[25] A "grass widow" is a divorced woman.

State College in Clarksville, Tennessee, to be near her boyfriend, Lewis Hancock. She had soon thereafter married Lewis—a nephew of my Russellville friend Pete Hancock—during her sophomore year. But she had still managed to graduate near the top of her class with a degree in education.

"I wanted to go to medical school," she told me. "But I didn't have the courage to buck my mother's insistence that I should teach." Her mother had told her that "women in medicine are a bit strange." (Admittedly, in the 1950s, medicine was still a man's world.)

Martha Helen's interest in medicine, and science in general, was no surprise. Her father, the son of an Alabama country doctor, was a senior on scholarship at Vanderbilt Medical School when he met and married Martha Helen's mother, Virginia Evans, who was a secretary in the medical school.

Hugh Beauregard Disharoon, Martha Helen's father, first practiced in Lewisburg, Tennessee, a small town south of Nashville. Anticipating America's entrance into the war, he enlisted in the Army Medical Corps in early 1941. He was a lieutenant colonel when he died at Fort Benning, Georgia, in 1943, at age thirty-three, of viral pneumonia.

Hugh's untimely death left Virginia a widow with two young children: Martha Helen, who had just turned six, and Ginny, who was three. They moved to Hopkinsville to live with Martha Helen's adored grandmother, Helen Evans, and her bachelor uncle, Jess.

That first afternoon, before Martha Helen left for the drive back to Hopkinsville, I persuaded her to drive me to my apartment at Bobbie's Martin's[26] house which I'd begun renting earlier in the year. Fortunately, it was a lot more impressive than the Kaintuck. Reluctantly, I left her sitting in her car with the motor running as I dashed upstairs to grab a scrapbook of my prize-winning stories.

---

[26] Bobbie Martin, the mother of Bob Kirkpatrick,had been widowed twice: when Robert Kirkpatrick Sr. died and, later, when her second husband, Dr. William Joseph Martin, died.

When Martha Helen drove away with this homework, the motor that was my heart was beating in overdrive.

That night, I called her in Hopkinsville and proposed.[27] She didn't give me an answer, but she admitted she had enjoyed the afternoon and would like to see me again.

MARTHA HELEN AND I WERE ACCOMPANIED on our first "real" date by her children from her eight-year marriage to Lewis—Catherine, six, and Carter, five. We attended the Shaker Pageant in Auburn, an annual re-creation of the Shaker story about Mother Anne and her followers.

The evening went well, considering that Catherine spilled a grape snow cone down the front of her brand-new white dress, and Carter—leaning over the front seat on the drive home—candidly offered, "I don't think my daddy would like you very much."

On our second date, Martha Helen and I took the children for a picnic and history lesson to the Jefferson Davis State Park at Fairview, Kentucky, between Russellville and Hopkinsville.

In the restroom, Carter presented a detailed explanation of the plumbing. Waving his arms as he turned on first the hot and then the cold water faucets, he gave me a lecture right out of the playbook his Great Uncle Pete Hancock surely wrote when he was Russellville's water commissioner. After Carter switched to the sewer business and showed me how to flush a toilet, there was no doubt about it. Carter's mother might change her name to Smith, but that kid was a Hancock for life.

As we rode the rickety elevator to the top of the towering monument, I noticed the skinny operator—dressed in a plaid shirt, blue jeans, and suspenders—winked at Martha Helen. He did the same thing on the trip down.

"A friend of yours?" I asked, once we were safely on the ground.

---

[27] To this day, Martha Helen says I have it wrong. She says it was at least a week before I mentioned marriage. In truth, it seemed a given from the start.

"Sort of," Martha Helen said. "He's a former patient of mine from Western State."

ONCE MARTHA HELEN AND THE CHILDREN MOVED to Nashville not long after we met, my new sweetheart was living a life of minimum subsistence. So the collapse of the transmission in her Chevrolet Chevelle that first month in graduate school was a real calamity.

I saw the transmission's demise as an opportunity to demonstrate that I'd be a good provider. I went to Bob Kirkpatrick at the Southern Deposit Bank and borrowed the repair costs.

By the time Martha Helen and I were setting a wedding date six months later, Bob was financing all of the college expenses that her scholarship didn't cover.

Life that first year was thrilling but exhausting. Several nights a week I drove to Nashville and back, sometimes getting home at 1:00 or 2:00 in the morning. Perhaps I was kept alive on those dark roads by Martha Helen's prayers to a guardian angel.

Money was scarce, so our dates were simple: a trip to the park or an occasional movie. A big weekly outing was a visit to the Burger Chef. At her tiny duplex near Vanderbilt, we lived on fish sticks, Chef Boyardee ravioli, and other quick-fix meals. A bag of Keebler cookies was a once-a-week treat. Catherine, showing the first of her fine skills in the kitchen, surprised us one night with a tuna casserole, an ambitious undertaking for a seven-year-old.

Martha Helen and I began taking Catherine and Carter to the Vine Street Christian Church. I had not been a churchgoer since I was a teenager, but I was determined to be a dutiful parent and expose the children to a Christian upbringing.

To our surprise, the Reverend Wayne Bell, the minister at Vine Street, was a Kentuckian. His services were crowded with what appeared to be the Vanderbilt Divinity School at prayer. I liked

Wayne's sermons that "afflicted the comfortable" and urged the congregation to strive for social justice.

Those first months of our foursome, Carter was forthright about my overtures, rather bluntly assessing my good qualities and shortcomings. Catherine maintained a stoic, unsmiling assessment of me, even when I plied her with frequent gifts. She would accept a new doll or a book, but there would be a painful wait while she examined the bribe to decide whether it was worth a softly voiced "thanks."

In February 1967, I bought some expensive tickets to a Nashville concert by the Monkees, a rock group Catherine adored. Martha Helen and I planned a stop at an ice cream shop on the way home to tell the kids of our plans to marry.

Driving to the concert, Carter leaned over the front seat (which should have been a clue) with a request.

"Al," he said, "Catherine and I have been talking. We like you, but we want to ask you something."

"Sure, Carter. What is it?"

"Do you think you could quit hanging around Mama so much?"

We got the ice cream cones that night but postponed our announcement.

Slowly, though, we wore down their resistance. When we were ready to exchange rings and swear fidelity, Martha Helen's dowry was the Chevelle and two kids who were resigned to a new man in the house. Her mother, Mrs. Disharoon, had taken a liking to me, but did have one question:

"Why would you want to marry a divorcee with children?"

"I've been divorced fourteen years, and I'm tired of sleeping single in a double bed," I told her. "The kids under the roof just make it cozier. I've waited a long time for a family, and I love all three of them."

For my part, I was giving Martha Helen four years of sobriety from an alcoholic spouse who wanted a family to share his new life. I had a salary of $128 a week, plus a mortgaged 10 percent interest in *The News-Democrat* that she could help me pay off.

I had bought a used car of my own and was now driving (some said dangerously) for the first time in ten years. Martha Helen encouraged me to give away a green suit from Leedom's and buy a blue one. And she threw away my bottle of Vitalis.

I would do anything she asked me, of course. With her big eyes, her pretty brown hair, that engaging voice, her oh-so-smart mind, that slender frame, and loving arms that embraced me when we listened to Billie Holliday after the children were asleep, she was the transforming figure in my life: the woman I would always love.

When Wayne Bell married us in the Vine Street chapel on June 17, 1967, Martha Helen was just twenty-nine. I was forty. Everyone in Logan County approved of the match. Their crazy editor had married a woman who worked in an insane asylum.

I should mention that Martha Helen and I gave each other a special wedding present: We swore off cigarettes. It made for a somewhat jittery honeymoon, but more than forty years later, we're alive to tell our story.

BY THE END OF 1967, MARTHA HELEN AND I were exhausted from pondering what would or should happen in 1968. I would retire the balance of my debt to Mrs. Evans in January, and Martha Helen would receive her master's degree in the spring.

Her future soon was settled. Once she and the kids moved to Russellville, she would commute to Bowling Green, Kentucky, for her job as a psychiatric social worker at the Comprehensive Care Center, a mental health facility. Her salary, fortunately, would be more than mine.

My situation was more difficult to resolve.

Mrs. Evans and I, along with Dan Knotts, depressed over a divorce but still our ad manager, had spent a year discussing how to modernize the printing plant. It was time to convert to the photo offset process, but she couldn't, or wouldn't, decide what to do.

Mrs. Evans appreciated my successful efforts to increase *The News-Democrat's* revenues. After all, that was one of the reasons she sold me an interest in the business.

But my efforts bothered Dan. He remained as reliable as he'd been when he was married to Mrs. Evans's daughter Dorothy, but he only moved at one pace, doing the same thing every week and making time for golf every possible afternoon. Dan's discontent was shared by some other employees, who liked the same old dependable routine better than my ideas for more special sections and the ads to support them.

And unfortunately, my aged partner, who had done so much for me, was getting on my nerves. The more I fretted about how much I was doing for her, the more my resentment of her grew.

Both Bob Kirkpatrick and Judge Noe had separately advised me that I could buy the rest of the paper if Mrs. Evans would agree to reasonable terms. But when I first presented the idea to her in January 1968, she was unhappy about it.

Today, I understand her hesitance. Making decisions is difficult when one is seventy-plus, and even harder if the question is whether to sell the farm or business, move to a smaller home, or live elsewhere with a child. Yielding possession, power, and control is often a bitter experience.

ON JANUARY 9, 1968—MY FORTY-FIRST BIRTHDAY—my father died of a heart attack while in Marathon, Florida.

My mother would not travel by airplane, so I flew to Miami to accompany her and my father's body on a train back to Nashville. My Uncle McGregor paid someone to drive my parents' car back to Hendersonville.

Mother and Dad had enjoyed several winters on the Florida Keys after they sold the farm, carefully planning their drive down to avoid Sarasota.

My parents' days in Florida were finally over. But I had no idea where—or what—my future would be.

38

The Logan Leader

WHEN I FIRST MET HER, VIRGINIA PAGE was a Logan County farm wife who had been working modest clerical jobs in Russellville to bring some cash home to her hardworking husband, Les. My decision to hire her as circulation manager for *The News-Democrat* was one of the most inspired of my life.

Virginia had missed out on college because of the Depression. It didn't matter: She was still my brightest employee.

How smart *was* this small, dark-haired, soft-spoken woman?

Smart enough to marry perhaps the best young farmer in Logan County when they were both teenagers. Virginia and Les, whom most people called "Junior," were tenants who ran Joe Copple's farm while they saved money to buy their own land. Twelve- to fourteen-hour days never daunted Virginia, who always did more than she was asked at her "town job," then went home to drive a tractor in the fields, sometimes until nearly midnight.

To top it off, Virginia could write. A column on personal finance that I coaxed her to write won a state Farm Bureau award.

Virginia had been working for me four years when my negotiations to buy *The News-Democrat* stalled in February 1968.

Mrs. Evans had valued the paper at $150,000 when she sold me my ten percent interest in 1964. Four years later, when I offered to buy it, I appraised *The News-Democrat* at $135,000. She promptly refused my offer.

I don't think my bid was rejected because of its size. Mrs. Evans just didn't want to sell.

I gave up. I asked for a return of my 10 percent investment at my appraisal price. My friend Jim Lyne started drafting the buyout papers that meant the end of my ten-year employment with the paper.

Within a few days, a disgruntled Harry Whipple summoned me to his office. When I entered, I saw to my surprise that several other men were gathered there: the mayor, Wallace Herndon; Rockwell's local attorney, Sam Milam; the banker Earl Davis; and wise Marvin Stuart, who called the shots in local industries' dealings with the rest of us in Logan County.

"What's this about you leaving?" Harry grumbled.

When I told him I couldn't work out an agreement with Mrs. Evans to buy the paper, Harry commanded Earl, her banker, to make it happen.

The next day, Earl reported back that Mrs. Evans was intransigent.

What could I do? Where would we go?

That night, I called Martha Helen (she and the children were still living in Nashville as she finished up school) and told her about the meeting.

"Then why don't you start your own paper?" she asked.

The following day, Virginia Page asked me the same thing.

"Start my own paper?" I asked, stunned at the thought.

"That's what I said," Virginia whispered.

I told her that Martha Helen agreed, and that she thought Whipple had called his little meeting to send a signal that the county would support me.

"She's a smart girl," Virginia said.

I made up my mind then and there. It was time to fight. I had been run out of New Orleans. It would not happen again.

I told Virginia I would start my own paper only if she would come with me. With her help, a new paper just might work.

"I'm with you, Al," she said.

And so began a new adventure.

I CALLED MY BANKER, BOB KIRKPATRICK, to tell him my decision. That evening, he came to see me, bringing along a financial plan scribbled on a piece of paper.

Bob figured my $13,500 would be 52 percent of a new company we would call Logan Ink, Inc.

The outside investors were all mutual friends: Bob himself; Bill Fuqua, the city attorney; Lillian Noe, Judge Tom Noe's wife; and Bosworth Grier, a Connecticut transplant who managed two hosiery mills in Logan County for his father-in-law. Inside investors would be Virginia, Tookey Kemp, Wanda Scott, our bookkeeper, all of whom left *The News-Democrat* to join my staff, and Charlie Snyder, an experienced printer from Adairville, who would boss our production.

All the investors except me would loan the new company a figure equal to twice the price he or she paid for the stock. The staff investors could borrow the money they would loan to Logan Ink from Bob's bank, if need be.[28]

"You won't loan anything," Bob explained. "We're taking all you have for this startup, and if we crash, you lose everything."

The total capital of Logan Ink, Inc. was about $25,000. But the loan to the company provided a little operating money. We would lease the production equipment, buy a station wagon, and print our newspaper on an offset press at Franklin, twenty-two miles east of Russellville.

I rented the lobby of a shuttered hotel two blocks off the square as our temporary office and assigned Virginia, our new managing editor and vice president, to work out the details. Then I bought time on WRUS to advertise a contest. Participants who mailed in $2 for a subscription could "name Al Smith's new newspaper."

Don Neagle, the radio reporter, and Lon Sosh, the station manager's son, recorded a commercial pretending to be two hicks

---

[28] One investor who didn't need Kirkpatrick's help was Virginia. She had a net worth of $75,000 compared to my $13,500, an impressive lesson for me on the worth of farmland in Logan County.

who were speculating on the competitive situation and professing puzzlement over the new printing process the start-up would be using.

"Don, what's an offset?" Lon asked.

"I don't know, Lon," said Don."But Al says he'll tell us just as soon as they mail him the instructions."

ONE NIGHT NOT LONG BEFORE OUR DEBUT, I panicked. Shaking with anxiety, I switched on the lamp in our Nashville bedroom at 3:00 a.m. and buried my head in Martha Helen's lap.

"Everything's going to be all right," she said as she stroked my head.

She kept repeating this assurance, reminding me that people wanted me to stay in Russellville and to succeed. Finally I calmed down and got back into bed. I gave Martha Helen a big hug and went back to sleep.

I realized another good reason why I loved Martha Helen. She could stay calm in a crisis.

THE LOGAN LEADER APPEARED FOR THE FIRST TIME on May 1, 1968. A cartoon in the first issue showed local citizens looking at an ascending rocket labeled Logan Leader. One of them speculated, "Do you think that thing will fly?"

That night, I borrowed Bos Grier's jeep and drove all over town after midnight, proudly distributing my new paper.

At dawn, I called my graduate school star of a wife in Nashville and told her we were "on the streets." Then I fell asleep in my apartment, only to wake up startled, two hours later.

"Oh my God!" I shuddered.

"I've got to do it all over again next week!"

ALTHOUGH I HAD PROMINENT INVESTORS, and three of my stockholders had left The News-Democrat staff to join me, I was only pretending to enjoy the fight.

We were waging a battle against a family who had given me a job a decade before when I was down and out, and who had even sold me an interest in their business. We were earning admiration for taking on the older paper and its increasingly troubled owner. But that didn't drown out a tiny voice I could still hear that would forever whisper, *"She thinks you betrayed her."*

Regardless of the merits of our dispute, Logan countians seemed to relish watching the competition. We sold two thousand subscriptions while the entertainment lasted. Still, when two grocery chains declined to advertise with *The Logan Leader*, I wondered how long we could hold out.

THE OTHER SIDE BLINKED FIRST.

A few months after *The Logan Leader* began publishing, a Florida newspaper broker named Bill Matthews[29] showed up one day to inform me that Mrs. Evans had hired him to sell her paper "to anyone in this wide world except you."

"If she won't sell it to me," I asked, "then why are you here?"

"Because you're the logical buyer."

After about a week of persuasion from Matthews, the Evans family relented. We agreed on a price.

The News-Democrat was ours. Embittered, Mrs. Evans moved away from Russellville.

The war was over, but no one called to congratulate me. Were our readers disappointed because Russellville was once again a one-paper town?

To the surprise of many, we announced that the community would still have two newspapers. *The Logan Leader* would publish on Mondays and *The News-Democrat* at the end of the week.

Then it was my turn to be surprised. The folks at the Kroger grocery store, who resisted my new newspaper before the merger,

---

[29] Not to be confused with William Matthews, the Shelbyville, Kentucky, newspaper entrepreneur.

loved the new arrangement. They started running extra ads—in *The Leader*, to draw customers early in the week.

Matthews earned every penny of his commission. He taught me lessons I used as I bought other papers through the years—how to recapture prices I paid through "writing up" the depreciation of acquired assets; by using "no-compete" agreements in which payments are deductible expenses for the buyer and taxed as ordinary income to the seller; and by replacing a once-a-week paper with twin weeklies to increase ad sales.

I learned about "balloon notes" that allowed me to pay interest only for a few years before the principal was due as a lump sum. As we contemplated buying more papers, Bob Kirkpatrick taught me to use signature notes[30], signed by our stockholders, who gave simple statements of individual net worth (without detailed financial information), as collateral to secure bank loans for operating expenses in towns where we bought papers.

Within the next four years, Logan Ink bought three more small Kentucky weeklies, at Morgantown, Leitchfield, and Cadiz, all rural county seats close enough to Russellville to allow their editors to mail or physically bring their news and ad copy to Russellville to be printed. Once we purchased the newspaper in Cadiz near Lake Barkley, Kirkpatrick calculated we had sufficient cash flow from our papers to finance our own building and high-speed press.

IN BUSINESS, I NEVER HAD MUCH TALENT FOR DETAILS. I left the nuts and bolts of operations to a loyal and patient staff. My zest was for the hunt, and my skill was at trading.

My most notable real estate success was to persuade the Ryan family—who were absentee owners of several blocks of Russellville real estate—to break their rule against selling their property. Impressed by my plan to adapt a beautiful nineteenth-century former

---

[30] Banking regulations today likely prohibit some of the practices accepted in the 1960s.

hardware store on the square to a printing plant, they sold me the building for a reasonable price.

My architect was Bailey Ryan (no relation to the building's owners), a leading Louisville professional who was a Logan County native. Until I asked him to design our renovation, he said, he had "never received a commission for as much as a chicken coop" from Russellville.

Ryan's renovation plans were exciting and just what we'd hoped for. Things were going well until the bids on his design came in at twice our budgeted expense. We were stunned.

I recruited Fount Shifflett, a former jailer who owned a lot of low-income rental property, as an adviser.

He recommended a work crew coordinated by a family of out-of-town carpenters who had just built the new Assembly of God church. I became my own contractor. The work was completed at half the cost of those early bids.

The renovation was a proud addition to the buildings around the square. The restored Victorian façade was a handsome contrast to the interior, which had exposed brick walls and bright colors. And the building worked. It accommodated the needs of both the newspaper and the pressroom.

Our "new" old building won Bailey Ryan's architectural firm first-place awards for best adaptive design and for environmental preservation.

By the time of the renovation, Whipple's company, Rockwell International, had bought Goss International, one of the country's leading manufacturers of printing presses. Through Whipple, I was able to wheedle a generous discount on a four-unit Goss press. The unloading expense, however, was not part of the deal.

The solution?

Harry sent three forklifts and drivers down the highway from Rockwell to the square to take the machinery off the trailers, *at no cost*. We featured the pictures of the operation on the front page.

The unloading of the press was a sentimental moment. Without Harry Whipple, I might not have made it, in more ways than one.

WE PAINTED AN ENORMOUS AMERICAN FLAG on wallboard and hung it on the red brick wall behind the new press. Under floodlights after dark, the flag could be seen from the street, symbolizing that this was a First Amendment business known as "Freedom of the Press."

Sharp young kids like my son Carter were earning money and learning a trade by catching and binding inky papers inside the pressroom, developing sports photos in the darkroom, and hawking headlines on the corners. Others, like my daughter Catherine, wrote stories for the paper.[31]

I guess some were slightly underage (Carter said he wasn't the only one who had to stand on Coca-Cola crates to catch papers coming off the press) and thus worked illegally. But I had coached all of them: "If any strangers in blue suits, white shirts, and ties ask who you're working for, tell them 'my parents'!"

As the name of the expanding company changed to Al Smith Communications, I was proud of the wonderful folks who worked many long hours at our new building. Their wages may have been low, but there were tasty press-night suppers, when we brought barbecue or fried chicken dinners in to feed a work force reluctant to claim overtime. For many years, until inflation got the better of us, the best benefit we offered was full payment of employees' health insurance.

Several of our high school students became achievers in the printing business, including Virginia's son, Leslie Page Jr., and Shelley Barrett, the girl he met in our composition room and later married. Robert Stuart—whose marriage to his wife, Jodie, also

---

[31] My younger daughter, Ginny, never worked at the paper because she was too young, having been born in 1971. She earned a Ph.D. in psychology and now works as a business consultant and executive coach. I call it "catching up."

resulted from an office romance—first came to work as a teenager, riding a bicycle.

By the time he was twenty and in college, he had become almost indispensable to us. He once boasted to me that he had mastered every job in our company except mine.

"Then why couldn't you be the publisher, Robert?" I asked him.

"Because I don't know how to talk on the telephone."

39

The Gentleman Reformer

I FIRST MET GEORGE STREET BOONE in 1965 at the cemetery in Fairview, Kentucky. Granville Clark and I had gone over to the tiny Todd County town to hear a speech about Kentucky and the Civil War. After the remarks were over, Granville introduced me to George, who was standing in the shadow of the Jefferson Davis monument with Barry and Mary Bingham.

I didn't really know the Binghams, except by reputation as Louisville royalty and owners of one of the best newspapers in America.

In the cemetery that day I also met Thomas Mabry, a writer and former museum curator who was Barry Bingham's classmate at Harvard. Mabry and his wife, Ethel, lived with their daughters on a six-hundred-acre farm near Guthrie, some of the richest land in western Kentucky. When the Army Corps of Engineers revealed plans for a dam on a nearby river that would flood those acres, Mabry had hired George Boone to challenge the dam.

As he took on the formidable job of blocking the dam—which my friend Nat Caldwell supported—George and I became friends. (The Mabrys also warmed to me as I conceded that Caldwell wasn't always right.) Once George succeeded and the engineers were in retreat, he generously began introducing me to his impressive roster of friends.

IT SEEMED GEORGE STREET BOONE KNEW EVERYBODY.

I was the token country editor he drove to out-of-town conferences of do-gooders and dragged to after-hours cocktail parties for introductions to power brokers and his intellectual and artsy friends.

It was George who introduced me to Len Press at KET and perhaps said the kind words that suggested to Len that I might be the right host for a public affairs program.

George was a man of parts, as the saying goes, and a man of the community, which, in his case, was the commonwealth. He was a former Navy officer, a serious reader, a political liberal, and a constitutional scholar with two law degrees.

George was also a partygoer and a party-giver, welcomed everywhere for his wit and social skills, not the least of which were recipes for killer martinis and mint juleps.

His other friends and I were certain George could have starred in a big-city law firm, as a top judge, or as a professor at either of his universities, Vanderbilt and Columbia University Law School. But that was not to be.

George was indentured for life to his birthplace, the sliver of land—some of it the most fertile in Kentucky—wedged between Christian and Logan counties on the state line across from Montgomery County, Tennessee.

In his solo practitioner's office near the Todd County Courthouse or at his historic home, perhaps George dreamed of political and intellectual success to rival that of other Todd countians, such as U.S. Supreme Court Justice James McReynolds or the poet and novelist Robert Penn Warren. But those were figures who left the land that George called home. That was a price he wouldn't pay.

A descendent of the Boones who pioneered Kentucky and one of seven children of a country doctor, George was forever rooted in Elkton. Whether it was the legend about the statesman Henry Clay and the theologian Alexander Campbell playing cards all night at a Todd County tavern in the nineteenth century, or the tales of the authors Caroline Gordon and Allen Tate[32] making love in a Guthrie cemetery in the early twentieth century, the mystique of Todd County held George an enduring and endearing captive.

Indeed, simply to elect George to one memorable term in the Kentucky House of Representatives required an earthy political finessing of which I was probably the prime earth mover.

Before his death, Doc Beauchamp told me that George, although admirably equipped in brains and character, lacked "the common touch." Besides, Beauchamp said, "He just isn't one of the boys."

I knew that was a reference to George's to-the-manor-born style of speech and his Tidewater Virginia-like vowel sounds, which were unique to cultured Todd countians. Never mind that he had won the Founders Medal, the highest honor a Vanderbilt graduate can receive, or that he could drink Beauchamp under the table. Doc, who could have elected a Jersey cow to the Kentucky Legislature, meant that Boone was too independent politically.

It turned out not to matter.

Doc was called to the Great Precinct in the Sky in the spring of 1971, just before the May primary for state representative. With a swiftness that Doc would have admired, I suggested to his pallbearers—Doc's most trusted henchmen—that they forsake the hack candidate to whom Beauchamp was committed and join George's Russellville friends and my newspapers to elect him.

After we got George elected, the veteran Logan County tax assessor, Karl Dawson, told me he had one regret about helping to make it happen. Just before Election Day, honor dictated that Dawson drive to Daysville, on the line between Todd and Logan counties, to give back a $500 contribution that the Todd County gentleman, endorsed by Beauchamp, had given to the Beauchamp gang.

"Doc never did nothing like that," Dawson said ruefully.

---

[32] Allen Tate, poet, critic, preeminent representative of the Southern Agrarian school, married Caroline Gordon, novelist, native of Todd County. They divorced in the 1950s.

IN THE TWO BRIEF YEARS that George served in Frankfort, he joined a band of young rebels who championed reform, which included Vic Hellard, Joe Clarke, Bobby Richardson, David Karem, and Nick Kafoglis. George became, according to one of these men,[33] their "intellectual-spiritual leader."

Although the Frankfort press corps named George Street Boone Kentucky's outstanding freshman legislator, he served only one term. Then the folks back home retired him, sending to Frankfort in his place someone more like "one of the boys."

After the death of his brother Ben, who owned the *Todd County Standard*, George married for the first time. His bride was the impressive Joy Bale, the widow of Dr. Garnet Bale of Elizabethtown. Joy was also a civic leader and later became poet laureate of Kentucky. They worked together for useful projects, but George never ran for office again, and he never left Todd County.

The governors who could have appointed him a judge and the law schools that could have named him a professor never did so. Perhaps this is because Kentucky is a state that has trouble honoring intellectual excellence.

But if George felt defeated, he never bellyached about it. And he never stopped championing progressive causes.

---

[33] Clark and Richardson became speakers of the Kentucky House of Representatives and Karem became Senate Majority Floor Leader. Vic Hellard went on to direct the Legislative Research Commission where he instigated the Long-Term Policy Research Center. After eighteen years of invaluable guidance on public issues, the Center was killed by the legislature in 2010, a reactionary, anti-intellectual move, allegedly for budgetary reasons.

-40-
Graeme's Flag

I TOLD PEOPLE I PUT THAT FLAG IN THE PRESS ROOM so that, no matter how many Cold War paranoids, racial bigots, and Watergate scoundrels wrapped their craziness in Old Glory, there would always be *one* flag, somewhere, that stood for truth and justice.

This was true, as far as it went. By the 1970s, I had become an officer in the Kentucky Press Association, and I *was* all fired up about "sunshine laws" that guaranteed the press's First Amendment rights to open meetings and records.

But there was something else about that flag.

In many unspoken ways, it was a memorial to Granny Graeme, the woman who'd coached me when "we" won the eighth-grade county prize with a speech titled "The Spirit of the American Flag."

When Graeme died in a car accident in 1949, she was still disappointed in me for the choices I had made—to slip away from the family, to give up the Legion scholarship, to leave college on a bus for New Orleans, and to become a reporter, not a governor.

After I had left Vanderbilt and gone to New Orleans, I saw my grandmother only one more time before she was killed when her car plunged off Lookout Mountain. We were in New Orleans, at my Aunt Dollie's house.

My grandmother barely spoke. I didn't say I was sorry, but she didn't either. She just gazed at me with a sad, curious half smile as I tried to report some achievement at *The Times-Picayune*. To me that accomplishment was just like earning all A's in the eighth grade, but she wasn't buying the message.

My grandmother and I had lost trust in each other. I was the son of the son she loved, the one who went to war in 1917 and came home broken. Despite new beginnings and a chance to fix mistakes with another "Albert," it had all gone wrong again.

That experience with the new flag on the pressroom wall was a long time ago for the old man who writes this book. But now I know.

At the open house to dedicate the newspaper plant, all of my new family—including a baby, Ginny—and two from the old—Dollie and Uncle Lad—were standing with me. The bishop for the Episcopal Diocese of Kentucky was praying.

But it was Graeme I was thinking of when those first papers rolled off our new press.

I was picking up her flag.

JOHN ED PEARCE was already one of *The Courier-Journal's* best-known reporters when he came to see me in the fall of 1973. He was writing a piece about changing small towns and wanted to talk to me for background.

Who knows how much I was channeling my grandmother as I showed John Ed around my new plant. We talked about Logan County that day, and I'm sure my enthusiasm for being its editor no doubt showed.

I told John Ed about the fight to maintain local control of our hospital when Hospital Corporation of America (HCA) wanted to buy it. I don't recall if I mentioned the poll *The Logan Leader* conducted by way of postcards inserted in the paper. Shamelessly biased, the poll's main question was: *"Do you want your hospital controlled by outsiders?"* The answers came back shouting a clear *"No."*

A brief digression: Dr. Thomas Frist, who was then president of HCA, and I ultimately came to an agreement in the 1970s. He would withdraw the offer to buy the hospital, and I would agree to let him know if the time ever came when the community wanted to give up control.

Dr. Frist and I both kept our promises. In 1982, the Logan County Fiscal Court decided it wanted the hospital to be part of a larger system. I contacted Dr. Frist and told him. "They've lost the will to run the hospital," I said. "My newspaper will not oppose you."

Within months, HCA bought Logan County Hospital. The company built a new building at a different site, and the old Hill-Burton hospital, once the pride of the community, was closed. It now sits empty on the hill.

No doubt I also told John Ed of my tough-but-unsuccessful campaign to consolidate Logan County's high schools and my efforts to help elect George Street Boone as a representative in the Kentucky Legislature.

And I'm sure I got rather windy when I told him of my role in the community's frenzied sales job to land E.R. Carpenter, a major manufacturing company, in Russellville. But landing that urethane pouring plant took persistence, and more than a little luck.[34]

After John Ed returned to Louisville, he phoned to inform me that the plans for his story had changed. Instead of a piece on small towns, he would write a profile of me in the Sunday magazine.

UNDER THE HEADLINE "Gadfly Editor—the Devil and the Darling of Russellville," a color photo of me standing beside my press appeared on the cover of the February 10, 1974, magazine. Inside, Pearce's seven-page story just about "told all," including my drinking problems and my decision to make Russellville my home.

---

[34] In 1968, Russellville's leaders were excited when word got around that Carpenter was looking for a site in either Russellville or Hopkinsville, Kentucky. Russellville had two favorable potential locations, but after much haggling, the owners of the favored location wouldn't budge on their asking price. The Carpenter site selection team headed for Hopkinsville, and it looked like the deal was off.

Hating to lose this good prospect, Lawrence Forgy and I called his son, Larry Forgy, who at the time was Governor Louie Nunn's budget director. Larry put us in touch with the governor.

"Governor Nunn, we're trying to land the E.R. Carpenter plant in Russellville," I explained. "We need some help from the state to sweeten the deal."

The governor offered to run an access road to the property at state expense if the landowners would give a little on the price. "I want to see that plant in Russellville," said Nunn.

I quickly relayed this information to the Carpenter team, and they headed back to Russellville. Under pressure from the governor, the landowners lowered their price, and the Carpenter plant was built in Russellville.

Reporting that I was stirred by Logan County history that "reflected the frontier and the whole country," John Ed wrote of those early years in Russellville when I was still dreaming of another career in big-time journalism, hoping someone would call:

"And finally, one night, Al came face to face with reality and with himself.

"'If you are going to make anything of your life, it's going to be right here.' And from that moment I started to change. I don't want to make a big thing of it. It's happened to a lot of people. But I know there's a road to Damascus. I've been on it."

I was thankful John Ed noted that I told him I had a lot of help, first from Mrs. Evans and then from Martha Helen, my staff, Bob Kirkpatrick, and other journalists, such as Nat Caldwell of *The Tennessean* and George Michler, a *Courier-Journal* state editor who ran my stories from the region with my byline.

JOHN ED TURNED OUT TO BE THE AGENT who pulled me beyond the county line and onto a larger stage in Kentucky.

Strangers wrote letters thanking me for my candor about my drinking. Prominent citizens I hardly knew wrote approving notes. It was great fun to hear from old friends in New Orleans to whom I unashamedly sent copies of the story.

Then came two visitors who had read the story. Each brought a proposal that took me into television.

The first was Alfred Shands, a filmmaker, writer, Episcopal priest, and husband to Mary Norton Shands, who with her mother owned Louisville's WAVE-TV and several other broadcast properties.

Shands planned a bicentennial documentary about Kentucky, told through the experiences of three contemporary families with ancestral roots deep in the state's beginnings. He contacted me to suggest a family in western Kentucky.

After Shands and I had talked awhile, he asked if I would like to narrate the show. The job meant I would visit with the three families—the Clarks in Russellville, the Hancocks in the Bluegrass, and the Bowlings in eastern Kentucky's Leslie County—all while television cameras rolled.

The next visitor was Len Press, the executive director of KET. Len wanted to create a public affairs program about politics, education, and business. Would I be interested in a part-time job as host and producer of the show?

My answer to both men?

An emphatic "Yes."

On the Road

THE YEAR 1974 MIGHT ALSO BE CALLED "the year I hit the road."

It was the beginning of a frenetic period in my life. I realized that alcohol had, in a sense, cost me twenty years. I was back on a fast track, to recover what I drank away.

I'd been free from the grip of alcohol for ten years, but the old underlying desire for attention was still there, as was the compulsion to say whatever went through my mind. The hand of my dead Grandmother Graeme was pushing me back to the stage. But this time, there was a difference. I was paying attention to the needs of people in the broader world, not just my own.

THE TELEVISION VENTURES WITH SHANDS AND PRESS meant I would be leaving Russellville on frequent trips across the state to produce programs. As I waited for that work to begin, my calendar for the summer of 1974 rapidly filled.

The Kentucky Press Association (KPA) had reformed its annual convention customs. Where previously we solicited contributions from the alcohol beverage industry, the association stopped that practice. The state press itself, under the influence of *Courier-Journal* publisher Barry Bingham, Jr., was committed to higher ethical standards for newspapers in reporting and business relationships.

I was a new officer of KPA, which was campaigning for open meetings and open records laws that guaranteed more public access to government. KPA board members traveled to every region of the state. We preached about the reforms we'd made at our own papers and explained the need for "sunshine" laws to fellow journalists. I was in a small group that negotiated with the governor's aides and legislative leaders for the greatest transparency possible.

Meanwhile, Nat Caldwell, the reporter hero of my youth, was dragging me into projects to promote TVA's cheap electricity as a resource for new jobs and Kentucky coal as an answer to the energy problems that the 1973 Arab oil embargo had caused.

Tall, lanky, wise-cracking Nat[35] was perhaps the most famous journalist in the mid-South. The editors at *The Tennessean*, in awe of Nat's national achievements as an investigative reporter, let him go wherever his nose for social and economic trends took him. Those editors expected him to "make things happen"—that is, to write stuff that would boost the TVA region, the paper's avowed editorial mission.

Nat commandeered me to help him spread the news that Wendell Ford, Kentucky's new governor, was investing more state money in coal research (at the University of Kentucky) than any other governor in the country. After I told Ford that Nat's reporting was creating favorable headlines about him in Tennessee, Ford agreed to give Nat an interview. I went along but Nat did most of the talking. Ford's message was that Kentucky deserved more attention for making coal "an ace in the hole."

In the early summer of 1974, Nat talked me into organizing a grandiose promotional event in Russellville called "Goals for Coal," a daylong fest of speeches in a county where no coal is mined. Russellville's Mayor Wallace Herndon, who had been entranced by one of Nat's spellbinding pitches, raised the money for the barbecue to feed the faithful hundreds who flocked in from several states.

---

[35] Nat had won a prestigious Nieman Fellowship for journalists at Harvard in the 1930s and many other awards for his writing, including the Pulitzer Prize in 1962 for articles on antitrust violations by both management and union labor leaders, which had squeezed small companies out of the coal mining business. His coverage of the TVA was credited as the inspiration of the dam at Kentucky's Lake Barkley. He also was a principal reporter in *The Tennessean*'s campaign against the Crump political machine in Memphis.

Across the back of the stage at the Russellville High School auditorium, a banner proclaimed: "We have more coal than the Arabs have oil—so we should dig it!"

On the stage were Governor Ford, Kentucky's U.S. Senator Marlow Cook, former Tennessee U.S. Senator Albert Gore Sr., and others. In their speeches, these leaders spun out dreams of coal converted to liquid energy and a new U.S. energy policy that would thwart Arab gaming of oil prices—goals, of course, that have yet to be realized.

I was master of ceremonies at the event, and I don't remember any talk of environmental concerns. Voices across the region were already warning about the multiple problems of heedless coal production, but none were heard that day.

Within the year, however, Nat told me he had listened to the environmentalists and decided they were speaking the truth. He became a convert.

It was then that he grew critical of his old friend, Aubrey "Red" Wagner, the longtime TVA chairman. Other reporters jested that Wagner broke out in a rash when he saw "the new Nat," but a later TVA chair, David Freeman, would say, "The TVA is alive today, in large part, because of Nat Caldwell." [36]

I WOULD LIKE TO WRITE THAT I MET ALL THE DEMANDS of these new activities and travel without neglecting my family and business. But I can't. At home, Martha Helen was the nurturing parent. At the office, Virginia Page was the iron woman who kept the papers rolling off the press and our business profitable. Our dedicated

---

[36] Twenty-six years after Nat's death in 1985, coal provides 46 percent of the nation's electricity and produces nearly a third of the carbon dioxide and other gases responsible for warming the planet. Coal produces millions of tons of other pollutants that are harmful to humans and the environment. Most Kentucky writers and artists now join poet, writer and conservationist, Wendell Berry, in opposing mountaintop removal for coal mining. Kentucky officials, however, including Governor Steve Beshear, demand that the regulators "get off our (coal's) back." — Political pandering, not problem solving.

staff met our deadlines, often more efficiently when I was away and not delaying the press by writing last-minute opinion pieces.

Confronted in our later life with this repentant mea culpa, Martha Helen conceded it was true. But she insists that I had a talent for leadership and a zest for identifying solutions to social problems.

"You enjoyed the struggle to help work things out and improve our lives," she says. "That was *you* as well as your grandmother's ghost." As I made new friends around the state in the 1970s, death was claiming friends and leaders in Russellville.

Judge Tom Noe died in November 1971, a few weeks before our daughter Ginny was born. Tom's impulsive invitation to that AA meeting had changed everything for me.

Former mayor Taylor Fuqua and businessman Marvin Stuart also died. Each man was a small-town success, though they were very different: Fuqua, plodding but tenacious; Stuart, glib and always smiling. Both were always open to the next deal that would benefit Russellville. When there was opportunity to improve the community, they showed me how to develop it.

When Doc Beauchamp died in April 1971, all three candidates in that spring's Democratic primary—Bert Combs and Wendell Ford, who were running for governor, and Julian Carroll, who was seeking the lieutenant governorship—were at Beauchamp's funeral, giving it the pomp of an event of state.

Laid out in an open casket, the old warrior wore a red tie, as all "loyal Tom Rhea men" did on Election Days. I don't know how many angels were needed to loft Doc to the heavenly gates, but if more were required, I'm sure extras were available from the Tennessee cemeteries where, it was said, the "Rhea men" found extra voters when needed.

Harry Whipple died at age fifty-nine, but not before giving me one last push, this time in Russellville's little Trinity Episcopal Church. For several Sundays in 1968, after Martha Helen decided this would be our place of worship, I sat stiffly through the service until one Sabbath, when I heard a whispered "Kneel, Goddammit!" grumbled from behind me. A violent shove from Harry pitched me forward.

BY MIDSUMMER, AL SHANDS WAS READY to begin work on his documentary. Shands's wife, the backer of *Three for Kentucky*, wanted "the best" for the project. Al recruited a fine film crew that introduced me to filmmaking as art as we went "on location" to the mountains, the Bluegrass, and just down the street.

We started in Russellville, where Granville Clark's family gave us an appealing inside story of life in a small town, including a fried-chicken dinner and an inspection of the pistols that a great-grandfather had fired while chasing the Jesse James gang in 1868.

We visited Granville's law office in a historic building. As we spoke, Granville pondered on camera whether Joe Gran, his bright teenage son, would find satisfaction as a lawyer if he came back to practice in Russellville as his father had for many years.[37]

At Claiborne Farm in Bourbon County, I interviewed Secretariat's groom as the frisky Triple Crown winner, who stood at stud at Claiborne, galloped in the paddock. This was the domain that A.B. "Bull" Hancock, Jr., who dominated the thoroughbred industry in his time, left at his death to his family, under the management of a trust. The trustees selected the younger son, Seth, as president, bypassing the older son, Arthur III.

Arthur broke away from Claiborne and set up his own stable at Stone Farm. He talked to me of his ambitions to win the Derby (which he later did) and write Bluegrass music (which he also did). The film closed with a scene of Arthur sitting in a porch swing at the little cottage where he lived, picking his guitar and singing.

No less compelling than the Hancocks and the Clarks were the Bowlings, representative of families that had lived in the mountains

---

[37] The answer was "Yes." Gran, as he is now called, practices law in Russellville, much as his father did. He is in the same building, using his father's desk and chair.

of east Kentucky for generations. The family patriarch, Ott Bowling, had a dozen children who were safely delivered by Frontier Nursing Service nurses who came on horseback. He recalled when Hyden, the Leslie county seat, had no paved roads, and remembered cutting logs to tie into rafts to float down the Kentucky River to sell at sawmills at Frankfort.

Ott showed me—the former Boy Scout who couldn't tie a knot—how to shoot a long rifle he had made. Tamping down that rifle for another firing, Ott gave me the best quote of that summer.

"Well, Al," he said, "me and Miss Rachel, we've had a good life.

"Twelve children we've had, six boys, six girls. All of 'em's living, nary one's a whore, nary one's a rogue, and they never been on food stamps."

Unfortunately, Ott said those memorable words off camera.

IN AUGUST 1974, after the shooting of *Three for Kentucky*, Martha Helen and I were invited to bring the kids to Florida for a visit with my cousins. We were to stay at Seven Springs, the wilderness preserve my Uncle McGregor had saved for his family from the purchase of a thousand acres of Florida forest and thicketed scrubland near Ocala, Florida.

Uncle McGregor had died two years earlier, but his widow, my Aunt Elizabeth, was there with her sons, Wilson and McGregor Jr., and the latter's family.

Catherine, then 14, grew suspicious as we pulled off the highway onto a path through tall grass. She and Carter started complaining as we jolted our way a mile through the field to find some rough family cottages under mossy oaks near the hidden springs. Slapping at mosquitoes, both of them looked at me, indignantly.

"You mean *this* is our Florida vacation?" they whined.

"Well, it's *free!*" I replied.

No matter what Catherine and Carter thought, the site was beautiful, with glass-bottomed boats to use in the crystal-clear spring. Canoe trips down the stream were fun for the families.

The other entertainment, however—at least for the adults—was the black-and-white TV. We were awestruck as Richard Nixon resigned the presidency over the Watergate scandal.

Two days later, surrendering to my older children's demands for a "real" Florida vacation—meaning something a little less remote, with a pool—we left my family and the birds, snakes, squirrels, alligators, and fish at Seven Springs and headed for Fort Pierce on Florida's Atlantic coast.

We would never have found our way out of "the wilderness" had my cousin McGregor not guided us back to the interstate. McGregor, by then teaching at Miami-Dade Community College, was returning home. But on his way, he led us to a trailer park where he unlocked two Airstreams for us, relics of his trip around the world years earlier with his family. The Airstreams were ours to use for free until we returned to Kentucky.

It was not until we bedded down for the sweltering night that we realized they weren't air-conditioned.

There was more discomfort coming.

Mosquitoes poured through the open windows. So did an overpowering stench from the nearby Indian River. The plumbing was unconnected, so we had to go to a bathhouse for toilets.

At 3:00 a.m., Martha Helen and I were still awake. We started laughing. The alternative was to cry.

The next morning, McGregor gave us final operating instructions for the Airstreams, which I couldn't understand, while he snacked from a sack of peanuts. Then he was off to Miami.

As soon as he was out of sight, I went across the street to a Sheraton Hotel on the beach.

"Got two rooms?" I asked the clerk.

"How about five for the price of three?" the clerk replied.

"Nope. Two will do."

He handed me the keys.

I tried not to inhale the marijuana fumes as I left the nearly empty hotel. By breakfast, we were installed in two air-conditioned rooms, and family dispositions were rapidly improving.

Two days later, the ex-president was safely back in California, and the new president, Gerald Ford, had moved in at the White House. My older children and their little sister had splashed for hours in the Sheraton pool. Martha Helen had acquired a suntan. I was still pale-faced, but I had finished writing the script for my narration of *Three for Kentucky*, sitting beside what seemed the most wonderful air conditioner the Carrier Company ever made.

THREE MONTHS LATER, ON NOVEMBER 7, 1974, I went on the air with the first *Comment on Kentucky* program.

My guest was U.S. District Court Judge Mac Swinford. Neither of us had been on television before, and it showed. We each sat in rocking chairs and bobbed like corks on a fishing line.

Swinford, one of the longest-serving federal judges in U.S. history, had been appointed to the federal bench at age thirty seven by President Franklin D. Roosevelt. Respected for integrity, wisdom, and knowledge—all attributes of a great judge—Swinford recently had written a book, *Kentucky Lawyer,* published by the University Press of Kentucky. Full of folklore, rural humor, and country lawyer wisdom, that book was our topic.

We discussed juries and the aggressive conduct of U.S. District Judge John Sirica during Watergate. (Sirica had ordered Nixon to turn over the secret tape recordings of White House conversations to the Watergate special prosecutor and congressional investigators, which ultimately led Nixon to resign.) Swinford closed that episode of *Comment* with a stirring defense of both Sirica's conduct and the jury system.

The next week, I received a warm letter from the judge, expressing his satisfaction with the program. A few months later, he died of a heart attack. KET replayed our interview on the day of the funeral.

Four decades later, I am still proud that this was our initial program. I doubt that any living Kentuckian in public life in 1974 was more respected than Swinford, with the possible exception of former U.S. Senator John Sherman Cooper.

Each of these men—Swinford, a Democrat, and Cooper, a Republican—ascended the political ladder on the rungs of partisanship. But at the pinnacle of their careers, each earned a reputation for fairness by putting the common good above party affiliation.

-42-
Courts Hall

MY *COMMENT* WEEKENDS STARTED WITH A DRIVE to Lexington on Friday afternoon. I would do the show that evening, overnight at a cheap motel, and then drive back to Russellville on Saturday morning.

Martha Helen was patient about those absences. But one Saturday afternoon in the fall of 1974, I arrived home to find her in tears.

"Oh, Al," she wailed. "You won't believe this. Mrs. Covington called. They're moving back to Russellville and they want their house back!"

This was a huge blow. For five years we'd rented a nineteenth-century house owned by the Covington family of Paris, Tennessee. The house had once been owned by Thomas deGraffenried, the man who had left Russellville a million dollars in the 1960s.

Though we'd always known the house wasn't really ours, the Covingtons had been gone from Russellville for forty years when we moved in. We assumed we'd be able to rent as long as we wanted.

BACK IN 1969, the Covingtons had been renovating the house in absentia when we asked to rent it. Tommy Williamson, the expert carpenter the Covingtons had hired to handle the work, was dragging on the job; he frequently took off to work for others, assuming the Covingtons were in no hurry. The Covingtons let us move in and, before long, they put Martha Helen in charge of the renovation.

My wife reveled in the opportunity. She designed the kitchen, chose the paint colors, managed other improvements, and pushed Tommy into high gear.

We moved in with great expectations. "They've been gone so long, they'll never come back," Martha Helen predicted. "Sooner or later, we'll be able to buy it."

The house was a spacious place to raise a family, and we decided it was time for another child. Over a steak dinner in early 1971, I had read a poem which ended with the words *"We're going to have a baby."* Catherine and Carter, then eleven and ten, were excited, or perhaps they were just stunned. After all, none of *their* friends had a baby in the house.

"I should have known something was up," Carter later said. "We *never* got to have steak."

VIRGINIA LASSITER SMITH WAS BORN on November 22, 1971, to the great delight of our family, friends, and the newspaper staff.[38]

So it was particularly troubling in 1974 when we learned Martha Helen was wrong about our outlasting the Covingtons. The elderly couple had decided to reclaim their homeplace.

Faced with this setback, we searched for another old house. Day after day, we took Ginny for a stroll around the residential section of Russellville. Catherine and Carter joined the hunt. Nothing was for sale.

One day at lunch, Granville mentioned that his wife had suggested we should consider the Gorrell house.

The *Gorrell* house? What was she thinking?

That three-story Victorian manse, on the corner of Ninth and Main, had been closed up for five years. The owner, Mrs. Roy Gorrell, was bedfast and being cared for at the residence of Mrs. Bess Martin, her sister-in-law.

---

[38] I suppose many of our friends were surprised that, at forty-four, I was the father of a new baby. "Al, I guess it was the yogurt," my friend Granville Clark said. I was dieting in 1971.

Though I couldn't imagine that the house was still habitable, I called Bess. She agreed to let us look at the house, but she said it would have to be after dark. She wasn't sure she could legally sell the house, and she didn't want to set the neighbors to talking.

With little Ginny in tow and flashlights in hand—the house had no electricity—we sneaked in.

Room by room, floor by floor, our flashlights shone on high ceilings, ornate fireplaces, stained glass windows, and shrouded furniture. We swept aside cobwebs as we tried to envision what the house might look like, stripped of five years of dust.

Bess, holding Mrs. Gorrell's power of attorney, won permission to sell, and we took a chance. By Thanksgiving 1974, for the grand sum of $28,000, we were the owners of the town's red-brick "white elephant": all 8,500 square feet, three floors, and ninety-five windows, not to mention a coal furnace for heat and plumbing that hadn't been used in five years.

This was the first house that either of us had ever owned. It may have been the biggest in town.

It was indisputable that it needed the most work.

RESEARCH SHOWED that the house was built by Winn Courts, a banker who wanted to rival another banker's house at the north end of town back in 1883. The Rhea family—the same one that had controlled Logan County politics for so long—purchased the house from Courts and owned it until the Depression, when they sold it to Lilburn Gorrell. Frank Gorrell, one of Lilburn's children who went on to become lieutenant governor of Tennessee, remembered keeping a pony in the huge, cut-stone basement.

We decided to give the grand old house a name: Courts Hall, in recognition of its builder.

"Does that sound ostentatious?" Martha Helen asked.

"Maybe not," I said. "I just hope people don't get the idea we're rich."

Maude VanCleve, our housekeeper and Ginny's caregiver, eyed the house with reservation.

"Folks, this is no little cottage," she said sorrowfully. "This is a *man's* house."

She was right. I loved the house. Maybe it fit my expansive personality.

I especially liked the big front porch, which Thomas Rhea had added when he owned the house. I could imagine him expecting to make his acceptance speech as governor.

That glorious moment never happened, but Catherine and Carter soon realized there were benefits to the porch. You could sit on the swing and see every teenager in Russellville as they drove by.

Martha Helen went to work planning a second renovation. Still a social worker in Bowling Green, she juggled the needs and activities of our three children as she organized her project. Downed by a timely case of the flu, she designed the kitchen. Wallpaper books covered our dining room table. With little money for this huge project, she acted as the contractor.

We were relieved when the furnace appeared sound; the plumbing worked too, with remarkably few leaks.

Workmen began to appear. This was our ecumenical house: The roofers were Jehovah's Witnesses; the carpenters, Baptists; the electricians, Pentacostals. As the Amish women paperhangers, clad in their long dresses and caps, stood on scaffolding to hang long streamers of creamy white paper, they resembled graceful cranes. Their husbands, who built the scaffolding, stood below and watched.

BY MOTHER'S DAY 1975, Martha Helen had her "new" old house.

The rooms sparkled with new paint and paper. The oak woodwork and the hardwood floors shone. We were a little self-conscious about succeeding the elite bankers, political leaders, and builders who had lived in the house, but I was very proud of the historic mansion. No longer a drunk in a firetrap hotel, I now lived across the street from a marker that proclaimed the area "Governor's Corner.[39]"

The house was a palace for make-believe; Ginny had a playroom under the staircase and another in the "tower room" off her bedroom. Catherine and Carter had a great space to entertain friends. When the Episcopal Bishop of Kentucky came to install a new priest at our church, we invited the congregation for a potluck lunch. At Halloween, teenagers took over the basement for a very spooky haunted house.

With no money left to repair the garage, our cars sat out front: a yellow Volkswagen Rabbit and a gold Volkswagen Scirocco. We were saving gas before that was popular.

In Lexington, I asked advice from the head of the UK College of Architecture, who also owned an old Victorian. "How can you remove the red paint on the brick economically?" I asked.

"You can't," he said.

"Just let it peel off. That's what I'm doing."

---

[39] John J. Crittenden, fifteenth governor of Kentucky, served as attorney general under three presidents and five terms as U.S. Senator. He was noted for the Crittenden Compromise, a futile effort in 1860 to avert the Civil War.

Mister Chairman

GOVERNOR FORD, A DEMOCRAT, AND SENATOR COOK, a Republican, had a cordial relationship when they appeared at the "Goals for Coal" conference in Russellville, but when Ford announced a few days later that he would contest Cook's reelection, the friendship fell apart.

Ford didn't really want the U.S. Senate term that would begin in 1975. It would mean leaving the governor's office a year early. For that and other reasons, Ford had tried to persuade Lieutenant Governor Julian Carroll to run for the Senate seat with his backing.

But Carroll, hoping for the five-year stretch as governor that likely would be his if Ford went to the Senate, resisted the case that he should seek the Washington office.

So when the Democrats couldn't find another candidate, Ford bowed to party pressures and announced for the Senate. From that moment on, he had no greater cheerleader than Julian Carroll.

Marlow Cook had a reasonable record as a moderate Republican, but he had no chance against Ford in a state where the number of registered Democrats dwarfed Republican registrations. Although he was not complicit in Watergate or the associated scandals, he was heavily damaged by their fallout. It was just a tough time for Republicans to run.

Ford won, but Cook—who resigned a few days early to give Ford a leg up on seniority—prospered afterwards as a Washington lobbyist until he retired to Sarasota, where he became a popular civic leader. Ford quickly won respect from Senate Democratic leaders, earning key assignments until he retired after twenty-four years in the Senate.

I BECAME CHAIRMAN of the Kentucky Press Association at its winter convention in 1975.

Carroll, the new governor, who joined us for a speech, was rightly thrilled over prospects of an improving economy and added revenues. He promised improved spending for education as a centerpiece of his legislative program, and later delivered, pulling Kentucky's teacher salaries from the lowest in the country to the middle of the list of states.

In just a few months, I would have another encounter with Carroll, this one prompted by an idle chat I had on Russellville's town square.

On Memorial Day, I walked from my house down to the newspaper office, which was closed for the holiday. (I worked a lot more holidays than my family would have liked.) On my way in, I stopped to speak to Walter Collins, an old, down-and-out friend who was slumped on a park bench, dozing off a little early-morning wine in the sun.

Shaking himself awake, Walter yawned. "Hi, Al," he said forthrightly.

We had the downtown to ourselves, but Walter said it hadn't always been that way. He could remember a time when the square was crowded on Memorial Day, with speakers, bands, horseshoe throwing, and barbecue that he prepared.

Walter missed those days. "Everybody knew I was the best barbecue man in town," he said.

"Ever barbecue a goat?" he asked.

"Nope," I replied.

So Walter told me how.

I proceeded to the office. I had other work to do, but I decided that first I needed to tell Governor Carroll about that goat.

I wrote the governor a letter about my conversation with Walter. I told him about the "old days," the music, the games, the public prayers, the flirty young people, the speeches, and everything else Walter had so vividly described.

"Who will know this story when Walter is gone?" I asked Carroll.

Noting that he and I were recent fathers of girls—my Ginny and his Ellyn (the first child born to a sitting Kentucky governor since 1905)—I proposed to Carroll that he set aside some funds to record the memories of older Kentuckians, like Walter, for those girls and the state's future generations. I told Carroll we also should tape interviews with political movers and shakers such as himself, as well as business, education, and arts leaders who were changing Kentucky.

The post office was closed, but I put a stamp on my letter, walked there, and mailed it that very day. When a tepid reply arrived from Frankfort, written by an aide on behalf of the governor, I called John Ed Pearce.

I read both letters to John Ed. He was in Frankfort, writing about the legislature, but he "got it."

"Let's go see Julian," he said. "I'll call and get an appointment."

I was soon glad I had called John Ed. The governor was so quickly enthused about my ideas for an oral history commission that I knew he had never even seen my letter.

Carroll—tanned, trim, and prematurely white haired, with a smiling mouth full of pearly teeth—was the last governor for whom legislators would jump through hoops. Within a few months, Kentucky passed a law creating the nation's first taxpayer-supported commission dedicated to the collection of oral histories.[40]

ALTHOUGH NEITHER JOHN ED NOR I HAD ASKED to serve, I was appointed chairman and John Ed vice chairman of the Oral History Commission. We elected an executive committee that

[40] More than thirty years later, the Commission is still the only fully government-supported oral history project in the country, but its tax support has dwindled. Nevertheless, the oral history collections contain some 50,000 interviews—a lot of stories for Ellyn Carroll, Ginny Smith, and future Kentuckians.

included Dr. Robert R. Martin, the president of Eastern Kentucky University; Dr. Thomas Clark, the prestigious Kentucky historian; and Dr. Forrest Pogue, a Kentucky native and Washington, D.C., resident who had written a biography of General George C. Marshall.

We received one hundred applicants for the job of commission director, among them ten Ph.D.s. But we surprised ourselves by hiring a perky, twenty-two-year-old woman who was working in a Danville, Kentucky, gift shop. Debbie McGuffey, who had grown up in Stanford, Kentucky, had graduated with honors from Western Kentucky University with a degree in French. She could type well, was widely read, smiled a lot, loved baseball, and brimmed with friendliness. She impressed all of us with her intellect and sparkling personality. She was the right person for the job.

Others in state government found her personality and skills the right combination. When she retired from state government at a young age, she was the Kentucky Council on Higher Education's lobbyist with the state legislature.

Taking the minutes at executive committee meetings, Debbie sometimes had to tolerate digressions from the matter at hand, when the old-timers wanted to share an indiscreet story about a scandal from the not-so-distant past.

Glancing at the tape recorder whirring on the table, Dr. Martin would ask, "Debbie, is that thing on?"

"Yes, sir," she'd reply.

"Then cut it off!"

JOHN ED AND I WERE POTENT LOBBYISTS. But Carroll had also been quick to respond to a request for more state funding of the arts brought to him by Barry Bingham Jr., the publisher of *The Courier-Journal*, and Hudson Milner, the chairman of the Kentucky Arts Commission, who was CEO of Louisville Gas and Electric.

Just as quickly as he had formed the Oral History Commission, Carroll responded to Bingham and Milner on the spot, proposing a state challenge grant to match private donations to the arts. This was a significant boost of dollars for cultural and creative efforts in Kentucky, never rivaled by any other governor.

Meanwhile, Carroll also appointed me to the Kentucky Arts Commission.

Moving to Russellville from New Orleans had meant a precipitous drop in my exposure to the arts. There were few concerts and there was no Dixieland jazz in Logan County; no Faulkners walked the streets. But there *were* arts activities in our small town, and maybe Carroll appointed me because I had done what I could to promote them.

Several years earlier, for example, I had produced a special edition of the newspaper to welcome the Louisville orchestra to a concert celebrating the opening of the splendid 1,000-seat deGraffenried Auditorium at the Russellville High School. (The auditorium had been built with a portion of the $1 million that Thomas deGraffenried had left his hometown of Russellville when he died in the 1960s.)

Packed with ads and pictures featuring all the musicians, stories extolling their artistry, and an editorial imploring our rural readers not to embarrass us by staying home, the paper's appeal to local pride had an effect.

That concert occurred on a foggy night, but I had never seen such a line of cars as inched toward the school, not even for football playoffs at Rhea Stadium. Extra state troopers and deputies parked them all. Every seat was filled when the music began.

Whatever the reason, in late 1975, after Hudson Milner died, Governor Carroll named me chairman of the Kentucky Arts Commission.

This was less than two years after the Pearce article about me in *The Courier-Journal.* I was chairing three state organizations, hosting a weekly TV show, publishing five papers, and about to start a suburban[41] weekly near Nashville. Twelve years after I sobered up my life was moving pretty quickly in the seventies.

I wasn't the only busy family member. Martha Helen had changed to part-time status as a mental health counselor, but she still sometimes drove seventy miles round trip as she visited clinics. At home she mothered a four-year-old and two teenagers in high school. They were active kids who deserved more of a father's time than they received. I regret I was so much a part-time dad. I used to think they were blessed because I was sober; they never saw me drink—but for too many days when they were growing up, they never saw me.

---

[41] The *Harpeth Herald* was the paper I started in affluent Brentwood in Williamson County, Tennessee.

-44-

Comment,
Those Happy Hours

AS I CRANKED UP FOR A SECOND SEASON of *Comment on Kentucky* during the summer of 1975, I invited Governor Happy Chandler to tape two one-hour interviews that I could divide into four thirty-minute shows.

I was still a nobody to a statewide television audience, but Chandler was a "somebody," with a robust personality and a famous name. As a two-time governor, a former U.S. Senator and baseball commissioner, and a colorful campaigner on the stump, Chandler had impressive achievements to talk about. He was the kind of star *Comment* needed to build an audience, and I told him so in a letter. Soon thereafter he called me in Russellville, and it was clear he agreed.

In the KET dressing room, Chandler, then a vigorous seventy-two, was pumped to go before the cameras.

He was the only guest in the show's thirty-three-year history to decline makeup. I guess he thought powder and paint were sissy, but he gave a different reason. Pointing proudly to his ruddy visage, he smiled at the makeup assistant.

"You see this complexion?" Happy asked.

"God gave it to me, and I don't want to mess it up."

Happy was elected governor for the first time in 1935, defeating Thomas Rhea to become, at age thirty-seven, the "boy governor" who reorganized state government. He served for a time as a U.S. senator and baseball commissioner before he was elected governor for a second time in 1955. During that second term, he built the University of Kentucky Medical School and the appropriately named Chandler Medical Center.

As expected, Happy gave memorable answers to my questions.

"Which was the better of your two terms as governor?"

"They were equally good!" he said.

When I solicited his thoughts on other Kentucky governors, he had to reach all the way back to 1901 to find someone to praise: J.C.W. Beckham, another "boy governor," who was sworn in at age thirty-one when he was barely old enough to assume the office. But for his contemporaries, Happy had few kind words.

He was scornful of project bonds that other governors had issued, insisting "I'm allergic to debt." When I asked for his thoughts on the civil service law Bert Combs had instituted during his 1959 to 1963 term as governor, Happy put a pox on it.

"Albert Benjamin," he said, "it is a fraud!"

(Thus began the governor's practice of calling me by his own given and middle names, which he said he enjoyed hearing occasionally instead of his nickname, Happy. Chandler could never deny, however, that "Happy" was the most politically valuable credit he earned at Transylvania University, where he famously arrived as a student with only "a red sweater, a five dollar bill, and a smile.")

Happy was justifiably proud that as commissioner of baseball, he had approved Jackie Robinson's contract with the Brooklyn Dodgers, helping to integrate the sport. He was proud of his decision as governor to dispatch troops and tanks to west Kentucky to protect students who were integrating public schools there.

Explaining those decisions, Happy told me, "I was afraid to face my maker when He asked why I wouldn't let Jackie Robinson play baseball or let those black children go to school with white kids."

DURING THOSE INTERVIEWS, HAPPY TOLD ME that his well-known political split from his boyhood friend Earle Clements was rooted in misunderstanding. Happy and Clements had made peace once, but then fell out again in struggles over power at Frankfort.

It was said, to the annoyance of Chandler, that Clements didn't care who was governor as long as he could run the state, and that Chandler didn't care who ran the state as long as he could be governor.

But when the cameras quit rolling, Happy urged me to invite Clements to sit for a similar interview.

"I'll come with him," Happy offered excitedly. "You can seat us side by side.

"We'll give you a helluva show."

I loved the idea. So when Clements, arthritic and on crutches, showed up to present his official papers to the University of Kentucky, I was in the audience, waiting to make "the ask."

Happy was there too, guffawing from the second row at Clements's attempts at light humor with the event's guest of honor, Lady Bird Johnson, widow of the president.[42] But that evening at UK, while Happy mixed with Clements' friends at a reception following the dedication ceremony, Clements was not pleased to meet me, nor enthused with my report that I came as an emissary from Happy, from KET, and from the new Oral History Commission.

"Would you be interested in doing an interview with …"

Clements cut me off, letting loose an oath.

"I know you," he snarled. "You're a friend of that goddamned little John Ed Pearce and those goddamned Binghams!"

So much for Happy's great idea.

---

[42]When Lyndon B. Johnson (LBJ) was hospitalized with a heart attack in 1956, he was Majority Leader of the U.S. Senate. Clements stepped in as acting leader to execute LBJ's wishes. The time he lost from his reelection campaign in Kentucky, plus Governor Chandler's support for his Republican foe, Thruston Morton, cost Clements his Senate seat that year. When Johnson became president, his friendship helped the wounded Clements become among the most powerful lobbyists in Washington.

CLEMENTS AND CHANDLER WERE THE GIANT OAKS of Kentucky politics in the mid-twentieth century. They were such strong characters that their tempestuous fights with one another sometimes obscured their extraordinary accomplishments.

Happy was always talking, shaking hands, and ever eager to seize the spotlight; Clements, big and bluff, was a brilliant strategist and domineering manager but a poor speaker who was often cold and unforgiving. I think the funny stories about their different personalities and the colorful gossip discourage understanding of how much each of these men from rural Kentucky did to advance the state.

Regardless of their rhetoric, both Happy and Clements made impressive improvements in roads and schools, as well as health, welfare, and penal institutions. Each was innovative in modernizing state government.

Chandler presented himself as a fiscal conservative. Happy won support for opposing a sales tax, but he raised revenues by increasing excise taxes and income taxes. A $1 billion upgrade of the Chandler Medical Center in the first decade of the twenty-first century reminds us of Happy's brave fight to build it in the first place.

Clements was a New Dealer, with an activist streak like his heroes Franklin Roosevelt and Alben Barkley. He built or funded eight thousand miles of roads, took over maintenance of six thousand more, and launched a massive agriculture and industrial development effort.

Under Clements, Kentucky outspent every state but New York in developing parks. Today's complaints that budget battles in Frankfort have allowed the parks to deteriorate suggest that Kentucky once had the best parks in the nation. They were that way because the visionary Clements set out to make them so.

IN THE SECOND OF TWO CAMPAIGNS that former governor Clements managed for him, Bert Combs was elected governor. Grateful, the new governor appointed the old one highway commissioner. Since Kentucky needs only one governor in Frankfort at a time, this was a bad idea.

When Clements and Combs botched a response to press criticism of highway department contracts for used trucks, their friendship ruptured. The break was so severe that Clements went on to support Happy's unsuccessful bid for a third term as governor against Combs' handpicked choice, the estimable Ned Breathitt. Imagine my surprise, then, when Bert Combs told me, after an interview with him later in my TV career, that I should press hard for an interview with Clements.

"He was the greatest governor of the twentieth century," Combs said. We were standing in the parking lot after our taping.

"That's what a lot of people say of you," I replied.

"I know," Combs said, with a thin smile.

"But it was Earle." And then he drove away.[43]

IN 1975, KET WAS AWARDED AN UNUSUAL GRANT from the Kentucky Humanities Council to fund *Comment* for another season. The funds came with a requirement that a humanities professor appear on each week's episode along with the journalists to "illuminate" the discussions from the perspective of his or her discipline.

As we needed the money to keep the show on the air, I did not suggest that a Vanderbilt dropout might not be the best person to head such an endeavor.

Instead, praising the perspicacity of the Humanities Council director, I assured her of my enthusiasm for the idea and promptly called Dr. Thomas Clark, the eminent state historian and professor

---

[43] On a lighter note: Once when Clements was in Frankfort on business during his time in the U.S. Senate, he reportedly was impressed to see that the New Capitol Annex he had broken ground for as governor was open for business.

"How many people work there?" Clements asked his friend Doc Beauchamp.

"About half of 'em," Doc replied.

emeritus at UK with whom I served on the Oral History Commission board.

From my end, the conversation sounded something like this:

"Would you like to join a weekly TV panel of grubby reporters like myself and your old student, John Ed Pearce? You would? Well, great!

"Say, Tom … history is one of the humanities, isn't it? … I thought so.

"What about political science? … No? Well then, what about economics? … No?

"Well, Tom … do you know any other historians who can talk about Kentucky as well as you can? … No?"

So that was why Dr. Clark appeared on a lot of shows that season. He had forgotten more history than we reporters ever knew and had already written more books than any of us ever would.

From time to time other humanists would appear when we gave the professor a night off. But Len Press became jittery watching me try to frame perspective on suspected kickbacks to mine inspectors or the state highway department's five-year plan from theologians and philosophers. The following year, he scrounged up funding from other sources for a full season and didn't ask the Humanities Council for any more money.

MEANWHILE, I EXCITEDLY ACCEPTED AN INVITATION from Earl D. Wallace to be his guest for a weekend at Shakertown at Pleasant Hill near Harrodsburg, Kentucky. I would also go to the Derby as his guest.

The courtly Mr. Wallace, a retired oil executive and Wall Street investment banker who was in his late seventies, was the founding chairman and leader of Shakertown, a restoration of nineteenth century buildings and three thousand acres of grounds in Mercer County.

Wallace had obtained a $2 million federal loan for the project, the largest ever made for historic preservation in U.S. history. After many rebuffs from Kentucky banks and national foundations from which he sought additional funding, he struck gold when Mr. and Mrs. Eli Lilly of Indiana saw the work in progress and became the first of several out-of-state philanthropists to write him very substantial checks.

Wallace often cultivated journalists for get-acquainted visits to Shakertown. During my weekend there, I was fascinated as my elderly host sat up until midnight telling me stories of his life as a boy in the mountains and as a UK engineering student.

In college, he and other students had picnicked among the ruined buildings he was restoring with the millions of dollars he had raised. Although he scoffed at the Shakers' religious practices, including celibacy, he admired their craftsmanship.

Wallace never accepted a nickel in salary or expenses for his Shakertown work. His interest in the project grew out of his volunteer work with the Blue Grass Trust's preservation efforts in Lexington, Kentucky.

Wallace ultimately intended to establish a center for meetings at Shakertown and a series of conferences on public issues that would provide the village a modern use beyond tourism.

Neither of us could imagine that first weekend how close we would become as we worked through the years to bring this dream to reality, or that I would run the Shakertown Roundtable, a forum on public policy and educational issues, for ten years after his death. I take that back—maybe Wallace imagined it. He was quite the visionary.

Next morning, the old gentleman drove me to Louisville for an early lunch before the Derby with his friends Mary and Barry Bingham Sr., who were enthusiastic patrons of his restoration efforts. Jokingly, Wallace insisted that when he decided to add a representative weekly editor to the cross section of journalists invited to learn about the Shaker project, "Barry told me that you, Al, were the countriest country editor in Kentucky." Mary laughed, while Barry blushingly demurred, but I suspected that John Ed Pearce's magazine story was the source of Earl Wallace's interest in my career.

When I said goodbye to Earl Wallace on Sunday, I was awed, of course, but I was also hooked. As we became friends, he opened to me his wider world of access to leaders in business and finance, society, and politics. And I joined the ranks of those who would do anything for him because he did so many selfless things for others.

JULIAN CARROLL HAD BECOME GOVERNOR when Wendell Ford ascended to the U.S. Senate in what would have been his fourth year in office. In 1975, Carroll set about winning a four-year term for himself.

In what was sort of a "sham" primary, Carroll was challenged by young Todd Hollenbach, the boyish county judge from Louisville. The campaign was a chance for Todd to get out of town, tour Kentucky, meet and greet the country folks, kiss their babies, and hug their women.

For Carroll, Hollenbach's contest provided an excuse to tap the pockets of coal operators and road contractors, squeeze certain state employees, alert insurance brokers with state contracts that there was a new governor, and promise favors to all who stuffed his tin cup with campaign cash.

After Carroll easily disposed of Hollenbach in the Democratic primary, Len Press encouraged me to try to set up a gubernatorial debate to be televised on KET during the fall general election campaign. With the help of Terry McBrayer, a Democratic member of the state House of Representatives, and Larry Forgy, a rising star in the Kentucky Republican Party, I was able to make it happen.

The Republican nominee was Robert Gable, a coal and timber magnate who had a rather patrician air. His critics unkindly called him "stuffy," but Gable and I were friendly, and he had been an early guest on *Comment*.

As the debate got underway, Gable pulled out a big dinner bell, which he said he would ring "whenever the governor tells an untruth."

Citing the rules against props, I firmly requested Gable put down the bell.

He did. But not for long.

After a few more remarks from Carroll, Gable began ringing the damn bell.

I stopped the debate and told Gable we wouldn't start again until he retired the bell from action. Gable then meekly slid it under his seat.

My little confrontation with Gable got as much press attention as the serious points each candidate made.

The event was a bit of a history maker—the first statewide televised debate in a Kentucky governor's race. But it will be forever remembered as "The Truth Bell Show."

And Carroll later told me that when he returned to the Governor's Mansion that night, his wife and four children were lined up on the stairs, each holding a little dinner bell and merrily ringing away.

President Jimmy Carter congratulates his new
ARC co-chairman, one of the first Kentucky
editors to endorse his candidacy.

U.S. Senator Jennings Randolph of West Virginia, a father of the ARC.

Len and Lil Press, heroes of education and public service in Kentucky, our dear friends.

All smiles to be together: Terry Birdwhistell, dean of U.K. libraries, Len Press, founding director of KET, and Jim Host, sports broadcasting entrepreneur and civic leader.

Renee Shaw, my plucky
co-producer of *Comment*,
who never hesitated to
straighten me out.

Associated Press reporter Sy
Ramsey, who helped launch
Comment on Kentucky.

Virginia "Ginni" Fox, Len Press's successor at KET, who kept *Comment* strong and free.

Talented KET producer George Rasmussen and I in Leningrad after shooting a documentary in Moscow. (My proudly purchased Russian hat was made in Mexico City.)

Nat Caldwell, the legendary Nashville reporter who won a Pulitzer Prize and taught me how to make things happen.

My mentor and great friend Earl D. Wallace, who led the restoration of Shakertown at Pleasant Hill where I filmed a documentary about him.

Two mentors, Owensboro attorney Morton Holbrook and historian Thomas D. Clark, with Chancellor emeritus of Vanderbilt, Alexander Heard. They were at a Shakertown Roundtable which I chaired.

Media magnate Roy Park, left, meets my partner Virginia Page, as he reviews one of our newspapers which he bought in 1985.

Two stars I befriended when they were young: Al Cross, left, and Jack Lyne, each named to the U. K. Journalism Hall of Fame.

Dinners after our shows were occasions to share stories behind the stories. Such an occasion in the last month of my TV career was with guest, Robert Novak, far right, and others including, from left, Kay and Tom Loftus of The *Courier-Journal*, chef Kevin Toyoda of Bella Notte Restaurant, Jack Brammer of the *Herald-Leader*, and Ronnie Ellis of CNHI Newspapers.

For my last *Comment* show before a live audience, I was joined by former governors Brereton Jones, John Y. Brown, Jr., Paul Patton, and incumbent governor Steve Beshear.

(Top) Family members turned out for a dinner in Lexington at which I was given the first Al Smith Award through Community Journalism. Martha Helen and I stand proudly behind table that included, from left, granddaughter Lauren Hancock and her father, Carter; son-in-law Bill McCarty, his wife Catherine, and sons Connor and Evan; and son-in-law, Bill Major. The award was sponsored by the Bluegrass chapter of SPJ and the Institute for Rural Journalism and Community Issues.

(Left) Daughter Ginny Major with her husband Bill and, from left, daughters Susannah and Ava.

(Right) Martha Helen and I enjoy the festivities at my retirement show and dinner at KET on November 16, 2007. Four years later, she inspired me to finish this book.

-45-
Presidents

AFTER GINNY WAS BORN, we had recruited Maude VanCleve to be our nanny, cook, and housekeeper.

We were a bit of a comedown for Maude. Born in Adairville, Kentucky, in the southern part of Logan County, Maude had moved away and spent most of her life in domestic service to several affluent families, including the William Ruckelshauses of Indianpolis before he went to Washington as the first head of the Environmental Protection Agency.

But when Maude's ailing elder sister Addie needed her, Maude had moved home to Adairville. She paid a sitter for Addie from the modest salary she earned with us.

Maude, who could be openly snooty, soon mentioned to Martha Helen that she had never worked in a family where the lady of the house worked "out." In response, I told Maude that I had never known a black woman who was a Republican.

Maude's skepticism about whether we were "the right kind" of white people began to ease when she met Governor Ford and Senator Cook at our house after the "Goals for Coal" event.

And her distant attitude dissolved completely when the Gerald Ford White House sent a transcript of an interview that some other reporters and I had with President Ford.

I had mentioned Maude by name to Ford, remarking that "Mrs. VanCleve" was a southern lady "of color" who was a Republican, which made the President smile. I explained that Maude was past sixty-five but that she couldn't retire because she had to scrape up the money to pay health care costs for a sister who was bedridden as the result of a stroke.

The transcript showed that President Ford had sympathetically assured me that government relief was on the way.

Reading the transcript reassured Maude that the President of the United States personally felt her distress. It also convinced her that the Smith family was an acceptable employer.

After that, Maude—already becoming Ginny's black grandmother—began to spare some affection for us.

Addie died around the time Ginny entered first grade. Preparing to leave us and return to a church-owned retirement home in Indianapolis, Maude came back from my friend Granville Clark's office shaking her head.

"Mr. Clark wouldn't charge me for drawing up that deed on my sister's house," she said.

"That was nice," I said.

"He just said, 'Maude, I know what you did for Addie.'"

BY THE TIME JULIAN CARROLL WON HIS OWN FOUR-YEAR term as governor in 1975, just a year after Watergate, the Republican Party was reeling nationally from the fall of Richard Nixon. While Governor Ronald Reagan prepared to challenge President Ford in the 1976 Republican primaries, Kentucky Democrats began to hear appeals from the Jimmy Carter campaign, which was organizing in Georgia.

The Carter folks were calling friends in other states to expand the former Georgia governor's national network. One such friend was Dale Sights of Henderson, the owner of a uniform rental business. Sights in turn asked his friend Walt Dear—the publisher of Henderson, Kentucky's *Gleaner* and a friend of mine—to invite me to Carter's upcoming Kentucky kickoff in Louisville.

"It's turnabout time," Dear said, reminding me that Sights had attended the "Goals for Coal" program in Russellville.

I went to the meeting, but I wasn't expecting much. So I was surprised to see Ed Prichard on the front row of the hotel conference room, sitting with Bill Cox of Madisonville, Kentucky, who had been Julian Carroll's campaign manager. The dark horse Carter was better connected than I thought.

Because of my new commitment to government-funded KET, I wanted to avoid appearing partisan. So I attended the meeting in the role of an interested reporter, which I certainly was.

A few months later, when Carroll called a press conference to endorse Carter, most of the state's former Democratic governors were there to meet the beaming candidate.

Also present was Todd Hollenbach, the county judge-executive of Jefferson County, Kentucky. Dressed in a jumpsuit and sporting a deep tan, the toothy Hollenbach whispered to me that he had interrupted a Florida vacation to fly back for Carroll's endorsement.

"That was quite a sacrifice, Todd," I said.

"Well, Julian asked me to," Hollenbach said. "We're good friends."

Which I had thought was so, all through that primary when they ran against each other.

"I promise an administration as good as the American people," Carter said. Happy Chandler and Bert Combs, sitting side by side, smiled approvingly.

There I was, at Louisville's Galt House Hotel, with the Governor of Kentucky, the chief executive of Jefferson County, and a former Georgia governor who wanted to be President of the United States.

Looking at Carter, I felt we had both come a long way in Dixie. Like Carroll, Carter was a governor for the new South. And my life in journalism was changing again, and I liked it.

When Len Press, the new grand master of my career, hired me for *Comment*, he gave me the lights, sound, and cameras necessary to talk to thousands of Kentuckians on Friday nights. Each week as I drove home from Lexington, Kentucky, to my little papers, I felt like Cinderella. My coach was really a pumpkin, but I didn't care.

I had the best of two worlds.

-46-
The Talent Pool

THERE ARE SOME EIGHT THOUSAND WEEKLY PAPERS in our country, covering events of importance to America's rural readers. Yes, the rural population is dwindling, but at fifty to sixty million people, it is still too significant to be ignored.

Community journalism is a challenge. The wages are low; there is never enough help. Talent, such as it is, is where you find it.

If you are lucky, there will be romantics who love the country, young people who want to work in their hometowns, or everyday folks to whom you can teach the business.

I was lucky. I found all of those types and more.

If I didn't radiate the glamour of a big city editor, I generated enough excitement to keep together a staff that kept me going.

JEANNIE LEEDOM, THE DAUGHTER OF WALTER LEEDOM, who owned a downtown clothing store in Russellville, was a student at the University of Kentucky when she phoned me in 1970 to report that Governor Louie Nunn had sent the National Guard to the UK campus after an old ROTC building was burned during an antiwar protest. Jeannie soon became my first full-time reporter with a college degree in journalism.

Good-natured, cheerfully versatile, and well-informed about our county, Jeannie was a mainstay at our papers for twenty-three years. She wrote news, sold ads, did page layouts, and, until she married, traveled to other towns to edit papers I had just bought until I could hire permanent management.

Long after she left our paper (for a job with better benefits) Jeannie wrote me a letter telling of her memories of nights spent at the Goodnight Motel in Cadiz, Kentucky, planning her wedding. The wedding was scheduled for the fall of 1972 in Russellville, but Jeannie was stuck in Cadiz that summer, working on the *Cadiz Record*, which we had just purchased. She also wrote movingly of the love she felt "from my newspaper family" when her father died and when her twins were born, and of the maternity leave I gave her so she could stay home with those twins before any special laws required employers to do so.

JEANNIE'S DESK MATE for many of his forty years in journalism was Jim Turner, another Russellville native. Jim also taught at Russellville High School off and on for twenty-seven years, specializing in speech and drama. He coached many students to statewide awards, and my daughter Catherine to a third-place finish at the 1977 National Forensic League national tournament.

Energetic and versatile enough to be a sports columnist and, finally, an assistant managing editor (while teaching), Jim also worked part-time at the local radio station broadcasting sports and news after school for five years. In his sixties, Jim began an online digital newspaper, *The Logan Journal,* with his son.

Not long ago, Jim shared with me his recollections of our years working together.

"I have only positive thoughts about my days with you, although I was frustrated often about how late you started writing," Jim wrote me. "You tended to be more interested in community, state, and national affairs than you were in getting out a good newspaper on a regular basis.

"What and who you knew, though, made us a better paper when you got around to us. ... After you left, I spent most of my remaining years wishing you would walk through that door again."

IN MY FIRST YEAR IN LOGAN COUNTY, Charlie and Dottie Snyder bought *The Enterprise,* a very small weekly at Adairville on the Tennessee border. They befriended me when I was lonely. I would sometimes take the bus south to join them for supper, and then Charlie would drive me the twelve miles back to the Kaintuck.

By the time I started *The Logan Leader* in 1968, the Snyders had sold *The Enterprise* to the Barretts of Ohio County, Kentucky. Charlie became the *Leader*'s composing-room foreman.

Charlie had an easygoing disposition. Everybody loved him, with one exception: Eugene Carnall, our press foreman. Gene probably resented Charlie's popularity, but he tolerated him. He even understood when I rehired Charlie after I'd fired him.

Charlie became an alcoholic. When he didn't respond to treatments I paid for, I fired him, even though he was a stockholder.

The firing worked. When Charlie came to see me after going to thirty AA meetings in thirty days, I sent him back to the composing room as boss again. That time, he truly *was* in recovery, and that's how he stayed for the rest of his life—not only sober, but a pillar of help for other alcoholics trying to whip their addiction to booze.

As a deputy jailer in his retirement years, Charlie ran AA meetings in the jail. Wilnah Upton, our receptionist, played the piano in a little Baptist mission in the Bottom, where Charlie and I once bought whiskey from the black bootleggers. When Wilnah told Charlie she needed a man at the church on Sundays to keep order and clean up after services, he came.

Those two friends from the paper ran that mission until they died. At Charlie's memorial service there, the church was packed with people he had helped with different problems.

Dear to me in memory are loyal people like Eugene, the press foreman, Judy Murphy, who set the first type for *The Logan Leader* and hung onto that job long after I left, and Virginia "Gin" Lloyd, an Army widow who was a sharp proofreader.

Gin used to fuss at me when I cussed too much. "Such a vocabulary you have," she said. "You can talk better than that."

But at ninety, Gin seemed to have forgiven me when I saw her at a company reunion.

Yes, she said she still remembered trying to clean up my language. But she also recalled the advice I'd given her one day when she was complaining—in her own genteel way—about problems we were having with the staff at the post office, where we mailed our papers every week.

Gin said, "Al, I told you 'People can be such a bother.' But you cooled me off."

"You said, 'Yes, Gin, but they're all we have to work with.'"

WHEN JO MOTSINGER, MY MAKEUP PERSON AT KET in Lexington, told me that Larry Craig had been the smartest boy in her class at Todd County High School, that was enough for me. Back in Russellville, I hired Larry as a part-time reporter.

Larry was a stout lad in overalls with a chew of tobacco in his jaw and a shotgun in his pickup when he began to cover the Logan County school board, whose members detested me. At the time, Larry was also pastoring a rural Baptist church in south Logan County and helping his wife Patty pay her college tuition.

As soon as the board members concluded that Larry shared my enthusiasm for consolidation of the county high schools, they used their influence with Larry's elders and got him fired as pastor.

Over in Todd County, where his father had a barbershop in town and a farm in the country, there were no employment calls for Larry. But the Lord soon called Larry to pastor a little church at Logan County's northern border. The congregation there was mostly Muhlenberg County coal miners, including several of the top union leaders.

My friend Nat Caldwell, from *The Tennessean* in Nashville, telephoned me in November 1974 about the stories Larry had written about the national bituminous coal strike. Nat said Larry's stories were the best portrayal of the miners' problems and their side of the strike that he had read in any paper.

The next night, Larry was sitting in my living room, being interviewed about the strike by Nat and Rudy Abramson, the national correspondent for the *Los Angeles Times* Washington bureau. (Rudy was a former *Tennessean* reporter who had broken into the big time.) On assignment to explain the coal strike issues to readers, Abramson had touched base with his old friend Nat, who dragged him up to Russellville through a thick fog to hear Larry Craig shine light on the miners' side of the strike.

At the time I got to know him, Larry didn't have much education. What he had was good sense and a pithy style of writing and talking. Larry eventually got a degree, bought my Morgantown paper, and became a journalism instructor at Western and president of the Kentucky Press Association. (With support from Larry, Patty ended up with a doctorate in education.) He achieved statewide attention when a vengeful Ku Klux Klan burned down his church over a scornful anti-Klan sermon.

IN THE SPRING OF 1976, I hosted a *Comment on Kentucky* show with three of the state's college newspaper editors as panelists. By that fall, one of those graduates—Al Cross—was temporarily living on the third floor of our house and sharing a room and bath with my son, Carter.

Al, who was from Albany, in Clinton County, Kentucky, had edited the *College Heights Herald* at Western Kentucky University in Bowling Green. His contribution to that episode of *Comment*, and our conversation on the ride between Bowling Green and Lexington, convinced me he was smart. When I got back to Russellville, I knew I wanted Al to edit one of my papers the minute I could hire him.

That summer, having just graduated, Al was running a second paper in a one-paper town, Monticello, Kentucky. I phoned him with a job offer as a reporter.

To my astonishment, he turned me down.

Al explained that he intended to buy that second paper and compete with the existing weekly in a town I believed was too small for two papers. Amazed and a little offended, I concluded that maybe the kid wasn't as smart as I thought.

Nevertheless, I called his father.

Perry Cross owned a farm and part of a real estate firm, ran a one-man loan office, and had been a Chevrolet-Buick dealer and a Republican member of the Kentucky House of Representatives. He was forty-nine when Al was born, which likely accounted for young Al's maturity. Al spoke as if he had never been a kid.

"Mr. Cross, do you know who I am?" I asked Perry.

"I've heard of ye, Al."

"That's a smart boy you have, but he's just done a dumb thing."

"Why, did he turn you down?"

"Mr. Cross," I said, "you've worked hard for your money."

"Sure have," Perry said.

"Your son doesn't know it, but that paper he wants to buy is already bankrupt."

Perry Cross didn't say anything.

"He'll likely want you to invest," I added.

Silence.

"At your age, that's a risk you don't need to take ..."

More silence.

"Especially since I've offered him $110 a week, and he can live free at my big old house for two months, to get on his feet."

Still nothing from Perry.

"Talk to him, Mr. Cross," I urged.

Two days or two months later—Al and I still can't agree—I answered the phone and heard the surliest words imaginable from a new hire.

"So when"—Al let out a deep sigh—"do I"—another sigh, and then a snarl—"come to work?"[44]

"How about the first of September?" I proposed.

"That's Labor Day," Al said with disdain. "You don't take holidays?"

I said it would be okay if he waited until Tuesday.

Thus began a long association with the kid who became the man I thought he could be—first as my reporter and editor for a few years, and then *The Courier-Journal's* man for twenty-six years, nearly seventeen of them as chief political writer.

I will note, with pride, that when Perry Cross was dying in 1993, he often could see and hear his bright son talking politics on TV with the Al who wouldn't take "no" for an answer.

---

[44] The real story, according to Al Cross, is that his father didn't interfere in his plans. Al says his small paper's largest advertiser quit advertising, and he could see it was time to close down. A happy coincidence for all. Others besides Cross who left and found success elsewhere included John Barnes, who became a financial reporter and then a stockbroker in Little Rock; Cathy Zion, magazine publisher in Louisville, and Larry Wilkerson, editorial writer, The *Atlanta Constitution*.

-47-
TV, TVA, and the ARC

WHEN WE STARTED *COMMENT ON KENTUCKY,* Len wanted it to be a journalists' show. He proposed we call it *Kentucky Week in Review.* I countered with *Comment on Kentucky,* and he yielded.

Len envisioned that the show would feature reporters talking about government and politics, but I broadened that mission to include authors, professors, filmmakers, even poets. *The Wall Street Journal* had thrived by reporting on many endeavors under the rubric of "business," and I took the same liberty with "politics," expanding our reach to include business, health, and the arts.

In weeks when Kentucky suffered major disasters, though, we were flexible. I did some memorable shows about coal mine fatalities, plane and school bus crashes, a nightclub fire, droughts, and floods.

THE THREE OR FOUR PANELISTS I CHOSE for each week's *Comment* usually featured some of the best talent from the state's larger papers, broadcast stations, and the wire services.

Because I didn't live at Frankfort, I kept close phone contact with the news bureaus there all week. By Tuesday, I usually had settled on the week's guests. Then I called those reporters to assign them the topics I wanted them to discuss on Friday night's show. On Friday afternoons, I'd stop somewhere on the drive from Russellville to KET's Lexington studio to phone in the headlines to lead off that night's broadcast.

The guests who appeared on my show received modest fees, but the payments came from a production fund fed by so many different sources that no guest's check could be traced to a particular special interest.

A *Comment* audience favorite for many years was Sy Ramsey, from the AP's Frankfort bureau. A tough, infantry veteran who had seen combat in World War II, the humorously cynical Sy could write or dictate a story faster than any reporter I ever knew. No matter how complex the news of the day, Sy always wrapped it up in time for his late-afternoon tennis matches.

When I first invited Sy to be among the initial guests on *Comment,* he declined. "The AP has no opinions about the news," he explained in a patronizing tone.

"Oh, I just want background and your insight," I told him. "KET is neutral, you know."

That satisfied Sy. He went on to become the most opinionated reporter ever on *Comment.*

Our viewers loved Sy's cranky, sometimes outrageous asides.

When Lt. Governor Thelma Stovall vetoed the state legislature's repeal of support for the federal Equal Rights Amendment, Sy enraged the feminists by speculating that the idea occurred "while she was washing the curtains at the mansion."

A perennial candidate for governor to whom I was required to give airtime each election cycle once accused Sy during a broadcast of making fun of her.

"That's all right," I reassured the woman as the cameras rolled. "He talks to everyone that way." (There was loud and appreciative laughter on the set that night.)

I was a frequent target of Sy's dismissive remarks. Using descriptive language never before heard in a *Comment* broadcast, he once wearily described a candidates' debate I had moderated as "so much crap."

Sy died in 1983 of a heart attack. At his memorial service in the House chambers at the state capitol, AP's new Kentucky chief, who lived outside the reach of cable and had never seen *Comment*, seemed pleased when I explained that Sy treated every governor just alike.

"That's wonderful to hear, Al," the bureau boss said.

"Yes," I said. "With utter contempt."

FROM THE FIRST *COMMENT* SHOW on November 11, 1974, until the last, on November 16, 2007, I selected the guests and the topics. No one ever told me which guests to invite or to blacklist, mandated topics we should or shouldn't discuss, or censored me. If there were governors or lawmakers who complained about what was said on *Comment*, the KET managers must have taken the heat, because I never heard about it.

Obviously, I was discreet enough to create boundaries, as Len and the KET staff trusted me to be. I sought advice from the panelists on sticky issues. They were some of the best reporters and editors in Kentucky. We worked by *my* few, responsible rules—no one else's— and I think most viewers would agree the programs were generously unfettered.

The tradition of an independent *Comment* that Len established was protected by his successors as KET executive director: Ginni Fox, Mac Wall, and Shae Hopkins. *Comment on Kentucky* was and is a public television showpiece for the First Amendment.

WITH *COMMENT*, LEN HAD GIVEN ME the opportunity to explore a different kind of journalism. During America's Bicentennial in 1976, I was able to expand my television ambitions a bit farther.

I applied for and received a grant to produce seventeen documentaries about people whom I viewed as representative Kentuckians two hundred years after the birth of the nation. Long on imagination but short on details, I was clueless about how to complete the project. Len assigned a creative young director, George Rasmussen, to bail me out.

Those bicentennial programs, aired on KET, included an interview with Colonel Harland Sanders of KFC fame, who fried a kettle of chicken for me and confided that "the wing's my favorite piece." Another documentary featured Lyman Johnson, the venerable black teacher of Louisville who integrated UK and broke the color barrier in Louisville public places such as the public library and movie theaters.

The subjects of another of the bicentennial films were Tom and Pat Gish, the courageous publishers of *The Mountain Eagle* in Whitesburg, Kentucky, who fought corruption in the courthouse and the coal industry. And I had a memorable interview with Harriette Simpson Arnow, the author of *The Dollmaker*, a book about a displaced Kentuckians set in World War II Detroit. (With its focus on the home front, not the battlefront, that novel is my pick for the best American novel about that conflict.)

THE "GOALS FOR COAL" RALLY at Russellville in 1974 established my interest in energy issues. Two years later, that demonstrated interest led to an interesting development and, ultimately, a new chapter in my life.

During Christmas week in 1976, I joined Kentucky's governor, its two United States Senators, and the state campaign manager for Jimmy Carter, who had just been elected President, on a conference call.

The message from the callers, all of whom were Democrats, was that as soon as Carter was inaugurated in January, they would ask him to name me to a vacancy on the Tennessee Valley Authority's three-person board of directors.

This was heady stuff.

The TVA, which serves seven states, is the country's largest public utility. Since its New Deal beginnings in the 1930s, TVA has been charged with developing the 650-mile Tennessee River system and its great valley. The utility's programs have included navigation, flood, and erosion control; improvement of fish and wildlife habitats; economic expansion; reforestation; and even malaria control.

As important to me as the TVA's impact on the region where I'd spent most of my life was the personal connection I felt to it. It was the TVA that had turned on the lights at Here We Are Farm in Hendersonville when I was in high school. It was the TVA that my grandparents, Graeme and the Major, had seen as a beacon of progress and that my uncles McGregor and Lad had called "socialistic" when I was a boy.

By 1976, that boy had become a man who was ready to keep the lights on, the rates low, and provide all those services.

THE CALL FROM THE POLITICAL LEADERS—Governor Carroll, Senator Ford, and Senator Walter "Dee" Huddleston, and Carter's friend and state campaign manager, Dale Sights—was exciting, but not a surprise. I had hinted—more like strongly signaled—that I was available.

After Carter was elected, I asked Carroll to support me for the TVA appointment. In retrospect, I should not have, out of ethical concerns for my role with *Comment*.[45]

There were plausible reasons for these influential Democrats to offer my name to the new president.

I was a Kentuckian, and TVA was Kentucky coal's largest customer. TVA supplied electric power to some thirty counties in western Kentucky, where I owned several papers, among them *The Cadiz Record*, in a town near the vast TVA-managed recreation area known as the Land Between the Lakes. And I was familiar with the politics of public power, having grown up on family disagreements about the New Deal generally and TVA specifically.

---

[45] I don't recall ever shading a story on TV or in the papers to favor a governor, least of all for Carroll, who took endless raps on the *Comment* show. The best reference for my fairness is the memory of our viewers, as well as of the reporter/panelists on the show, who would have been furious—and said so—had I ever tried to slant the program. Nevertheless, my awareness of what was ethical grew, turning me back to the conscience of a reporter from the ambitions of a publisher.

Besides, I was probably the first newspaper publisher in Kentucky to endorse Carter for president.

Because Carroll endorsed Carter early in the presidential campaign, many Kentuckians assumed that the new president owed the governor. So was the TVA appointment in the bag?

No. Months before the vacancy was filled, I knew the job was not going to me.

IN EARLY 1977, MY HOMETOWN FRIEND LARRY FORGY asked John Sherman Cooper, who by then was retired from the Senate and practicing law in Washington, to scope out my prospects. After taking me to lunch, Cooper sent me to Lee White, his former aide and a former chairman of the Federal Power Commission (now known as the Federal Energy Regulatory Commission).

"It's not going to happen," White told me. "Jimmy Carter is an engineer. He thinks the TVA is about electricity, not politics. David Freeman will probably be the new director and then the chairman after Red Wagner (who was then TVA chairman) retires."

Freeman was an engineer, a former TVA lawyer, and a friend of Carter's who at that time was working for a Senate committee on energy matters. He had authored a book that promoted energy conservation and the protection of the environment from the pollution caused by burning coal for electricity. TVA's critics admired Freeman as a conservationist; the boomers in the Tennessee Valley feared he was a too much an environmentalist.

I had learned a few things over the years about getting past grudges. So that day in Washington, I didn't head for home until I had gone to see Freeman at his office. He was friendly, but he disavowed any ambition for a TVA appointment, a lie so amusing neither of us could keep from smiling.

Ultimately Carter appointed Freeman director of the TVA, and he later became its chairman.

Freeman impressed me as a good choice to stand up to the old guard at TVA. His views were antithetical to those of Wagner, who once told me that clean air regulations didn't apply to TVA.

Wagner's critics said he had tackled a nuclear power expansion as if he were building more dams. This clumsy approach went awry and plunged TVA into billions of dollars in debt. I was mercifully spared responsibility for resolving that problem when Carter appointed Freeman instead of me.

AFTER FREEMAN WENT ON THE TVA BOARD, Martha Helen and I invited him to a dinner at our Russellville home to meet some of the prominent western Kentucky friends who had supported my appointment. Freeman was to fly to the gathering from the TVA's headquarters in Knoxville, Tennessee.

Over an hour into the party, the guest of honor was a no-show. The welcoming committee—Russellville's mayor and the local TVA manager—reported there were no signs of an incoming plane at Russellville's little airport.

About 7:30 p.m., our phone rang. It was Freeman.

"I'm at the airport, Al," he said. "There's no one here. Can somebody come get me?"

"The mayor and another man are waiting for you, Dave," I said.

Then I heard Freeman talking to the pilot. "Where are we?" Freeman asked him.

"Russellville, Alabama," the pilot said.

"Oh, my God," said Freeman.

"No wonder TVA is screwed up!"

TWO YEARS LATER, IN SEPTEMBER 1979, Senator Ford called me from Washington.

"How would you like to be chairman of the Appalachian Regional Commission (ARC)?" he asked.

I replied with a question of my own.

"Is that the one with all the money?"

"Yeah," Ford said, "And the White House says they won't jerk you around on this one like they did with the TVA. This time the job is yours."

"That's encouraging," I replied.

"There's just one hitch. You have to convince Senator Jennings Randolph that it was his idea."

Ford explained that every county in West Virginia was part of the Appalachian Regional Commission's (ARC) territory, which comprised parts of twelve other states, including Kentucky. The ARC was a survivor of President Johnson's War on Poverty. Designed to improve the economy and quality of life in Appalachia, it was still spending millions of dollars in the region.

"Randolph wants a West Virginian as chairman, but the White House is not going to let that happen," Ford said. "None of those other states will tolerate West Virginia having the key to all those dollars."

"But I don't even know Senator Randolph," I said.

"Well, you will," Ford replied. "He's also chairman of the committee that will have to confirm you.

"You're a fast talker. Come up here and get acquainted."

And that was how Mr. Smith went to Washington.

-48-
Going for It

THE APPALACHIAN REGIONAL COMMISSION was officially created in 1965. Two senators sponsored the authorizing legislation: Jennings Randolph, the West Virginia Democrat I had to court for the nomination, and John Sherman Cooper, the Kentucky Republican I'd long admired.

Governor Bert Combs had proposed a multistate attack on Appalachian poverty at least five years before the ARC was established, after he traveled eastern Kentucky with John Whisman, his assistant who figures in the history of the ARC as one of the chief planners who made it happen. Combs also rallied other governors to seek action.

The creation of the commission also had its roots in the make-or-break 1960 West Virginia Democratic primary campaign between presidential candidates John F. Kennedy and Hubert Humphrey. On his way to victory during that campaign, Kennedy became familiar with the state's poverty. Floods in Appalachia in 1963 reminded Kennedy, who by then was President, of the commitments he had made to the region, and he appointed a committee to recommend a long-range solution that became the ARC. Harry Caudill's *Night Comes to the Cumberlands: A Biography of a Depressed Area,* which was published in 1963, also is credited with making the region's problems a compelling issue for the conscience of the nation.

By the time I flew to Washington sixteen years later for an October 1979 meeting with Senator Randolph, the commission had invested $5 billion in the thirteen-state area it served.

Despite the big bucks, it wasn't long before I realized that many Appalachians were critical of the ARC. Its critics claimed that the commission was responsible for little economic development in the area aside from road building, that it wasn't bringing new industry to the area. A call to my friend Tom Gish, the newspaper publisher in east Kentucky's Whitesburg, produced a scathing indictment of the agency.

"Those people in Washington are out of touch," Gish said. "They treat us like an Indian reservation." Gish railed against managers who, he said, were obsessed with funding "growth centers," ignoring the plight of truly poor communities that might grow with better infrastructure and social services.[46]

"The ARC neglects mine safety, black lung, and other issues," Gish said. "It's just a road builder."

Gish's friend Caudill agreed. He called the ARC a "blind and toothless" watchdog for the region.

Shaken, I called Jim Branscome, a former reporter for Gish's *Mountain Eagle* newspaper who by then was a regional reporter for McGraw-Hill business publications.

"Tom's wrong about those roads, Al," Branscome told me. "I couldn't do my work and the region could never diversify without fixing those horrible road problems.

"Take that job and make the ARC better."

Also pleading, almost tearfully, that I accept the appointment was Sue Lewis. Sue was Senator Dee Huddleston's assistant for eastern Kentucky issues and had done the same work for Senator Cooper when he was in office.

"Take those criticisms as a challenge to fix the problems," Sue said. "Don't run from them."

---

[46] A "growth center" was a town that Whisman and other planners believed had the potential to develop many jobs if given help with its infrastructure. These larger towns would soon pull population out of the smaller towns, ultimately ruining them, Gish feared.

A FEW MINUTES INTO MY MEETING IN WASHINGTON with Senator Randolph—during which we mostly talked about Franklin D. Roosevelt—he declared that I was his kind of guy.

"I like the way this fellow talks," Randolph told an aide who was sitting in on the meeting. I think the senator saw me as a fellow New Dealer.

Promising a speedy confirmation by the Senate Environment and Public Works Committee, which he chaired, Randolph also said he would ask the White House to expedite my FBI security check.

"I want you on the job as soon as possible," Randolph said.

When I left, I called Wendell Ford and told him that, sure enough, I was now the West Virginia senator's choice. My appointment was *his* idea.

And the old man had made up my mind for me. I was sure I wanted the job.

BECAUSE HE CHAIRED A COMMITTEE, Jennings Randolph was one of the most powerful senators. But background checks for a presidential appointment take awhile, no matter how impatient a member of Congress may be.

The process began with a pile of forms about my personal finances. I didn't need a blind trust for my modest assets, mostly newspaper stock, but I had to resign as head of my company. Virginia Page succeeded me as president of Al Smith Communications.

The FBI also wanted every address where I had lived since birth and the name of every employer for whom I'd ever worked.

There were also questions about my health, which I tackled head-on. Remembering my friend Mac, the mail carrier I'd met through AA years earlier for whom I had such respect, I volunteered that I was an alcoholic recovering in AA who had not had a drink in seventeen years. I never hear a word of challenge on that.

A pleasant surprise came from the letter I wrote to George Healy, my one-time managing editor at *The Times-Picayune* back in

New Orleans. I told him to expect some government callers asking questions about me. I added that I was a different person from the kid who walked out on him in 1954 and staggered over to the rival *Item.*

Healy replied with a cordial letter but went further. When the news of my appointment and confirmation went out on the wires three months later, he wrote a story for *The Times-Picayune*, connecting the stronger points of a young man's New Orleans newspaper career to that of the fifty-two-year-old Kentucky journalist who was going to Washington. He sent me a clipping with a letter of congratulations.

That letter ended for me what many recovering alcoholics living a sober life have experienced: nightmares about being fired for drinking. Healy never again appeared in my dreams as a shadowy, angry authority figure. With the letter and article, he had removed himself from my subconscious, but not my gratitude list.

MY CONFIRMATION before Senator Randolph's committee came in late December 1979. Until I was sworn in, I had newspapers to run and a TV program to prepare. On *Comment* that year, there was much discussion about a governor's race that was turning out to be a lot more exciting than expected.

John Y. Brown Jr., the Kentucky entrepreneur who had catapulted Kentucky Fried Chicken into a global enterprise, married former Miss America Phyllis George in March of that year in a service conducted by Dr. Norman Vincent Peale in New York.

The day of the wedding, I had a lengthy phone conversation[47] with Ed Ryan, the Washington correspondent for *The Courier-Journal.*

Ryan told me that, after talking for two hours with Brown the night before the wedding, he was convinced that Brown was about to

---

[47] The credit card bill for that phone call was my only expense account item that KET ever challenged. "How could you and Ed spend $90 talking about a celebrity wedding for a show about politics?" asked Sid Webb, a KET deputy director.

jump into the governor's race against five announced candidates a mere ten weeks before the primary.

Ryan was about to tell his *Courier* readers and my *Comment* viewers that Brown, the supercharged multimillionaire, would be interrupting his honeymoon on a gamble that he could catch up and beat the field of other Democrats.

When the story broke, my teenage son Carter, the jock in our family, was already an admirer of Phyllis, by then a high-profile sports broadcaster. I cautioned him to keep his enthusiasm to himself. As moderator of KET's candidate debates, I could not afford to take sides. Carter nodded that he understood.

That was all forgotten when John Y. and his new bride helicoptered into Russellville in search of votes on a weekend when Martha Helen and I were away. In the middle of Riley-White Drug Store on the downtown square, Phyllis Brown hugged Carter. By the time Martha Helen and I got home, Carter had delivered the Sunday *Courier-Journal* all over town in a car with a bumper sticker that read "Brown for Governor."

IN A BREAK FROM THE PAST that stunned county courthouse political machines, Brown ran what I called a 3-M campaign: *millions*, *media*, and *Miss America.*

He used his millions to buy new kinds of media support—phone banks for calls, constant polling, and videotaped press conferences— with the beautiful, personable Miss America at his side to dazzle supporters.

By the day of the primary, two of the candidates pulled out in favor of Brown. That left Louisville's millionaire mayor Harvey Sloane, who was supported by the Bingham family, Lieutenant Governor Thelma Stovall, and attorney Terry McBrayer, whom Governor Carroll endorsed, to lead the casualties.

Brown triumphed with a surprising total of 165,158 votes— 25,000 more than Sloane, his nearest opponent.

The commentators on my show that night were Ed Prichard and Larry Forgy. When the cameras shut down and the studio lights came up, Prichard, a Sloane supporter, slumped over the table on the set, head down on his folded arms. Then, sitting up and opening his blind eyes wide, he raised a rhetorical question:

"What have we seen tonight—the birth of a statesman, or the death of a salesman?"

IN THE RUN-UP TO THE NOVEMBER GENERAL ELECTION, Republican Louie Nunn, who was seeking a second term as governor, offered a hapless attack on Brown's glitzy "lifestyle" that went nowhere. Brown won by 176,000 votes.

Sometime before the inauguration, I had a chance to suggest to Phyllis Brown that after I got to Washington, she and I might partner to promote tourism in eastern Kentucky. Phyllis soon took up the tourism cause in a shrewdly focused way, promoting the sale of Kentucky crafts and the work of Kentucky artists in the state parks' gift shops.

In what I thought were my last months as chairman of the state Arts Commission, I sought a $10,000 grant from outgoing Governor Carroll to sponsor a two-day writers' conference at the University of Louisville. The event would be a reunion of writers who had left the state and others who still lived in Kentucky. With a contingency fund bulging with dollars from new taxes in a fair economy, Carroll was turning into what I called a "kind king," and was forthcoming with the money for the conference.

Anxious to leave a supportive image with Louisville voters, Carroll also invited me to join him in breaking ground there for a new center for the performing arts.

The dirt we turned was still fresh when the new governor precipitously cancelled the project. He wasn't against the center as such, Brown explained: He just wanted to have some input before it was built, especially to see if he could reduce the projected costs that Carroll had approved.

What was really going on was that the new governor was not going to let the old governor get the credit for a monument the new governor would have to pay for.

As an outsider looking in on the political scene for thirty years, I was getting a new perspective. I was up close in the kitchen, seeing how the sausage was made.

Washington: Carter's Man

AN OPTIMIST IN 1980 WAS A COUNTRY EDITOR in Kentucky who would accept a job from President Jimmy Carter, move to Washington in January with his wife and an eight-year-old daughter—and buy a house! I did all that. Of course, I expected Jimmy Carter to win a second term and thought we'd be in Washington for five years. I did not foresee that the Iran hostage crisis and a sick economy with extraordinarily high interest rates would make Carter a one-term president.

In my last weeks in Kentucky, I scrambled to learn about the ARC and the thirteen-state region it supported. Over lunch, I asked Ken Kurtz, a Lexington newscaster from West Virginia, to tell me about his home state.

"What's West Virginia like?" I asked.

"Like East Kentucky," he said. "Only more so."

At Lexington's posh Coach House, I hosted a dinner for author and activist Harry Caudill from Whitesburg in east Kentucky and his wife Anne. The Caudills were temporarily living in Lexington while Harry was teaching at UK.

When we broke up about midnight, after discussing poverty over an embarrassingly fancy meal, I offered them an apology for the government that called me to Washington.

"You know how the Feds are," I joked. "They know so little about Kentucky that they're sending a guy from the flat side of the state to run a program for the mountain side."

"That's all right, Al," Harry said, "You've had the rural experience—and that's what counts."

With that blessing from Appalachia's most influential writer, I never again apologized for my roots in Russellville. I considered my appointment to head the ARC as a return to my deeper roots on the Cumberland Plateau in Tennessee, where my father was born in Cookeville, and his parents and Confederate grandfather published a weekly newspaper and crusaded for a college, a railroad, and better highways to the Cumberland Mountains.

Of course, some picky folks might wonder what skills the owner of a few little country newspapers possessed that qualified him to run a government agency with a $300 million dollar budget.

I thought about that also. But after a few visits to Washington to get oriented, I calmed down.

Washington, I decided, was just another county courthouse, only bigger. It was still about people in pursuit of resources and patronage. The question there was the same the farmers asked about roads in Logan County, "Who gets the rock?" Only now, the "rock" was larger projects, and many more dollars.

I CONSIDERED THAT SIMILARITY as I flew to Washington for a meeting with President Carter. Still, this was a lot different from that first day at the Logan Courthouse in January 1958 when I'd met Doc Beauchamp, Jim Lyne, and Rayburn Smith.

"You were one of my first supporters in Kentucky," the president said, shaking my hand in the Oval Office.

"Yes, sir—that I was."

"I hope you can do some good with the ARC."

"I'll try," I said. I thought it best not to mention the leaked memo I'd seen, on which Carter had penciled a skeptical note describing the ARC as a "pork barrel for southern governors."

"I hope you can cooperate with David Freeman and the TVA."

"Yes, sir," I said again. I remembered that Lee White, John Sherman Cooper's former aide, had sardonically noted that this engineer president thought the TVA was just "about electricity," meaning he was a little slow on the political perspective.

But I wasn't visiting with the most powerful person on the planet to gossip about his criticisms or his critics.

"Freeman and I are already doing that," I said. "We've discussed targeting social programs together, since the seven TVA states are all in the ARC territory."

"I wish you well," he said with his famous grin.

"I hope I won't disappoint you," I said, sincerely. At that time I didn't suspect he might disappoint me in the upcoming November election.

The President and I shook hands and posed for a picture. As I left the White House, I would like to claim I gave a grateful but not gloating thought to how far I had come—from a tipsy reporter in the French Quarter, or a jittery editor buying booze in the Bottom, to this meeting in the Oval Office. I don't remember. For sure I was looking for my driver. I wasn't used to mornings with chauffeurs any more than with presidents.

BACK IN KENTUCKY, WHERE THE PAPERS CARRIED pictures of me with the President, I took the oath of office from a federal judge, Edward Johnstone of Princeton, Kentucky, at Granville Clark's historic law office in Russellville.

Standing with the judge in front of a cheerful fire, surrounded by family and friends on a snowy January day, I was proud to be a Kentuckian from this town and this county.

I no longer resented the fate that cast me out of New Orleans. I accepted my part for the hard times I suffered, and I was grateful for recovery and redemption. I wasn't wearing a uniform, but I had passed the highest of security clearances, and I was trusted.

I was pleased to have the chance to serve my country again. And just as Taylor Fuqua had said to Jesse Riley after winning the

Russellville mayor's race so many years earlier, "That's what I meant to do."

Joining the Carter Administration in some capacity was an ambition that struck me as I was driving home to Russellville from Lexington a few days before the election in November 1976. Sure that a progressive southerner was headed for the White House, I wanted to join in the action.

With half a dozen papers to manage, a TV show to produce, three children to raise, and a good chunk of debt on my back, I hardly needed another job. But I wanted to volunteer anyway. It was like my senior year in high school. I was crazy enough to think my country needed me and there was a reason I should enlist.

I'm not clear about the reason, but in those days, marveling at life's gifts since I overcame the compulsion that sabotaged my youth, I could get drunk on gratitude.

And that's why I sent a message that I was available and that's why I received a call to Washington three years later.

-50-
Saving Appalachia

MY FIRST DAY ON THE JOB IN WASHINGTON, Henry Krevor, the ARC's executive director, sought my approval of a projected highway budget of $214.6 million for Fiscal Year 1981.[48] I had never held in my hands a spreadsheet showing that many dollars, much less had the authority over spending them.

I had covered enough Logan County Fiscal Court and school board meetings, however, to know what I was supposed to look out for first: my own interests.

The proposed appropriation for Kentucky didn't compare favorably to the amounts allocated for states whose senators and representatives sat on committees that had oversight authority for the ARC.

West Virginia was slated to receive the lion's share of the funds, and that I could understand. This was the province of Senate committee chairmen, Jennings Randolph and Robert C. Byrd. Every county in West Virginia was eligible for ARC monies, a claim no other state could make. No problem there.

But Mississippi and Alabama? Those flat states were *Appalachia*?

I knew that some counties in those states, as well as others from unlikely locations such as South Carolina, had been included in the ARC's thirteen-state region back when the commission was organized in order to garner political support. Since those states were in Dixie, where seniority is highly prized, their senators and representatives were influential.

---

[48] The highway budget was 71 percent of the total ARC budget of nearly $302.4 million for my first year.

Nevertheless, I considered the disproportionate amount of highway dollars to be an insult to Kentucky's legislators and the state's forty-nine[49] ARC counties. I threw a mock fit with Krevor.

"Georgia!" I growled. "If Jimmy Carter needs all these extra dollars swiped from central Appalachia to carry Georgia in November, then he's in worse shape than I thought!"

I told Krevor that Senator Wendell Ford and Senator Dee Huddleston would be outraged at the miniscule allotment he had proposed for Kentucky, as would Carl Perkins, who had represented east Kentucky in the U.S. House since 1948.

Krevor, a tough, temperamental little lawyer from Boston, appeared disappointed. "Oh, my," he said, looking downcast. "This is a surprise."

Then, in a sad voice, he added, "I guess I'll have to accept that the new federal co-chairman[50] is as greedy as the congressmen from Mississippi and Alabama."

For that moment, I loved the man.

My predecessor in the job was Robert W. Scott, a former North Carolina governor who had resigned to go home and run again for that office.

"I want to be treated with the same respect you showed Governor Scott," I told Krevor.

He started to say something, but hesitated. I could read his mind. He and Scott hadn't liked each other.

"*Better* than the governor," I clarified.

The next morning, Krevor brought me a revised spreadsheet showing a $2 million increase in the allotment for Kentucky roads. He could see I was pleased.

---

[49] Today fifty-four Kentucky counties are part of the ARC.

[50] The Commission leadership is partnered by the federal co-chair who represents the President, and a Governors' co-chair (who is rotated annually). The federal co-chair uniquely has veto power in the voting process but, historically, avoids its use.

"That's such an improvement," I declared. "What will this money be for?"

Krevor smiled. "A project I'm calling 'Approaches to the Middlesboro Tunnel.'"

"Whatever works," I said.

WITH A COMMISSION STAFF of some one hundred planners and support folks, Krevor was responsible both to me, as the president's representative, and to the Appalachian governors in the federal-state partnership. Those governors and I were jointly charged by law with creating opportunities for economic development and improving the quality of life in a region where twenty million people lived.

The governors were represented in the ARC's Washington office by a states' designee. During the ARC's first decade, long before I was appointed, the visionary John Whisman of Kentucky held that post. Though each of the thirteen governors was a member of the commission, they were allowed to send an alternate of cabinet or near-cabinet status to routine commission meetings.

My personal staff of a dozen people included Lillian Press, the wife of KET's Len Press. Lil previously had served as an executive assistant to Kentucky's commissioner of mental health and health. I joked that I recruited her because that job taught her to "speak bureaucrat." (Lil's success as my special assistant brought her to the attention of Governor Brown. When Brown later decided to create a Governor's Scholars program for rising high school seniors, he named Lil its founding director.)

Debbie McGuffey, the state Oral History Commission's capable secretary, came along as my Washington secretary. Jim Tucker of Nashville, a planner from the Tennessee governor's office, became the first African-American to hold a major appointment in the federal ARC office. As my special assistant he was adept at smoothing out problems with individual states.

I had inherited from Governor Scott a congressional lobbyist named Linda Fuselier, a Ph.D. in English from the University of California at Berkley. A tiny young woman with a salty wit, Linda, on occasion, cursed like a Teamster. She was a force in the Washington power scramble, not least because of her ability to write an idea on one side of a piece of paper—clearly and concisely—then explain it in three or four minutes.

OUR OLDER CHILDREN WERE IN COLLEGE when we left Russellville. Ginny, then eight, was able to walk to her new school from the house we bought in Alexandria, Virginia.

At historic Christ Church in Alexandria, where George Washington had worshiped, we made new friends and enjoyed chats after services with an old friend, Hodding Carter III, my one-time New Orleans newspaper intern from Greenville, Mississippi. Hodding had gone on to make his family's newspaper, the *Delta Democrat Times,* even more liberal than had his noted parents. He partnered with black friends to form the Freedom Democrat Party in Mississippi.[51]

Hodding, no relation to President Carter, was an assistant secretary of state who appeared frequently on the national evening news to comment about the hostage crisis in Iran.

Speculating on President Carter's chances for reelection as we stood outside the Episcopal church where Robert E. Lee took his first communion, Hodding and I marveled that we had come so far in the South, and in the nation, from the world that Lee had left us.

BEFORE I CAME TO WASHINGTON, the enthusiasm for Lyndon Johnson's War on Poverty had produced significant investments by the ARC in its region: several thousand miles of construction of an

---

[51] In 1964, during the civil rights movement, black and white Mississippians started the Mississippi Freedom Democrats to challenge the whites-only U.S. Democrat party in Mississippi.

Appalachian Development Highway System, access roads for airports, industrial sites, and schools.

Sixty to seventy percent of ARC's budget had once been designated for highway construction, but by the late 1960s and 1970s, agency money flowed for water and sewer, mine reclamation, and solid waste projects as well. Supplemental funding combined with investment from other government agencies to construct health, recreation and tourism facilities; low-cost housing; community colleges; and three hundred vocational schools.[52]

Although the ARC had plenty of critics, small towns and rural counties valued its ability to provide the "first-dollar match"—that is, the initial local contribution to a project in which the largest piece of the pie came from federal and state matching funds.[53]

ARC's planners had flexibility to move quickly on construction work once partners were on board—and the ARC was adept at rallying partners.

An example was the response to the tragic 1967 collapse of the Silver Bridge,[54] which connected West Virginia and Ohio across the Ohio River.

The ARC pressured authorities in both states, as well as the Army Corps of Engineers, to get moving. Reconstruction of the bridge began within three weeks—far more quickly than the typical timetable, in which it might have taken as much as six years to begin the project.[55]

---

[52] Clusters of counties known as Area Development Districts (ADDs) or Councils of Government (COGs) provided input about how to spend ARC money. Those groups initiated wish lists of projects for governors to prioritize before sending them on to our Washington office.

[53] With its capacity to leverage $2 to $4 from other agencies for each ARC dollar, on certain projects, the ARC had had an impact greater than its own budget on the seventies. The ARC unique local match relieved poor communities in its nearly 400 counties from having to scrape up the required "first dollar" from their meager resources.

[54] Forty-six people died when the bridge collapsed while it was full of rush-hour traffic in December 1967.

[55] Cited in *Uneven Ground: Appalachia Since 1945,* Ronald D. Eller, University Press of Kentucky, Lexington, 2008.

Appalachian historian Ron Eller of UK says the best example of the goals, capacity, and energy of the ARC in its early days was the Pikeville cut-through project in Pike County, Kentucky. One of east Kentucky's designated growth centers, Pikeville's downtown business district frequently was flooded by the Levisa Fork of the Big Sandy River.

Inspired by Pikeville's dynamic mayor, William Hambley, the ARC coordinated the efforts of fourteen government agencies to reroute the river through a massive cut in a mountainside to get the waterway, the railroad, and the highway out of the downtown area. The recovered land was used for urban redevelopment.

In his superb book, *Uneven Ground: Appalachia Since 1945,* Eller says the $21 million of federal grants for the cut-through project "rivaled the building of the Panama Canal in the amount of earth that had to be removed. By the turn of the century, as a result in part of the efforts of the ARC, Pikeville had grown into a modern, comprehensive service center."

Eller notes, however, the low-income people in the sixty poorest counties in central Appalachia remained "almost untouched" by the commission's programs. The early "focus on growth" theory,[56] which so angered Whitesburg editor Tom Gish and reformer Harry Caudill, diverted too many dollars to populous areas such as Pittsburgh in northern and Huntsville in southern Appalachia.

Many antipoverty activists saw the program as a boon for the rich and entrenched interests. Although $8 million was spent on research projects before I became federal co-chairman, the research recommendations were rarely executed, Eller writes.

---

[56] Growth theory mandated social overhead and infrastructure investments toward large population centers to maximize growth. Large areas, such as eastern Kentucky, had no major urban centers within the ARC area, according to the early definition. Smaller towns were later included as growth centers. Almost from the beginning of the ARC there was contentious debate about growth.

ONE NIGHT DURING MY FIRST WEEK AT THE ARC, I stayed late at my office to write a letter to James Still, the revered author and poet who was perhaps Appalachia's foremost literary artist.[57] I knew Still, who lived in Hindman in Knott County, Kentucky, from my service with the state Arts Commission.

I told him that I was learning about both the ARC and the region it served and that I regretted the disappointments I'd heard expressed about the agency. I said that I would listen to all the voices in Appalachia, especially the social activists and artists who felt they had been ignored. I wanted to champion all the region. I don't recall how he responded, but it was the beginning of a friendship that involved letters and visits for his birthday parties in Hindman.

Meanwhile, I tried to puzzle my way through the paradoxes of coal mining. Increased demand for coal during the Arab oil embargo had contributed to another spell of relative prosperity for the region, whose economy was prone to boom-and-bust cycles. Per capita income had climbed as a result of the "mailbox" economy—that is, increased receipts of welfare and other government benefits. New roads and infrastructure investments meant increased employment for women in the service sector—low-wage jobs in tourism, finance, health care, and shopping centers—but yielded little of significance in manufacturing.

I got conflicting answers to my questions about how much of the region's spotty new prosperity resulted from the ARC's efforts and how much stemmed from the rising demand for coal. And I wanted to know why relatively little of the coal profits seemed to return to the region to improve its health and education services and facilities.

I was hearing early, explosive reports about research funded by the ARC and conducted by a task force from the Highlander Research and Education Center in east Tennessee (formerly the Highlander

---

[57] *River of Earth*, a slender novel about a coal miner's family moving from camp to camp, is James Still's best-known work. Still won many literary awards for his collections of short stories, poems, and juvenile literature.

Folk School). The study indicated significant absentee ownership of Appalachia's land and resources. The research substantiated gross underpayment of taxes on billions of dollars of mineral wealth and the land that held it. The study apparently confirmed activists' convictions that distant "outside" ownership of more than half the region's land resulted in the "colonial" relationship of an extractive economy. There was much more "take out" than "put back."

What would I do about that land ownership study? It was a back-burner issue but I decided to turn up the heat.

Citing President Carter's instructions to work together, I called TVA's David Freeman and asked for the loan of high-speed computers to accelerate completion of the land study, which he provided. When John Gaventa, then Highlander's coordinator, came to thank me, I teased him about telling *Newsweek* that he "couldn't remember anything" the ARC had done for reformers in Appalachia.

Meanwhile, old-timers like John Sweeney, the government economist President Johnson had selected as the first ARC federal co-chairman, advised me to go all out in support of coal mining. Sweeney said not a word about the side effects of that mining: safety issues, black lung, or land and water pollution. Nor did he mention the decline in mining jobs as coal mining became more mechanized.

Sweeney had been a strong liberal in his day. But he had become a railroad lobbyist, and trains carried coal. It was clear enough where his interests now lay.

"Just get the coal to market," he urged.

WHILE I WAS OPENING A WIDER DOOR for regional activists, I funded a research grant to Harry Caudill. I thought he planned to write a script for a documentary on the pioneer coal camps. Instead, he wrote another book attacking the exploitation of Appalachia, titled *Theirs Be the Power: The Moguls of Eastern Kentucky*.

The book included an interesting account of the development of Middlesboro, Kentucky, by British land companies. Caudill described

John C.C. Mayo's use of the "broad-form deed" to purchase thousands of acres of underground mineral rights for very little and then sell them for a high price, a practice that made him the wealthiest man in Kentucky at his death in 1914.

Caudill also scorched the big strip miners, principally William (Bill) Sturgill, and criticized Sturgill's lawyer (and Caudill's friend), Bert Combs. The University Press of Kentucky found reasons to reject the book, calling it academically deficient.[58] No mention was made of the fact that Bill Sturgill was chairman of the Board of Trustees of the University of Kentucky, the press's largest partner.

Leaving that denial to the judgment of history, I register my own plea that readers not make too much of Harry's acknowledgement of me at the front of the book as someone "who knows what an author appreciates."

Remember—I thought I was funding a historical film.

---

[58] The book ultimately was published by the University of Illinois Press.

-51-
Short-Termer

IN THOSE FIRST MONTHS OF 1980, a parade of Kentuckians visited my office at the ARC.

Dee Davis,[59] one of the most brilliant rural strategists in America, and filmmakers from Appalshop, an arts and education center at Whitesburg, Kentucky, came in search of money to build an auditorium for cultural and tourism purposes. They got the grant they wanted.

Canny old Henry Spalding,[60] an engineer from Hazard, Kentucky, came with a message. Spalding wanted me to remind Kentucky's new governor, John Y. Brown Jr., that highway contractors wouldn't have money to make campaign contributions to politicians unless they had highways to build.

What Spalding wanted was progress on a road that would run between Ashland and Alexandria, Kentucky, near Cincinnati, otherwise known as "the Double A Highway." The old man's message to Brown was "get cracking!"

When the elevator door closed on my guest, I wondered what a tape recording of our conversation would sound like to an FBI agent. There was no promise of a bribe. The old man was just running a tutorial on the facts of life between contractors and politicians, I guess. Yet he certainly fingered me to pass on the message.

William G. Kenton, the speaker of the Kentucky House of Representatives, stopped by the ARC to discuss the new ceiling on the rate of Kentucky state tax increases. Like the popular Proposition

---

[59] Still in Whitesburg, Dee now heads the Center for Rural Strategies.

[60] I liked Henry Spalding. He was the only Kentuckian I ever met who knew my grandfather, the Major. He had done a coal survey for my grandfather's railroad, the Tennessee Central, in Monterey, Tennessee.

13 in California, this was House Bill (HB) 44, limiting the growth of taxes in Kentucky. It was initiated by Lieutenant Governor Thelma Stovall the previous year, 1979. Kenton agreed with her and wanted to rebuff requests to mitigate it.

A big man with a voice to match, which earned him the nickname "Boom Boom," Kenton ended up getting his way.[61] Governor Brown, to whom the critics of HB 44 appealed, disdained spending time trying to control the legislature. The newspapers had long called for legislative independence, and it happened on Brown's watch—not as an exercise in governmental reform, but because he didn't care.

NONE OF THE NEW PEOPLE IN MY LIFE, not even Governor Brown, exuded the superpower that flowed from Senator Robert C. Byrd of West Virginia. A former Senate majority leader, Byrd had stepped down from that post so he could become chairman of the Senate Appropriations Committee and "do more for the folks" back home in West Virginia.

Senator Byrd called me to a meeting one day to do exactly that. The purpose of the session was to fix the flooding problems that had devastated little Matewan, West Virginia, in the narrow valley of the Tug Fork of the Big Sandy River.

Matewan had seen thirty floods in almost as many years. One of them, in 1977, had destroyed a third of the community's houses, its city hall, its fire trucks, its sewer and water services, and a medical clinic.

---

[61] I thought Kenton's advocacy of this anti-tax provision was a terrible idea, but then, I wasn't planning to run for governor in 1983. A year after his visit, when I was back in Kentucky, Kenton asked me to manage his campaign in that race. I was shocked; that was a worse idea than HB 44. Sadly, before I could turn Kenton down, he died suddenly on November 5, 1981. This was a loss for Kentucky. Kenton had many good ideas, among them the Kentucky Horse Park, for which he wrote the establishing legislation.

Senator Byrd wanted a half mile of flood wall to protect Matewan and $57 million to build it. You might say he was taking up a collection.

Representatives of each federal agency that potentially might write a check filled every chair in the room that day. The overflow lined up against the walls.

"Mr. HUD," Senator Byrd called out, "what can you do?"

"I guess $9 million, Senator," the representative from Housing and Urban Development responded.

"HUD: $12 million," Byrd said, and jotted something on a legal pad.

Moving down the line, Byrd said, "Mr. Army Engineers?"

"Twelve million, Mr. Chairman," a uniformed colonel replied.

"Corps of Engineers, $16 million," Byrd muttered, scribbling again on his legal pad.

"Housing Authority? ...

"Highway Administration? ..."

And so it went, around the room, until the chairman had recorded his raise-the-ante total of $32 million in pledges.

"That should get the project started," Byrd announced. The balance would be covered by an earmarked appropriation.

And I figured the ARC could plug some of the gaps.[62]

THROUGH THE REST OF 1980, I traveled the thirteen Appalachian states as a sort of cargo god, scattering modest grants from Portsmouth, Ohio, to Dalton, Georgia, always citing the support of President Carter for whatever project was proposed.

At every airport, there were men in suits proposing projects, including a former West Virginia chief executive at Beckley, Hulett Smith, who introduced himself as the West Virginia governor who had *not* gone to prison.

---

[62] These figures I give are from memory, not at all exact. But the sense of the session is accurate—Byrd raised every proffered amount.

In Pennsylvania, ignoring reports about Mafia links to the anthracite coal business, as well as to pizza shops, I introduced Jim Tucker, my aide from Nashville, to some thick-set gents in dark suits. (Jim later recalled that the market for anthracite, or "hard" coal, recovered "almost before I learned how to spell it.")

I flew a day of campaign stops on Air Force Two with Vice President Walter Mondale as he campaigned for Carter's reelection. My seatmate was United Mine Workers President Sam Church, who chewed tobacco and spit into a Dixie cup.

Mondale entertained us with stories about Jennings Randolph. The Vice President remembered that when he was a U.S. Senator from Minnesota, "The old man (Randolph) kept promising me assistance for my state if I helped with his."

Mondale smiled. "I always went along. And my votes turned out dollars for West Virginia and pennies for Minnesota."

On the ground in West Virginia, I was hazed by soot-faced miners, half-dressed when I visited their bathhouse with their congressman, Nick Rahall.

"Who's your friend, Nick—another crook from Washington?"

In a small commercial plane, I flew to Asheville, North Carolina, with Mondale's wife Joan and her social secretary, Bess Clements Abell. We were guests at a celebration of the ARC-funded cleanup of pollution in the French Broad River.

While we were in Asheville, Bess said something that startled me.

"You have the only other job I've ever thought I would want in Washington," she told me. "Giving out money to fix problems, helping where there had been no help ..."

Bess Clements Abell was the daughter of Earle Clements. She was as much a Washington insider as anyone could be. Her father had been one of LBJ's closest friends, and she had been Mrs. Johnson's social secretary.

I told Bess I needed her help to get an interview with her father.

"I'll fix that," she promised. "Dad has retired home to Morganfield. He needs conversation with someone like you."

Within a month, Earle Clements and I had become phone pals, thanks to Bess.

I called him several times for cordial conversations about politics. Each time, I'd ask for a date to televise an interview. Each time, he put me off, always promising "later."

After Bess called one day and said her father was ready, I attended a public tribute to Clements at the Seelbach Hotel in Louisville.

The ballroom was packed that day with old-timers from the Chandler wars, and there were many speeches.

Hobbling to the podium to respond, Clements was in poor shape, his body frail, and his memory faltering.

I realized then that the TV interview would never happen. We had waited too long.

AT COOKEVILLE, TENNESSEE, my father's boyhood home, my Aunt Dollie and I both spoke at a community lunch. Her nearby summer camps for children had been established during World War II; the first cabins were built by German prisoners of war. (The camps are now run by her son Malcolm and his wife Patsy, and remain an economic resource for one of the poorest areas in east Tennessee.)

Heading back to Knoxville for my flight back to Washington, my Tennessee host from the state highway department drove us over an extremely frail wooden bridge on a state road by my aunt's camps. "My God, this is awful!" I exclaimed as we eased our way over the rickety structure.

A year later, returning for a family visit, I found a replacement bridge, made of concrete. I swear I didn't ask for it, but perhaps I didn't l know my own influence in those days.

When I next saw Aunt Dollie's aging husband—"Mister Lad," as the camp kids called him—he said he appreciated the new bridge.

Ever the Republican, however, he grumbled, "It cost too much money.

"I could have built it for less, Al."

THE ARC WAS A COMPLEX ORGANIZATION, but after some time in office, I decided it processed projects more effectively than its critics would admit.

Director Henry Krevor's staff was almost a mirror of the federal government, with experts at desks for every program, such as education, health, economics—except war. I guess that was my desk: From the first day, I dealt with tension over policies and personalities.

In the fall of 1980, I decided to have a "sit-down" in Kentucky with a collection of mountain activists at the Hindman Settlement School in Knott County. These folks—well-intentioned people who drove on ARC roads, flushed their toilets into ARC sewer lines, drank clean water the ARC paid for, and got their pills at ARC clinics—had nothing good to say about us. They complained that the ARC was not sufficiently "transformative" of social ills.

My traveling companions for an overnight stay were Krevor—one of those Boston-raised bureaucrats that the activists Tom and Pat Gish complained about—and some of the best experts on health and education from the ARC. Richard Whitt, a Pulitzer Prize-winning reporter for *The Courier-Journal*, came along to record the dialogue.

Among the native Appalachians who joined us were the Gishs; Harry and Anne Caudill; Dee Davis and other filmmakers from Appalshop; Mike Mullins from the Settlement School; and James Still, the legendary writer. I don't think either side convinced the other, but as we left, Pat Gish had a request.

"Please don't bring these folks back here, Al," she said.

"We just might get to like them."

ON THE WAY BACK TO WASHINGTON, I stopped off to dine in Lexington with UK President Otis Singletary, his wife Gloria, and Robert Penn Warren, who was there for a lecture.

Kentucky's great man of letters, a Todd County native who had won two Pulitzer Prizes, asked if I had heard lately from his friends, the Sullivans in Nashville. Walter and Jane had been my closest friends during my Vanderbilt days.

The short answer was that I hadn't. My friendship with Walter had ruptured.

After graduate school, Walter had settled in as an English professor at Vanderbilt for the rest of his career. He wrote novels and literary criticism; defended the old Anglican *Book of Common Prayer* against efforts to revise it in the 1970s; and still championed the ideals of the original Fugitive Agrarians.[63]

In 1964, after I had sobered up in Russellville, I wrote Walter and Jane, inviting them to visit me in Russellville, only an hour's drive from Nashville.

A curious response from Walter ended our friendship. He wrote back that in that election year, he didn't believe he'd have anything to say "to a Democrat newspaper editor."

Robert Penn Warren, of course, didn't need to know all that. "Haven't heard from the Sullivans lately," was all I said to him.

As the dinner ended, Warren said he planned to vote to reelect Carter in that fall's election.

Back home in Alexandria the next day, however, I heard from Martha Helen, who reported on her own trip to west Kentucky to see relatives and friends.

---

[63] In 1930, twelve of the Agrarians—six of them current or former members of the Vanderbilt faculty and four former students, including Robert Penn Warren—published an anthology of essays that was called a "manifesto" against the destruction of Southern culture. *I'll Take My Stand: The South and the Agrarian Tradition* became a historic polemic. Although the writers did not all share the same views on race issues—they ranged from conciliatory moderates to stand-pat segregationists—they were united in a call for the region's people to go back to the soil.

"Al, nobody is for Carter," she said. "He is going to lose the race."

I didn't really believe her, until the bad news on Election Night before we went to bed. Then I conceded.

"We better make some plans," I said. "You and I are short-termers."

-52-
London, Reagan's Man

IT WAS NO SECRET THAT CARTER'S DEFEAT would be a blow to the ARC.

Reagan ran for office determined to reduce taxes and the size of the federal government. The ARC was just another unnecessary layer, his team declared.

The morning after the election in November 1980, Don Whitehead was in my office with a plan to help the ARC survive.

Whitehead was a moderate Republican who had held my position with the ARC during the Nixon and Ford administrations. By November 1980, he was a consultant with the conservative American Enterprise Institute (AEI).

Whitehead's plan was to use the AEI to convince the new administration that the ARC, as the sort of federal-state partnership the new president had promised his administration would promote, was more Reagan than Reagan.

While the Reaganites began to spread the word for all Democrats to be out of town by Inauguration Day, two leaders of a program they detested—Whitehead, from the new president's party, and I, from the Carter camp—were subverting the planned execution of the ARC.

Henry Krevor aided and abetted us by insisting that I not send in my resignation.

"The ARC can't operate without a federal co-chairman," he said. "Wait until the White House finds a replacement for you—or shuts the place down."

MEANWHILE, MARTHA HELEN, GINNY, AND I, along with an ornery pet cat, drove home to Russellville to meet Catherine and

Carter for Christmas week, 1980, at Courts Hall, the home we still owned there. We were all disappointed by Reagan's win, and the uncertainty of our future dampened our holiday spirit. But we were together—and a big tree was up, as usual, in the stairwell.

My old friend Lawrence Forgy called me the week after Christmas. He wanted to meet me at the Russellville Burger Queen with his cousin Theron.

Theron Forgy was a rural mail carrier in Butler County, where I owned *The Green River Republican* at Morgantown. Fount Shifflett, the former Logan County jailer who was the Republican Lawrence's Democratic pal, came along for the fun.

After gently expressing regret that his party's presidential victory was "costing you that old job," Forgy got down to business.

It seemed Theron wanted to be appointed to a paying position on the state Agriculture Stabilization and Conservation Service (ASCS) Board. But foes of the Forgys from within the state Republican Party were trying to block Theron. They were jealous of Lawrence's popular son Larry, who was about to leave a vice presidency at UK to join Bert Combs's law firm (which hired Republicans with promising futures). Lawrence thought I might be of assistance.

"Al," Lawrence said, "help us write something for Theron. Theron, bring Al a cup of coffee. Bring Fount one too."

"Cream or sugar, Al?" Theron asked.

"Black, thank you," I said. Fount took the same. Theron went to get the coffee.

The ASCS Board regulated allotment payments, land allotment and market quota programs, among other things. Theron thought the small salary he'd earn for serving on the board would nicely supplement his mail carrier pension, once he retired. Together with his income from a small farm, where he raised a little tobacco and ran some cattle, the combination would let Theron enjoy retirement, so to speak.

"Theron is what that board needs!" I exclaimed. "He will represent the little farmer!"

Lawrence lit a cigarette and handed me an Eagle tablet and a pen.

"Write that down, Al," he said.

By the second coffee, I had scribbled out the letter on two sheets. Lawrence folded it and stuck it in his pocket. "I'll take this to Granville Clark's office and get it typed," he said.

Theron got the job.

Back in Alexandria, believing my time with the ARC to be limited no matter what Whitehead cooked up, Martha Helen and I considered several options.

Of course, we could go back to Russellville. But I'd gotten interested in some of the growth areas of eastern Kentucky. When a call came from a newspaper broker that the largest weekly in the state—*The Sentinel-Echo* in London—was for sale, I talked to ARC's demographers to find out more about the area.

They pointed out that London, in Laurel County, lay at the intersection of north-south I-75 and east-west state Highway 80. And there was flat land in the area that could be easily developed. Those two features indicated much potential growth for the town and the county.

By the end of Ginny's school year in June 1981, we had sold our house in the Washington suburbs and moved to London, seventy-five miles south of Lexington.

Mortgaging our papers on the western side of the state, we had put our money where my mouth had been for a year: in an investment of several million dollars on the eastern side, in Appalachia. Thirteen years after buying *The News-Democrat,* this was the biggest acquisition Al Smith Communications had ever made. Bob Kirkpatrick in Russellville was still our go-to banker.

LONDON WAS A FINE MARKET in which to revitalize a long-established newspaper that had developed management problems that forced a sale. While London had a population of only four thousand, it was the county seat of Laurel County, whose population was ten times larger.

I remember being impressed that the local phonebook listed forty attorneys. They practiced in two courthouses: the Laurel County Courthouse and the U.S. Courthouse, with offices for U.S. marshals, court clerks, and FBI agents. The federal lawmen whispered they were kept busy with white collar crime and public corruption, most of it in nearby counties with intense competition for political jobs, where miners were losing out to machines as coal mining became increasingly mechanized.

Martha Helen and I remember the sense of vitality we found in London on our early visits. Everywhere we looked we saw constructions sites and new ventures. London was on the move.

London's location and good highway system made it a natural for distribution centers. The food industry, in particular, was very visible: two large bakeries; a dairy processing plant; Laurel Grocery Company; and Institutional Distributors, large wholesale grocers that distributed food and other goods all over Kentucky and several southeastern states.

Generally, we were welcomed to London, although some were suspicious of a Democrat publishing the paper in a very Republican county.

I explained to *The Sentinel-Echo's* readers that I didn't move to the mountains to convert readers to a different political party; I came there to give them a good newspaper.

One dissenter about our purchase of the paper was John David Dyche, then a Centre College student.

John David, whose relatives had owned the paper for a century, wrote a letter to the editor warning that I was a Democrat with insidious messages about false political gods.

I called John David and promised him a big headline on the letter that would suggest that the paper was "going to hell."

"Son, I need a conservative columnist," I added. "If you'll write something every week against what you think are my liberal views, I'll publish it and pay you."

John David said he was tempted but didn't have time to argue with me in print. He was studying hard so he could get into Harvard Law School.

Still, we stayed in touch. After he graduated from Harvard, I made John David a second offer, this time to appear on *Comment on Kentucky,* and he accepted. He was practicing law in Louisville when he became a regular commentator on the show. [64]

HOW DID WE MANAGE *THE SENTINEL-ECHO* while I was still with the ARC? With a good staff and a little sleight of hand.

From mid-1981, when we moved to London, to late 1982, most weeks I flew to Washington on Monday morning and back on Thursday night. Weekends gave me time to catch up with the news and write an editorial for the coming week.

The Reagan White House unwittingly did us a special favor by keeping me for two years after we moved to London. My absence left Martha Helen with her managerial skills free to take the paper to new levels of profitability without me in the way, dreaming up new projects and writing long past deadline.

As I awaited news of my replacement, I twice took unpaid leaves of absence from the ARC to reorganize the newspaper. But I kept in touch as the Washington staff fought to save the agency from Reagan's budget cutters.

As a Carter lame duck who had essentially become Reagan's man, at least until I was removed, I had to be very discreet. The White

---

[64] Republican readers of *The Courier-Journal* may be surprised that Editorial Page Editor David Hawpe and I later collaborated to persuade the paper's publisher to pay John David for a column. Hawpe and I valued his thoughtful opposition to our opinions. What we wanted was lively journalism.

House aides trusted me to answer all questions with "President Reagan feels his new policies for economic development will meet the needs of the people of Appalachia."

Reagan's people understood I didn't agree with that statement, but they trusted I wouldn't embarrass them in public, and they were right.[65]

Surprisingly, near the end of 1981, the Reagan administration asked me to serve in 1982.

That could be interpreted as a sign that the commission was about to be axed, the idea being that Reagan was retaining me, a Democrat, to throw on the funeral pyre. States that weren't in the ARC certainly supported this strategy.

But many Appalachian Republicans supported the ARC for the same reasons their Democratic colleagues did: Whether the program was a true agent of regional transformation or a vehicle for pork-barrel spending, it was a Golden Goose. Therefore, why kill it off?

Privately, during 1981, I sent the ARC staff in search of a moderate Republican woman to succeed me. The commission had never had a female federal co-chairman from either party, and I reasoned that the Republicans might like the credit for choosing a female.

It took two tries, but we found one. In late 1982, Winifred "Winnie" Pizzano of Pennsylvania was confirmed as the first of two Republican women co-chairs who presided over the agency until Bill Clinton brought in another Democrat.

LIVING IN LONDON WAS PLEASANT. New friends welcomed us. Whether my TV program had made me a fairly familiar face in the

---

[65] I didn't publicize my travel schedule during the time I continued with the ARC. But my Monday morning flights to Washington during that time were on the same plane with Congressman Carl Perkins. The irony wasn't lost on me: I was the president's man to kill off the ARC, and Perkins's agent to try to save it.

region, or my government position gave me a measure of respect, we never felt like strangers. Laurel County was a genuine growth center, with none of the hostility to the ARC that I experienced with writers, artists, and activists further east in the coalfields. My talented editor, Charles House, who grew up in Manchester, Kentucky, told me, "You don't really know where you are living."

"How's that, Charles?"

"You think you are in Appalachia, but you aren't," he said.

"Go thirty miles further east toward the mountains, to Clay County, where I came from. Now that's *serious* Appalachia!"

His point was that we had moved to a community that was much more affluent than counties to the east. Our bookkeeper, Judy McCowan, was cranking out positive reports that certainly justified our investment in the paper in *this* county.

The plants for food processing, data entry, the government services, and highway construction companies generated growing payrolls that boosted the retail economy. That, in turn, increased our advertising sales. The increased news content and commentary we added, including a second opinion page, with local columnists, attracted more readers.

The paper's energetic, cheerful workers seemed appreciative of us, and we were of them. Our London plant was a twin of the one in Russellville. As I frequently and happily told the London staff, they were the match of the employees on the west side of the state who had made possible our expansion to Appalachian Kentucky.

One day, proud of our growth, I called a strategy session with our managers to plan how we might convert our big weekly to a daily paper. Martha Helen was skeptical about the idea.

"Are we really ready for that yet?" she asked.

"Why don't we just double the cover price on the single copies to 50 cents and stay once a week for now? Ten thousand more quarters a week is a lot of money—and with no more work!"

I flushed with embarrassment, but the staff guys guffawed. I did take her advice, and, at 50 cents a copy, single sales of our 10,000 circulation weekly, most of them at grocery and drug stores, gave us our most profitable year.

WHAT SHOULD A "GOOD" NEWSPAPER DO to support better health care in Laurel and adjacent counties?

That question was asked—and answered—by Dr. William D. Hacker,[66] a thoughtful young pediatrician in Corbin, Kentucky.

In Hacker's view, Corbin and London—longtime rivals in business and high school sports that were a mere fourteen miles apart—should forget their differences and support construction of a comprehensive hospital to serve both towns and the surrounding area. And Hacker believed the newspapers in London and Corbin should endorse the idea and drum up backing in their communities.

The ARC was obliging enough to conduct a survey that showed Hacker was right about the need to replace the small, private hospitals in London and Corbin with a larger, comprehensive facility serving the general area. The State Health Department then endorsed the idea, and a citizens' committee organized to promote the new hospital.

The campaign, which Corbin's daily *Times-Tribune* joined, failed, narrowly, at the hands of a state hearing officer. But *The Sentinel-Echo* gained respect, and readers, for taking a stand for what we thought was progress.

BACK IN WASHINGTON, IN THE FALL OF 1981, the ARC was on life support. The most agile hero of the campaign to save the ARC was Henry Krevor,[67] the executive director, who devised two "finish-

---

[66] Dr. Hacker eventually left his pediatric practice and went on to serve two governors as state commissioner of public health. In a state with high rates of cancer, heart disease, stroke, and diabetes, related to smoking, obesity, and poor dental care, Dr. Hacker struggled honorably for change. It was a hard go.

[67] Henry Krevor taught me more about Washington than anyone else, but then I taught him a lesson I'd learned in Logan County—or was it New Orleans?

up" programs—one for highways and one for sixty particularly distressed ARC counties that needed additional monies for health and education.

These plans were legitimate, and they gave Congress cover to keep voting funds for the ARC, against Reagan's wishes, until George H.W. Bush became president and put the commission in his budget. Reagan never budgeted for the ARC, but when the Congress overruled him, he just waited and tried to defund it in the next budget cycle.

Although I was nominally Reagan's man, I remained a nimble advocate for the ARC and devised a plan I thought might save it.

I persuaded Senator Jennings Randolph to call his old friend, Kentucky's John Sherman Cooper, for a favor. Would Cooper, who by then was retired from the Senate, mind calling Howard Baker, the powerful new Senate Majority Leader from Tennessee?

My thought process went like this: Republican Cooper and Democrat Randolph went way back; inspired by Lyndon Johnson, those men had cosponsored the legislation that created the ARC. Meanwhile, there was an enduring relationship between Cooper and Howard Baker, which began when Baker's parents served in the U.S. Congress with Cooper and continued when Cooper introduced Howard Baker as the new freshman Senator from east Tennessee.

My idea worked the way I had hoped. Randolph made the call to Cooper. Cooper made the call to Baker. And Baker, who had originally supported Reagan's plan to deep six the ARC, changed his mind.

When the ARC state representatives gave him a bonus of only $5,000 for good performance, Krevor blamed me, though it was not my decision. He was furious, having expected more money and seeing himself as indispensible. Afterwards, he all but severed relations with me, which made it impossible for either of us to do our jobs.

In response, I sent a letter of resignation to the White House, asking to be relieved at the end of the month. When ARC governors began calling me for an explanation, I said I could no longer work with Krevor.

By the end of the week, the governors had fired Krevor, and all five ARC Republican governors asked Reagan to disregard my letter, which he did. I stayed until October 1982.

The lesson I hope I taught Henry: Don't forget who's boss.

On the Monday morning after those weekend calls, Baker spoke to Randolph in the Senate cloakroom.

"Jennings," Baker said, "John Cooper called me."

"You don't have to worry about the ARC anymore."

When Ronald Reagan went home to California, the ARC was still in business. Thirty years after he first tried to kill it, it was still operating on a reduced scale, but the approximate investment over the region, since passage of the Appalachian Development Act in 1965, was approximately $13.2 billion dollars, including $1.4 billion for Kentucky ($993 million for highways and 396 million for the non-highway program.)

Critics of the program seldom mention federal and state aid that comes to dynamic urban economies like Lexington's through tax credits and loop holes, outright government investments, or the enormous subsidies in the west for mining, grazing, and water rights.

In defending the program when I was the federal cochair, I made speeches saying " I never met a local official willing to give back an airport beacon, half mile of road, a yard of bridge, a foot of pipe, a flush toilet, a microscope, clinic, hospital operating room, or dental chair. "   In some poverty areas, these remarks earned a standing ovation.

At Senator Cooper's funeral, I smilingly confessed to Senator Baker that I had inspired the Cooper call to him about the ARC. Baker smiled back, "you knew I could never deny John Cooper, didn't you?"

-53-
Sold

OWNING A SMALL BUSINESS HAS ITS PERILS.

I may have wandered the darker parts of New Orleans and Russellville in a daze during my younger days, and I was confronted by some angry readers through the years. But I've rarely been as scared as I was the day in the fall of 1981 when Jake Butcher phoned.

Butcher was a high-flying Tennessee banker who later went to prison for fraud. How I came to be taking his phone calls requires a bit of a digression.

IN THE MID-1970S, MARTHA HELEN AND I became friends with the Gray family of Glasgow, Kentucky. Lois Howard Gray,[68] a beautiful widow with six children, was at the time struggling to save the small construction business her husband, James Norris Gray, had started not long before his death.

With the hard work of her four sons—Howard, Jim, Franklin, and Stephen—the Grays succeeded, over time, in developing the company into a major builder of industrial plants.

In 1977, when the Grays learned that I was a prospect for a TVA board appointment, they introduced me to Jake and C.H. Butcher of Knoxville, Tennessee, multimillionaire brothers who owned a bank in Glasgow from which the Grays had borrowed money. The Grays thought the Butchers, with their connections in the same city as

---

[68] Lois was the daughter of Dr. C.C. Howard of Glasgow, the leader of a crusade to eliminate tuberculosis in Kentucky. She served in the WAVES during World War II, where she used her artistic talents to map ship movements.

Lois was admired for her leadership, and all of her children inherited her spunk. One of them, Jim, running as an openly gay candidate, was elected mayor of Lexington after the company moved there from Glasgow.

TVA's headquarters, might have some influence over the selection process.

The introduction didn't help me get the appointment, but it did lead inadvertently to my own banking relationship with the Butchers. When Al Smith Communications bought *The Sentinel-Echo*, I had boldly (and optimistically) agreed to pay off several obligations of the paper's previous owners. One of them was a $600,000 note at the Butchers' Corbin, Kentucky, bank.

What I hadn't bargained for when I agreed to assume those debts was the various banks' insistence on increasing our interest to the astronomical rates of the inflationary early 1980s. After buying the paper when interest rates were in the high teens, Al Smith Communications was on the edge.

That day in 1981, Martha Helen and I were in Knoxville to attend the World's Fair, which Jake Butcher and other Knoxville businessmen had helped to develop. When we got to our hotel, a message was waiting for us: "Phone Jake Butcher."

I panicked.

"Oh, my God!" I gasped to Martha Helen. "He's going to call our note at his Corbin bank!"

It turned out Jake wasn't trying to squeeze me. He just wanted the names of some Lexington reporters.[69]

But that scare, and the bank debt that caused it, set me to wondering how long I could stand the pressure of owning a highly leveraged little newspaper company.

FOUR YEARS LATER, IN 1984, Al Smith Communications was prospering, thanks to Martha Helen and Virginia Page. But although

---

[69] Jake was drawing up the guest list for a press conference to announce his takeover of the Union Bank in Lexington. He said that he and C.H. hoped to someday have a bank in every major city on I-75 from Cincinnati to Naples. That was not to be—the brothers' financial empire collapsed, and both brothers served jail terms for fraud. Nevertheless, both brothers were always friendly and courteous to me.

interest rates had eased, I had a new fear: the United States Postal Service.

For chain retailers like Walmart, mailing advertisements directly to customers had become cheaper than paying to have them published in newspapers. As a result, papers everywhere—including my own— were beginning to lose significant chunks of their ad revenue.

I called wealthy Roy Park, a media magnate in Ithaca, New York, and suggested we talk about a sale.

I had first met Park, who owned media properties across the country, in Washington in 1981. I promised then to contact him if I ever decided to cash in.

Park,[70] then seventy-four, a bushy-browed man who was listed in *Forbes* as the fortieth-richest person in the United States, always dressed in gray pinstripes. He wore a watch on each wrist: one set on Ithaca time, the other for wherever his huge company jet swooped down, buzzard-like, to seize another "property." During our negotiations, we took turns saying grace at mealtimes. I wasn't as rich as he, but I could be just as unctuous.

MARTHA HELEN AND I, along with our accountant, Joe Cook of Bowling Green, went to Ithaca over Memorial Day weekend in 1985 to negotiate a sale.

Before the three of us boarded the plane for home, I told the president of Park's company that the purchase price his boss had just proposed was "a sorry unacceptable offer."

Then, to make sure there was no confusion, I added:

"Be sure and tell him I said 'No.'"

The man grimaced, but nodded.

But if I was unhappy, Martha Helen was pleased.

---

[70] Roy Park was a marketing genius. He made his first fortune in the cake mix business (Duncan Hines) that he later sold. He then began a communications company that acquired twenty-three radio stations, seven TV stations, and one-hundred forty-four medium size magazines and newspapers.

She had left social work while we still lived in Russellville, creating a successful new career as a portrait photographer that she pursued for nearly ten years.

But when we moved to London, she found herself solving business problems at *The Sentinel-Echo* in my absence. She worked with our staff to improve each department and, with Virginia Page in Russellville, tried to teach me the basics of cash-flow management and other principles important to our business.

She enjoyed those successes and really didn't want to sell the papers and give up the excitement of problem-solving—she liked making money!

When we got back to London, she showed me figures she'd written on a yellow legal pad substantiating her projection that the company would be worth ten million in five years.

I told her I thought Park's initial bid had been a deliberate low-ball offer. "He just wants to see how stupid we are," I said. "That old man wants to buy us."

Besides, I pointed out, her projection was optimistically predicated on a stable economy, no further problems caused by the USPS, and no competition from a yet-to-be-revealed rival.[71]

I wrote Roy a nice letter thanking him for the steak dinner in Ithaca and for the opportunity to see his collection of classic automobiles, worth millions of dollars. I wrote that I respected him, which was true, and that if I ever decided again to sell, I would call and give him another chance to bid.

Before I sealed the envelope, I slipped in the paper on which my wife had written her projection.

---

[71] That unknown rival turned out to be the Internet, which has all but wrecked the major newspaper industry and put a big scare into community papers like ours.

Before the week was up, Park called. He asked me to make another offer, lower than my first, and said perhaps he'd be willing to raise his bid.

I wrote back, cutting the asking price some.

Three days later, on a hot July day, Martha Helen and I were on our way from London to Russellville for a party. We had stopped in Bowling Green at a Ramada Inn to shower and change clothes.

I was coming out of the bathroom wrapped in a towel when Martha Helen handed me the motel room phone.

"It's Mr. Park," she said glumly.

I took the phone.

"I got your offer," Park grumped. "And I accept."

Standing there, clutching that towel in one hand and the phone in the other, I felt like I had won the lottery. It was a $5 million sale.[72]

TWENTY-TWO YEARS EARLIER, I had borrowed five bucks from *The News-Democrat's* cash register so I could hang on until payday. My mother had just driven me back to work, sober after what turned out to be my last binge.

It was Roy Park who made the offer that hot summer day.

But it was the recovery that started one autumn night in a church basement in Russellville that sealed the deal.

---

[72] Park bought the papers in London, Russellville, and Leitchfield; we had sold the other papers the previous year. We paid off loans and other stockholders out of that $5 million.

Martha Helen and I owned more than seventy percent of the business. But these were not large daily papers. Still, as Happy Chandler once said to me, "Mama and I have enough to get through the winter."

Epilogue

AFTER WORKING FOR THE PARK COMPANY for two years, Martha Helen, Ginny, and I moved from London to Lexington in 1987. Although I enjoyed having the "new money," I felt guilt pangs about selling out, as if I had abandoned the communities as well as the employees.

In Lexington I was an easy target for groups with ideas about reform. As the invitations kept coming, I couldn't say "no."

So many issues interested me, particularly those around education (revenge of a college dropout). The role of higher education in the state and "Bucks for Brains" to stimulate excellence in the universities were important if we were to have a better educated work force. (Ever wanting to consolidate, an urge that has now died, I even proposed merging UK and U of L.)

Bert Combs' winning lawsuit to reform the public schools and give more funding to the poor districts was a great victory. This became KERA, the Kentucky Education Reform Act, nationally acclaimed twenty years ago, but drained of much substance by the second decade of the new century.

The Governor's Scholars' Program, for which I begged the first dollars from Ashland, Inc., gave a special boost to bright rising high school seniors.

Pre-K and kindergarten, the best investment possible in economic development, were promoted by the Prichard Committee for Academic Excellence, led by the visionary Bob Sexton. Despite its importance, it is still slighted in favor of higher education and tax incentives for new industries.

I supported a stronger arts program and insisted on the economic benefits of cultural investments.

About these and other issues facing the state, I chaired a public forum, the Shakertown Roundtable (Earl Wallace's second great legacy), for ten years until 2000, when it was all but shut down.

Although in my sixties, I was still Graeme's boy—raising a public voice. I laughed at my civic compulsions. I said to Martha Helen, "If there is something I know little about that meddles in other people's business, doesn't pay, and I can be the chairman, then that's my line of work."

These heavy involvements began in London.

My friend and *Comment* regular, Associated Press reporter Sy Ramsey, joked that Governor John Y. Brown Jr. wouldn't appoint anyone to an office unless he knew them.

"And since he only knows twenty people in Kentucky," Ramsey said, "he appoints them over and over."

Coal baron Bill Sturgill admitted to me that he and W.T. "Bill" Young, another wealthy Lexington friend of Brown, flipped a coin over the chairmanship of the racing commission. Sturgill won, adding the tracks to his portfolio that already included head of the Energy and Agriculture cabinet and chairman of the UK board of trustees.[73]

So I wasn't too surprised when Brown appointed me to the Council on Higher Education to represent the state's Fifth Congressional District. This was in 1981, only a month after I moved into the district at London. Brown also reappointed me to head the state arts program, which had been renamed the Kentucky Arts Council.

That same year, Wilson Wyatt drafted me for the founding board of Leadership Kentucky. I later resigned, pleading the burden of a

---

[73] Young was one of Lexington's leading philanthropists, but he objected to donations for public institutions, lest those spare taxpayers their duty to support same. On behalf of the proposed new UK library, I argued fiercely with him at a breakfast that all great libraries became so with private as well as public funds. He relented and UK's W.T. Young Library now has one of the largest foundations of any public university in America. I don't claim I changed his mind, but I certainly tried to, and he did give generously and pressured friends to contribute to the endowment.

daily statewide radio talk show, *Primeline*, that I was hosting. Wyatt soon recalled me anyway to become the program's third chairman.

When we moved to Lexington, I did a three-year stint as an adjunct instructor in the UK political science department and at the Appalachian Center. About the first assignment, I called Larry Forgy for advice: "I've never had a course in political science," I said.

He laughed. "That's all right, Al, just don't read those textbooks. They will fog your brain." Forgy, my longtime friend from Logan County, lost the governorship in 1995 to Paul Patton by only 21,560 votes, or 2.2 percent. Although he privately blamed everyone but himself, it seemed to me his last weeks of campaigning were marred by his own foggy appeals to right wing extremists that turned off moderate Republicans and many Democrats who had admired him. Also, because the candidates accepted public financing, Forgy and Patton made many joint appearances. Patton improved by having to share the platform with Forgy, a superb stump speaker.

While I was sticking my hands in all the reforms of the day, the favored model for ethical journalism in the second half of the twentieth century was the detached, objective reporter.

That was never me. I was an engaged journalist.

I had two role models in my journalism career. One was drawn from *The Autobiography of Lincoln Steffens,* the story of a crusading "muckraker" of the early twentieth century. The second was a man I knew well, and loved: Nat Caldwell, the Pulitzer Prize-winning Nashville reporter who taught me how to make things happen.

Like Nat, I remained a New Dealer, strongly convinced of the role government has to keep the economy strong, education accessible, the laws equitable, and a safety net to protect all citizens. A pragmatic populist, I believe in following the Steffens example of exposing corruption in government and business, and the cliché about a great credo for journalists: "to comfort the afflicted and afflict the comfortable."

Advocacy was my thing. If I knew the facts, I formed convictions about the truth. Sometimes I stepped into the ring, becoming an active player in the narratives I told. But my practice was first to listen, to be fair, to report the opinions of others, to give them space in my newspapers, and always to be informed.

In the weekly newspaper business, when readers came into the office with a complaint about a story or editorial, I listened. I didn't hesitate to sit down with them and type their objections as they voiced them, then hand over a pen to sign their "letter to the editor."

From the time I returned to *Comment on Kentucky* in the fall of 1982, I was the host and producer for the next twenty-five years. With the exception of support for "better education," I dropped all political efforts and endorsement of candidates.[74] While hosting *Comment*, I paid Ken Kurtz, the retired news manager of a local TV station, to critique my programs. He was unsparing when he thought the show went off the track or a panelist showed bias.

I devoted many hours to selecting the best reporters and editors to explain the week's events. Other guests included professors, filmmakers, authors, even poets who can make sense of the complexities of our times if we but ask them.

Len Press suggested that I add brief editorial comments at the end of our programs. I called these "go outs." The segments irritated some of my reporters whose talking time was reduced. In fairness, perhaps they thought my opinions weren't that interesting. However, our audiences grew and, although we often received critical messages after a show, few viewers clamored for my head.

We talked about everything, but change was the underlying theme until and after I retired from *Comment* in November 2007. The changes that I have seen over the last fifty years have been enough to inflict grievous whiplash. And a lot of those changes, it seems, have come to stay.

---

[74] As the debate continues over testing and other metrics of educational achievement, I'm firmly for whatever it takes to keep a good teacher engaged with a child.

Walmarting damaged Main Street in our towns. Local stores gave way to big box chains; out-of-state corporations bought out local banks, real estate firms, hospitals, and media. Kentucky became a leading automobile manufacturing state. There were fewer but larger farms, as the tobacco program died. Agriculture became more diversified with poultry as the leading product, followed by horses, cattle, corn, soybeans, tobacco, and other crops, raised by a smaller population of farmers.

Industrial farming bore an environmental cost as Wendell Berry noted. Early on at *Comment* and on my radio show, *Primeline,* I called attention to Berry's concern about agribusiness, family farms, the food chain, and community life. Our "prophet in Kentucky," as *The New York Review of Books* called him, was always cordial, but I couldn't persuade him to join me for broadcasts.

Well-paid factory jobs gave way in numbers to low-paid ones in a growing service sector that should have been taxed but wasn't. As the revenue system became more dysfunctional, the state was less responsive to the need for more governmental support for education, human services, environmental regulations, and government's own pension and health care programs.

Coal was produced by fewer miners with more mega machines. Still a dominant source of low-cost energy, coal is increasingly under attack for sound environmental reasons.

The federal census in 2010 showed shifting demographics: an increasingly urbanized state of older citizens. Local governments are concerned about decaying infrastructure, especially utilities. Educational funding remains a serious issue as well as the desperate need to manage costs of overcrowded prisons. Health problems—from high rates of obesity, diabetes, heart disease, lung cancer, and addiction to pervasive tooth decay among children—are magnified for some 600,000 plus uninsured Kentuckians.

When Len Press and I started *Comment* in 1974, Kentucky was a different state politically.

Governor Wendell Ford, a Democrat, had just won a U.S. Senate seat from Marlow Cook, a Republican, and Richard Nixon had resigned the presidency over Watergate scandals. Cook's defeat left only two Republicans in the Kentucky congressional delegation. Economic and justice issues were the currency of our conversations, and few people demonized government. Cook, a one-termer, resigned early so Ford could benefit in seniority from an early swearing in. It's impossible to imagine such generosity in today's acrimonious political climate.

Ford was an able "constituent senator" for our tough-to-defend special interests (coal, tobacco, whiskey, racing), but he had the common touch with the voters, and it was thrilling to see him on occasion speak out for organized labor. I heard him tell a Rockwell manager, "I voted for your damn B-1 bomber [a military boondoggle], now it's labor's turn to get a vote from me [for union-influenced wages on public contracts]." When he said he hated nuclear power, I remembered he championed coal-fired electric power, but I believed his concern for his grandkids' safety from a nuclear accident was genuine.

Julian Carroll had a popular run until the scandals of pay-for-play politics (in which Ford was also a player) overtook him. The economy was strong, which gave him a generous purse with which to support improvements in teacher pay, kindergarten programs, the arts, and court reforms. Yet when he was the governor with a pitifully low salary, he accepted favors and bestowed some that were improper.

But he was the last New Dealer governor in Frankfort. When he shaped those budgets, he never forgot the meek and the poor. Liberals could cheer him in recent years for standing up as a state senator against able but stubborn David Williams, the Republican leader some called "the bully from Burkesville."

Within six years of Nixon's fall, Republican fortunes changed. Their party returned to the White House with Ronald Reagan, and *Comment's* reporters tracked the rise of Jefferson County's shrewd

Mitch McConnell from judge-executive, to the party's leader in the US Senate.

On the election night in 1984, when McConnell upset the incumbent Democrat Dee Huddleston, reporters swarmed the GOP Louisville campaign headquarters, but none reported the remarks of the mean-spirited Republican Congressman Gene Snyder. When the cheering stopped, Snyder allegedly commented to a small band of stragglers still in the room, "Well, folks, we've done the impossible. We've elected a U.S. senator—an S.O.B. who had no friends."

Al Cross suggests that McConnell is a modern, technological politician, far outside the personal approach that Kentuckians had typically required of their statewide political leaders. He and Brown were the first candidates of TV, not the courthouses. The elections of Brown, Wilkinson, Jones, and Patton as governors have been called "the rise of the rich amateurs." The old time courthouse machines were running out of gas.

Perhaps the most underestimated governor of my time as a commentator was Martha Layne Collins, elected in 1983. Respect for her continues to rise as historians and economists reckon the value of the Toyota investment in its Georgetown plant and Collins' efforts to bring it to Kentucky. Her aides, Larry Hayes and Carroll Knicely, deserve a salute too.

It was quite an experience to be at a gathering with Japanese executives whenever Collins entered the room. They jumped to their feet, bowing and applauding as if she were the queen of Kentucky. They knew her worth, perhaps before the rest of us.

WALLACE WILKINSON SOLD THE LOTTERY IN 1987 to an electorate that bought his sales pitch that it was a tax-free way to finance schools. The lottery was simply a gimmick to get votes. The 1990 school reforms required more than lottery revenues. Permitting the state to partner with organized gambling is a strategy that enables the rich to evade responsibility for legitimate taxes. Lotteries and slots (which now have their foot in the door through so-called "instant racing" machines) are a tax on the poor. What I learned about the lottery amendment in our state was that between whatever Kentuckians piously said about the "Good Book" and their pocketbooks, the latter was where their hearts were and how they voted. The poor, once again, voted against their own interests.

Before his death, horseman John Gaines appealed on the *Comment* show for expanded gambling at the tracks to save the breeding industry. Gaines was a creative thinker—he is credited with the idea for the Breeders Cup—but Arthur Hancock, winner of two Derbies, maintained that handicapping horse races is a skill, and he loathed what he called "the element" associated with Las Vegas gambling—the persons he feared would take over Kentucky racing if additional gambling were permitted.

Other state tracks with slots, however, have created a competitive disadvantage for Kentucky tracks. Many horsemen are taking their horses to those states. For that reason, most breeders agree with Gaines and want expanded gambling. Then, too, they recognize that Kentuckians spend millions betting with casino boats on the state's borders.

What do I think? I dislike government-supported gambling. I accept pari-mutuel betting as sort of a game of skill, with a piece of the profits supporting an agricultural enterprise, horse breeding.

When I urged the Lottery Board to give some money to the Council on Problem Gambling, they did so. I applauded this enlightened act, but was chagrined when they cut the ad contract for my radio program by the same amount. I fear the greed of casino bosses and all who run the legal games of chance.

The legislative independence that arrived on Governor Brown's watch eventually seeded temptations for corruption in the General Assembly. "Boptrot," a scandal involving harness racing (called "trots") and the Business Organization and Professions Committees, emerged. Conviction on a bribery charge brought a tough sentence in federal prison for House Speaker Don Blandford that dismayed many people, including reporters who respected Blandford's role in passing the school reforms of 1990. Before he was brought down, Blandford pushed the passage of gubernatorial succession and a law to provide public funds for gubernatorial campaigns[75] that limited their spending to reduce the pay-to-play syndrome.

When Wallace Wilkinson's term as governor was ending, I produced a program with the state's leading editors. None gave him any credit for passage of the Kentucky Education Reform Act and the billion dollars in taxes to administer it. The next week, the editors' top reporters, appearing with me, unanimously disagreed. They said KERA wouldn't have passed without Wilkinson's eventual support.

I agreed with the reporters, but some of the credit goes to Wilkinson's education adviser Jack Foster and his press secretary Doug Alexander who crafted the governor's campaign paper on education in 1987. Wilkinson said he wouldn't invest any new money in education "until the system is fixed." The underpinnings for KERA largely fixed the schools, but subsequent legislatures and governors lost their nerve and have chipped away at the reforms.

Wilkinson was followed by Governor Brereton Jones, a horseman who achieved reformers' longtime goal of succession, allowing governors and other officials to seek second terms, by leaving himself out of it. He won reforms in health care, but the lobbying and legislative process left the plan with flaws that kept it from being successful. Jones and his wife Libby championed the new Thomas D. Clark Center for Kentucky History at Frankfort, along with the appointment of Phillip Shepherd as environmental cabinet secretary, perhaps the best ever.

Governor Paul Patton reformed workers' compensation, then won an initiative to separate the University of Kentucky from the

---

[75] This law has since been repealed at the urging of Senator McConnell.

community colleges and gave UK a clear mission to be a leading research university. While dragging higher education uphill, he was perhaps the most effective of all those governors after Carroll. Then he dallied with a woman not his wife and ruined his chances to be a U.S. Senator.

When Steve Beshear, a Democrat like Patton, was elected governor in 2007, twenty years after he and Brown lost a primary to Wilkinson, I wrote an op-ed calling him a "hero of the second chance." Kentuckians love comebacks, and that was Beshear's story. Credit him also for encouraging Patton's return to public service in higher education[76] A governor who perhaps remembered the fall and rise of Ed Prichard deserves praise for offering a second chance to another smart leader.

Beshear disappointed horsemen by stumbling at the gate in an early attempt to expand gambling at the track, but he pleased me with a serious attempt to improve the problem of Kentucky's low standing in children's oral health. This was an issue I asked him to address when he ran for governor. And he kept his promise to do so.

The lackluster Republican governor, Ernie Fletcher, who lost his reelection bid to Beshear after a personnel scandal, was the only governor in my fifty years in Kentucky journalism with whom I had no relationship. I do remember his positive effort to create a Recovery Kentucky Program to house and treat addicts and alcoholics. This was the initiative of Fletcher's financial backer, the builder Don Ball, a longtime activist for care of the homeless and substance abusers. Beshear wisely kept this program, retained Ball as chairman, and named Jane Beshear, his wife, as co-chair.

AT CHRISTMAS 1985, MARY BINGHAM LAMENTED her regret that I sold my business. "Oh, Al, what will Kentucky do without your

---

[76] Patton is chairman of the Council on Postsecondary Education and president of the University of Pikeville.

voice in the newspapers?" I should have asked her the same. Less than a month later, *The Courier-Journal* was put up for sale.

The newspaper business was under siege by the time I retired from television in 2007. The impact of the Internet was already diverting ad sales, especially classifieds (about a third of metro papers' revenue) from print when major retail chains, indeed, nearly every segment of business lost profits in the deep recession starting in 2007. They cut their ad buys in all media: newspapers, magazines, and broadcast outlets.

After a long run of dependable profits, publicly owned newspaper companies especially suffered as they lost favor with investors, merged with other companies, and scrambled to keep their stock prices up by firing editors and reporters.

The Gannett publisher of *The Courier-Journal* boasted that newspapers are stronger than their own stories about media hard times might indicate. In Lexington, where the Knight Ridder chain sold the *Herald-Leader* with its other papers to the McClatchy Company of California, the publisher also made optimistic claims for the future of the business.

The Lexington and Louisville papers are profitable, but company headquarters suck out the profits, the curse of devil's bargains made with Wall Street when the companies became publicly owned. Both papers have fired many reporters and shuttered most of their news bureaus. *The Courier-Journal* is no longer a statewide newspaper. The *Herald-Leader* still circulates in the mountains, which have many Lexington shoppers. The Louisville paper may still care about Appalachia and western Kentucky, but their reporters are seldom seen away from Louisville and Frankfort.

As my life in journalism nears the end, I remain convinced that the future of the news business is still in content—where it has been from cave paintings to the iPad.

THERE WERE AND STILL ARE GRAVE PROBLEMS in rural areas. While having lunch sometime in 2000, I listened to my friend Steve Cawood, a respected lawyer in Pineville, recite his worries about life in Appalachia: kids leaving for lack of jobs, the school dropout rate, mining issues, rotten politics, divorce rates, Oxycontin abuse, and other health problems. He was in a funk. After he drove off, I wrote it all down and mailed the memo to my longtime friend Rudy Abramson, the Washington reporter I met during that coal strike in the 1970s. Rudy, who had retired from the *Los Angeles Times*, had a special affection for the mountains and was editing the *Encyclopedia of Appalachia.*

Rudy was so distressed over my letter he soon got a grant from the Alicia Patterson Foundation to validate Steve's report, and was on his way. When he stopped in Lexington a month later, Rudy added a new challenge to Steve's list. He said the press had grown dispirited in many small towns. Overworked, small staffs no longer had time to dig up the facts on the issues that were eating away at their communities. He noted low morale in the newsrooms and in their communities, and a pervasive distrust of authority everywhere— Washington, the state capitals, and the courthouses.

After writing several articles for the Patterson Foundation, Rudy returned to Lexington for an exercise in engaged journalism. We began a campaign to create an Institute for Rural Journalism and Community Issues at UK.

The UK president, Lee Todd, was open to our proposal, but where could we find the money to pay for it? It took four years, but after obtaining some small initial grants, we got a $250,000 grant from the Knight Foundation, and a $50,000 grant from the Ford Foundation. We were ready for work.[77]

---

[77] Hodding Carter, my intern at *The Times-Picayune*, was CEO of the Knight Foundation. Jim Host and Lois Mateus, friends from early times, helped raise an endowment for which Sally Brown, chuckling over my stories of drinking her Early Times whiskey then quitting, wrote the biggest check.

In 2004, UK and I recruited Al Cross to direct the Institute, taking him from a distinguished career at *The Courier-Journal,* which had stolen him from my papers twenty-seven years earlier.

The Institute's program is not about teaching students to craft "pretty" paragraphs. Instead, its mission is to help students and journalists at small papers understand and explain to readers policy issues—education, health, economic development, and the environment; to practice accountability journalism; and to champion to urban America the concerns of more than sixty million rural Americans.

The Institute now has twenty-eight academic partners in eighteen states. Cross has extended our reach from Appalachia to India and Africa. Our dream is to become a resource for rural people throughout the world, giving UK an international reputation for service that will strengthen the school and further diversify future generations of students.

Rudy Abramson, an Alabama dairy farmer's son, had been White House correspondent for the *Los Angeles Times.* Al Cross, who was raised in a small Kentucky town much like the ones Rudy and I knew when we were young, rose to become national president of the Society of Professional Journalists, a group of ten thousand editors and reporters. I remembered that Tennessee farm which saved my family in the Depression and the Kentucky county where I was given a second chance.

None of us had forgotten "where we came from," as the country saying goes. So, we went back to our rural roots.

Where we had started, we began anew.

Al Smith

HONORS

Honorary doctorates from University of Kentucky
and eight other colleges and universities

U.K. Journalism Hall of Fame (Charter Member, 1981)

Fellow of the National Society of Professional Journalists (SPJ)

Al Smith Fellowships, annual awards to Kentucky artists,
Kentucky Arts Council

Medallion for Intellectual Achievement,
University of Kentucky Library Associates

Distinguished Rural Kentuckian,
Kentucky Association of Electric Cooperatives

Rural Hero (for journalism), National Rural Assembly

Media Award, East Kentucky Leadership Foundation

Lewis Owens Award for Community Service,
Kentucky Press Association

Gabbard Distinguished Kentuckian Award,
Kentucky Broadcasters Association

Flame of Excellence Award, Leadership Kentucky

First Al Smith Award for Community Service
through Journalism, SPJ, Bluegrass Chapter

BOARDS

Co-founder of Institute for Rural Journalism and Community Issues

Chair, Kentucky Press Association

Founding Chair, Kentucky Oral History Commission

Chair, Kentucky Arts Commission (now Council)

Chair, Leadership Kentucky

Chair, Shakertown Roundtable

Acknowledgements

ANYONE WHO WRITES A MEMOIR IN LATE LIFE and tries to list the people who have helped with the book is inviting hurt feelings. The names left out through faults of memory are likely to be more than those recalled.

However, a non-inclusive account of support must begin with Martha Helen, the organizer of the hours of writing from start to finish. Daughter Catherine McCarty was the primary editor. A writer and lawyer, her gifts with words are enriched by a commitment to editorial rigor. She was generously assisted by Al Cross, who began correcting my mistakes when he went to work for me just out of college; Jack Lyne, editor of a major business magazine who grew up in Russellville in a family of the political players in my stories; and Michal Smith-Mello, who gave every page the final scan. The errors in this book are mine, not theirs.

Ginny Smith Major and Carter Hancock, my other children, kept up my morale in special ways as did three interested friends, Mark Neikirk, Don McNay, and Carl West. Of my five grandchildren, Lauren Hancock became a cheerleader after reading some early chapters and never let up the pressure on me to finish the book. (The others, Connor and Evan McCarty, and Susannah and Ava Major, were certainly on my side.) Bill Major, Ginny's husband, helped with the Introduction.

Others who encouraged me were Lil Press, Lillian Rhea Noe, Boardman and Lillian Stewart, my son-in-law Bill McCarty, Ward and Peggy Allen, Walter and Anna Durham, my sister Robin Smith Burrow and her daughter Rachel Burrow, Terry and Janice Birdwhistell, Jim Klotter, Tom Parrish and Nancy Wolsk, Joe and

Carol Lee, Devert and Judy Owens, Bill Bishop and Julie Ardery, Dee Davis, Mark Hebert, Ronnie Ellis, Nancy Green, Jamie Lucke, Jack Brammer, Ferrell Wellman, Pam Luecke, Randy Powell, Robert Brewer, Joe Graves, Steve Wrinn, and longtime New Orleans friends—Francis Weller, Elsie Halford, Tom Sancton, and Herman Kohlman.

The many fine journalists who appeared on *Comment*, and the producers, directors, and crews deserve much credit for the program's success. I am indebted beyond measure to Len Press who made it happen.

Bobby Clark, my publishing partner, Sid Webb, cover and photo layout designer, and Michal Smith-Mello put the book between its covers. Scott Mello created the Index. Jim Host, who I regret was not governor, jumped in to help market it. Mark Griffith and Evelyn Richardson cheerfully researched Logan County history. Pieces of my story occurred because of friends such as Tom Duncan, Wayne Bell, Pete Mahurin, Ginny and Brooke Lawson, David and Colleen Holwerk, Patti Cross, David Hawpe, Anne Caudill, the Byrne Evans family of Russellville, Carolyn Richardson, Bob Carter, Ralph Hacker, Steve Cawood, Sally Brown, Mary Bingham, Dot Ridings, Cindy Heine, Debbie McGuffey, Kim Burford, Judy McCowan, Charles House, Les and Shelly Page, Keith Runyon, Tim Kelly, and strong men now gone: Earl Wallace, Tom Clark, Phillip Davidson, A.D. Albright, W.T. Young, Morton Holbrook, Robert Houlihan, the Barry Binghams, Wilson Wyatt, John Ed Pearce, Ed Prichard, Bob Sexton, Governors Bert Combs, Ned Breathitt, Louie Nunn, Father Harry Burke, Otis Singletary, Tom Gish, John Stephenson, Rudy Abramson, John McClure, and Ken Gormin.

My spiritual life in Kentucky has been nourished by men and women in the recovery community in Russellville and Lexington. They know who they are, and that I love them.

This book is also published in memory of my parents, grandparents, the aunts and uncles who helped raise me, and all my cousins, including Marion Williams Kelley whose last words to me before her death, were "Al, Martha Helen is the best thing that ever happened to you." She was right, of course.

Index